The Castrated Family

THE CASTRATED FAMILY

Harold M. Voth, M.D.

SHEED ANDREWS AND McMEEL, INC.
SUBSIDIARY OF UNIVERSAL PRESS SYNDICATE
KANSAS CITY

Library of Congress Cataloging in Publication Data
Voth, Harold M
  The castrated family.

  Bibliography: p.
  1. Family—United States. 2. Sex role. 3. Parent
and child. 4. Mental illness—United States.
I. Title. [DNLM: 1. Family. 2. Social conditions—
United States. HQ535 V971c]
HQ536.V63   301.42'0973   77-10703
ISBN 0-8362-0730-3

CONTENTS

FOREWORD   vii

PREFACE   xiii

ACKNOWLEDGMENTS   xvii

CHAPTER ONE: THE NORMAL FAMILY   1

CHAPTER TWO: INFANCY AND CHILDHOOD:
    AWAKENING AND DEVELOPMENT   13

CHAPTER THREE: THE CAUSES OF FAILURE
    AND ILLNESS   46

CHAPTER FOUR: GUIDES TO MATURITY   89

CHAPTER FIVE: PSYCHOTHERAPY   131

CHAPTER SIX: CAREERS AND THE FAMILY   191

CHAPTER SEVEN: THE CASTRATION OF AMERICA   211

COMMENTS AND SELECTED READINGS   223

APPENDIX   235

FOREWORD

The author of this book, Dr. Harold Moser Voth, is one of America's most distinguished psychoanalysts and research psychiatrists and has made numerous experimental and clinical contributions to the understanding of human experience and behavior. What he has to say in what follows comprises the distillate of many years of work as a psychoanalyst and psychotherapist. It is at once substantive, forceful, and admittedly polemical; traditional and controversial; provocative and compassionate. It represents the views of a mature personality whose *modus vivendi* and clinical practice are all of a piece, whose conception of what he does as a physician and psychiatrist is pervasively congruent with how he conducts his life and gives expression to his role as the head of his own healthy family. Finally, it may be said to comprise a considered social commentary which emerges at a time when American society is reeling amidst a kaleidoscopic array of mutually antagonistic forces which, many of us believe, threaten us all with a progressive descent into decadence and social chaos.

The past twenty years have amply underscored the concept and predictions of future shock; indeed, the rapidity of social change, the revision and jettisoning of traditional folkways and social institutions, legislative and judicial efforts to promote major alterations in individual and social behavior have left the public with a pervasive sense of personal dislocation with perplexity and depression in their wake. We are daily treated to the erosion of traditional individual, familial, social, and religious values and ethics. Within this context the unusual becomes usual; the strange becomes familiar; the bizarre becomes commonplace; the perverse becomes the norm. God is dead, or demythologized or has undergone a change in sex; schools do not impart disciplined cognitive skills, but rather train the young to "adjust" to an increasingly confusing and polymorphous society; "equality" is legislated and adjudicated at the expense of individuality; there is no such thing as mental illness; legitimate authority is denigrated, even scourged; alcohol and drugs abound; crime continues to rise while divorce becomes commonplace and families disintegrate, leaving children in increasing numbers bereft of healthy parenting; illegitimate pregnancies burgeon in number, while abortion is just around the corner for any and all and the "pill" replaces individual responsibility for the conduct and issue of one's actions; civil rights zealots cloak their cruelty behind a facade of social concern, while assorted "queens," lesbians, fetishists, sadomasochists and other sexual unfortunates find new forums for the popularization of their illnesses while they clamor that theirs is either the right way or at least no worse than anyone else's.

Consider the following as backdrop against which Dr. Voth's book emerges:

1. Progressive disintegration of the nuclear family's responsibility to protect, nurture, discipline, and socialize its children, with resultant displacement of these duties to extra-familial substitute agencies, including child and day-care centers, schools, residential facilities, juvenile courts, and the like, none of which can adequately substitute for normal, healthy parenting and childrearing.

2. Progressive erosion of the male roles of husband and father, and of the female roles of wife and mother, with diffusion and blurring of familial gender, age, and intergenerational authority and structure, circumstances which are undeniably pathogenic for children. This situation has been abetted by many aspects of the so-called women's liberation movement much of which, under the color of a compassionate concern for genuine selfhood for women, has cloaked a hatred and envy of males based upon a failure of maternal identification, some of the basis for which Dr. Voth clearly sets out in this book.

3. Increasing failure of primary and secondary schools to

educate their students in literate cognate skills, with the result that
increasing numbers of graduates, including those who apply for
and expect to obtain higher education, are found to be subliterate,
unable to count, spell, or compose a properly written sentence,
much less reason logically and abstractly.

4. The emergence of a basically egocentric, adolescent view
of love and sex, epitomized in the phrase "Playboy Philosophy,"
according to which almost anything goes, or at least one should
feel free to "do one's thing" provided it is pleasing or satisfying,
or is concluded by the doer to be harmless to anyone else.

5. The broadcast and exhibition of ear-splitting, tasteless,
cacophonic noise called rock music, foisted upon young people by
unscrupulous promoters and purveyed by a plethora of electroni-
cally amplified, talentless, often drug-abusing gesticulators,
screamers, and gyrators whose dancing reflects a no-touch
schizoid condition.

6. The denial of the reality of mental illness, called by some a
"myth" perpetrated by strangelovian doctors bent upon imprison-
ing the socially undesirable. Associated either directly or indirectly with this cruel denial that sufferers really suffer has been the
politically inspired movement to empty out and shut down mental
hospitals, thereby to dump the chronically and severely mentally
ill into that will-o'-the-wisp, the "community," which is ill-
equipped to help them, where their illness was spawned in the first
place, and where unscrupulous operators often prey upon them.

7. Pervasive mistrust of any authority figures, reflective of an
underlying mistrust of parents ("If the President of the United
States is a crook, whom can you trust?"); the stupendous and
distracting burgeoning of litigation of all kinds reflective of a resort
to legalism as a substitute for discussion, trust and faith.

8. The ever increasing amount of legislation, and of civil
litigation arising therefrom, concerning civil and constitutional
rights, utilization and review of professionals, efforts to guarantee
honest elections and campaign expenditures, racial balance, etc.,
etc., which require a steady expansion of governmental bureauc-
racy for review and enforcement, resulting in turn in further
erosion of the very rights the legislation was designed to protect.

9 The development of the "equal opportunity" concept, with

the resultant emergence of reverse quota systems, disruption of seniority procedures and extreme efforts to guarantee racial or ethnic schoolroom balance which has nothing whatever to do with quality of education and has resulted in inner-city impoverishment and, in some areas, revolt by parents concerned with the welfare and education of their children.

10. The increasing emergence of the ill and distracted as influential social forces, stridently proclaiming themselves to be the wave of the future who, under the guise of civil rights and liberty, seek to legitimize their illness by means of such weirdities as homosexual marriages, lesbian childrearing and the like.

11. The burgeoning of supposedly self-enhancing pseudotherapeutic cults and quackeries, to which increasing numbers of alienated individuals turn in the face of the personal and social confusion and lack of identity from which they suffer; thus, we have everything from "primal scream therapy," swimming pool feelie groups, far-out pseudo-oriental mantra-chanting, charismatic guru-isms and various kinds of massage to the somewhat more scientifically legitimate methodologies, including sensate focus therapy, biofeedback training, some forms of transcendental meditation and the various "behavior" and "operant conditioning" procedures, the last oriented toward "retraining" or "reprogramming" human behavior with little or no regard for the subjects' inner thoughts and feelings.

What Dr. Voth sets forth here is best appreciated within the context of these and other related contemporary trends. What he writes will anger, even inflame some. Others, who will appreciate his statements as he "tells it like it is" will perceive in them a restatement of the urgent need of our society to experience a reawakening of the values upon which that society has traditionally been based, and more generally a reflection of any society's need for a manifold of coherent folkways, irrespective of their specifics, upon which to base its continued existence. Equally important, they will perceive in this book a statement of the necessary relationship of what one does to who one is, and of the work of the disciplined and compassionate physician to the viable social context within which he or she and his or her patients live.

Finally, I believe that the social ills with which we are presently beset, some manifestations of which I have enumerated above, will in time be cured, and that what good aspects of them have been present will endure. But we need to get back to basics, and that, in effect, is what Dr. Voth tells us. His book needs to be read and pondered by every literate person, in particular by those who presume to "shape," "change," or "treat" others, be they parents, educators, counselors, clergymen, therapists, politicians, or just plain citizens.

DONALD B. RINSLEY, M.D., F.A.P.A.

Topeka, Kansas

PREFACE

This book is born out of a deep concern for the future of our nation. Many great civilizations have collapsed, some at the very zenith of their growth, and the current trend in our own country is down; we are in a decline. A revolution is taking place in values, standards are being overthrown, and new guidelines for human conduct and for society as a whole are rapidly emerging which have not been tested but which are being blindly accepted by many. The character and moral fiber of Americans is changing—for the worse.

The divorce rate is soaring, with 50 percent of the marriages of the young ending in divorce. The stable heterosexual commitment is rapidly becoming a thing of the past. The authority of the male has diminished and increasing numbers of men show a marked irresponsibility toward their families and are heads of their households in name only. Not only is the status of males being diminished, but many men are becoming feminine in their appearance, attitudes, and behavior, and many women are becoming masculine in the same ways. Increasing numbers of women are avoiding their responsibilities as wives and mothers and believe their future lies in pursuing those objectives which once were the province of the male. Social and economic factors are forcing mothers to work and children into day-care centers or into the hands of unconcerned, and often transient, caretakers. For these various reasons children are being deprived of the most vital experience of all—good family life. The effects on children when their father is not a strong, masculine man and their mother a strong, feminine woman, when a strong family bond fails to exist, or when families disintegrate defies estimation. The cycle of sick or weak people who are the product of sick or broken families keeps repeating itself, the effects spread from one generation to the next and slowly but surely the sickness tears down the best traditions of mankind which made our society strong.

As a psychiatrist and psychoanalyst it has been my privilege for nearly thirty years to see a very personal, detailed and in-depth view of the human condition. It seems to me that there is a clear and definite link between the forces of sickness inside people and the current trends in society. A cyclical reinforcement exists between the individual and society. Sick people are "castrated" people, that is, forces within them prevent them from being competent and masterful men and women who can make a commitment to each other, create a family, and eventually replace themselves with healthy human beings. There is an alarming increase of such people in our land, a fact which, when seen in the context of the radical changes in norms and values, leads to my belief that ours is becoming a castrated land and therefore a land in great peril.

What I have written is by no means an account of all that is known about the ills of individuals and society. Indeed, it reflects only what I think to be valid as a result of my direct experience. In forming my conclusions I have been guided by the knowledge and experience I have acquired as a man, a husband, a father, a teacher, a researcher, and as a physician who treats the mentally ill. I sincerely hope this book will be of help to you. I have made no attempt to quote extensively from the psychiatric literature for purposes of supporting everyhing I have to say, nor have I attempted to include a scholarly survey of the literature on the topics about which I have written. To have done so would have produced an encyclopedia. A modest suggested reading list is appended.

Some of you will find parts of this book unsettling, or perhaps even shocking, disconcerting, and difficult to believe. I urge you to keep an open mind while reading the book, particularly when you notice a strong reaction in yourself. Changes in one's view of life, and personality changes, are often preceded by or accompanied by unsettled feelings or even deeper disturbances. Do not forget that people can change when they make a serious effort to do so.

I had several objectives in mind when writing this book. First, I hope to help parents achieve a deeper understanding of the principles of family life which, when applied, will insure better personality development for their children who will then be more likely to grow into healthy men and women. Secondly, I want to help individuals recognize the signs of failure and psychiatric disturbances and to teach them how they can help themselves, as well as recognize when they are receiving good psychiatric care should they require such assistance. These objectives are aimed at helping men become more masculine and women more feminine and at strengthening the cornerstone of civilization—the family. Men and women who possess the personal qualities which make solid family life possible will have no difficulty identifying and living by the best values and traditions. It will be their natural tendency to promote the growth of mankind by rejecting the sickness we see in our society today and also by discarding outdated traditions and creating new and better ones. This book is not a plea to return to "the good old days"; it is an effort to preserve the best we have in our national character and society, thereby providing a solid foundation for the future growth of both the individual and society.

ACKNOWLEDGMENTS

Various people have encouraged me during the preparation of this book. First on the list is my wife, who has repeatedly pointed out the good a book could do for families, for women (who are being bombarded by changing social and personal values), and for men (whose status is being weakened). She has also repeatedly endorsed my own belief that people should have a better understanding of the psychotherapeutic process. The pride my sons have taken in my writing and their encouragement (including the ten year old who writes his "book" while seated beside me when I am writing mine) have been a great inspiration and help to me.

Thanks are also due various friends for urging me to write this book. These include Dr. and Mrs. Roger Berlin, Mr. Andrew Smith, Miss Francis Gray, Mr. Sam Weisbord, Mr. and Mrs. Paul Mannen, as well as many of my former students.

I owe special thanks to my wife, Dr. and Mrs. Berlin, Mrs. Milton Chamberlain, Mrs. Andrew Bakalar, Mr. and Mrs. E. J. Erp, Mr. Theodore Weisman and Mr. and Mrs. Ben Voth, and Miss Gray for their assistance and comments, as well as encouragement.

I am especially grateful to Messrs. James Andrews and Lee Salem and Mrs. Donna Martin of Sheed Andrews and McMeel, Inc. who had the courage to publish this book.

CHAPTER ONE

The Normal Family

It is both practical and consistent with the basic qualities that Nature has given male and female that the woman who bears and nurses the baby should care for the young and for the dwelling in which the young live, and that the man, who is larger, physically more powerful and more aggressive, should provide the shelter, food and protection for his family. Even though the complexities of social life have vastly increased, this basic model of the family is as valid today and as consistent with the natural endowments of male and female as it was in primitive times. The family may reside on Park Avenue or on an isolated farm or in the jungle, but the basic qualitative differences between male and female remain the same. The integrity of the family, the care and proper psychological development of the young depend on the appropriate expression or living out of these differences. When environmental factors prevent the man and woman who make a family from living out the qualities with which Nature endowed them and from maintaining a family unit, serious consequences follow. These consequences are what this book is about.

All advanced levels of animal life show some form of organization with the male in the dominant position. Even very low forms of animal life reveal patterns of dominance among males and females, with the male dominant over the female. At higher levels the male is more dominant and powerful; he establishes his territory, competes for females. A very dominant male is the leader of the group. In primitive societies males were and are the leaders, with special powers given to certain ones. In modern societies males generally occupy the most powerful positions. For example, the greatest scientists, statesmen, politicians, professionals, artists, musicians and writers are mostly men; genius exists among men only. All organizations in modern society are hierarchically arranged with men in the most dominant positions with but rare exception. The family is an organization, and it is consistent with all known patterns of animal behavior, including that of man, that the male should be the head of the family. Konrad Lorenz (57, 58) describes male and female patterns within organization of lower animals. A scholarly account of why the male has always been dominant in societies and the head of the family is discussed by Stephen Goldberg in his *The Inevitability of Patriarchy*. (40)

Furthermore, it is consistent with the biological differences between male and female for the man to be the head of the family, its chief executive who has the ultimate responsibility and final authority. Gadpaille (38) summarizes the biological differences between male and female. Therefore, he should be responsible to see that members of his family are in psychological harmony with their own biologic roots, with each other, and with the society in which the family exists. Today, however, many new values are rapidly becoming social norms, eroding the traditional family relationships entirely or drastically changing the structure of the family. E. E. Lemasters (53) concludes that men have become passive and weak, women have become dominant, and that men are no longer heads of their families. Lesse (54) describes the same phenomenon and ascribes this change to industrialization. I agree with these observations. Furthermore, new social values and forces are stealing young away from their parents and destroying them or, if not that, so polluting them that the likelihood of their overcoming these effects and of becoming constructive citizens is reduced. A striking example of this is the wide social acceptance of the long-term use of marijuana and alcohol. There is an abundance of evidence which shows that marijuana breaks down the psychological strengths, particularly aggressiveness in the male, and especially in emotionally disturbed people, thereby impairing their effectiveness, and frequently leads to the use of harder drugs. Evidence now suggests that marijuana can damage the chromosomes in a high number of smokers. Nevertheless, smoking marijuana becomes rationalized in terms of "everyone is doing it so it must not be harmful" and thereby becomes a social "norm." Another example is the concept of "open marriage" or living together without the commitments generally associated with marriage. Another is the absurd point of view that men should remain in the home and rear young children while the woman works—in other words, that there is no basic difference between the impact of the father and mother on infants and children. Yet another is that homosexuality is a normal way of life. It is the responsibility of both the man and the woman, but of the man in particular, to ward off these erosive social forces which threaten to destroy his family or children just as males have always protected their families or, in lower animals, the herd from attack by a hostile environment. Society is governed by good values, rules and laws; these must be brought into the home today along with food, just as the primitive man brought the food.

The woman must reflect the best in human values too, but more of her time is taken up with rearing the young. She needs an authority standing sometimes beside her, and sometimes behind her, so that she can carry out her mothering role in the most effective way possible and so that she can impart certain other values to her children. So much of the woman's time and energy is consumed in the nurturing and caring functions that she alone cannot be expected to be the provider and the final authority as well. She cannot duplicate the man's functions, nor can he hers. Each can only approximate the other's. In her role as mother she will represent the finest in human values; from her the children will experience compassion, love, understanding, honesty, loyalty and care, and much more. She will be distracted from her basic tasks if she must both tame and guide the human instincts of her young and develop their potentials, and at the same time attempt to be protector of her family, the provider, and the authority which keeps it running smoothly. This is not to say that the woman should lack authority in the home, but it does affirm that the man should have more. Both the wife and children must know that.

To say that the man is the final authority in no way implies that he should be a tyrant, a dictator, a martinet, or have his way in all matters. What is best for the entire family should be the principle that guides the decision-making process within the family. The discovery of what is best may require much discussion among the family members. Someone must, however, have the final word.

The father should be loving, compassionate, understanding, capable of gentleness and the like—but all should know he is the protector, the one who is ultimately responsible for the integrity and survival of the family. It is known that the most successful families are those where all members, including the wife, look up to the father-husband.

Controlling and channeling the instincts and impulses of infants and children and developing their potentialities to the fullest extent, imparting the best in human values to them, require the best efforts of both the man and the woman. However, clear divisions of responsibility and labor must exist; some special responsibilities and authority are the mother's; other special responsibilities and authority are the father's. There must be no role confusion between the mother and father, and though these distributions of responsibility and authority exist, everyone in the family must also know, appreciate and respect the fact that the father has the overall responsibility for the family; he is its chief executive, but like all good executives he should listen to all within his organization.

No organization functions well with weak leadership—nor can the family. Strong and just leaders build strong organizations; this is equally true of the family. A really strong leader will evoke strength and bring out the best in everyone within his organization and at the same time maintain a hierarchic structure. However, we are rapidly becoming a fatherless society; if the trend continues I believe society as we know it will collapse. Families cannot exist without fathers. Without families society cannot exist.

There are those who say that parental roles are learned, that men and women have been forced into these roles by social conventions. I do not believe this. If this were true, then the consequences of male and female role confusion or reversal and the failure of the man to be the head of the family would not be as serious, productive of illness, and tragic as they often are.

Far-reaching and serious consequences result when internal family arrangements deviate from the norm. Virtually every patient I have personally treated, or whose treatment I have supervised, or whose treatment I have studied through a research endeavor, has revealed an aberrant family constellation. The most common pattern was the family in which the mother was domineering and aggressive and the father weak and passive. Some of these fathers were aggressive and assertive in their work situations but timid and weak in relation to their wives. The wives in these marriages clearly "wore the pants." Another pattern was that of a weak mother who tended to cling to her children, and a tyrannical father who was dictatorial but incapable of experiencing closeness to his wife or children. While it may seem that such a father is head of the family, actually much of the responsibility and authority falls to the wife except for periods when the father makes his presence felt by angry, usually irrational, outbursts. Some women are forced to fill the role of both mother and father by necessity. These women may be feminine but the absence of the father places all of the responsibilities on them; the effects of this family pattern on children as well as on themselves are not good. Fathers and mothers may be hostile, rejecting, overly anxious, or possessive. Some families lack any semblance of an authority structure. Some parents live up to their responsibilities sporadically. All of these conditions within the family adversely affect the child's personality development.

Strong fathers and strong mothers (in the feminine sense— strong femininity is not aggressiveness), who love each other, who cooperate with each other, and whose roles are clearly defined, produce healthy children. When this pattern is disturbed in any of a number of ways, emotional disturbances of a wide variety are the result in the children. Two studies illustrate this point. One is by Reinhardt (68) wherein he points out that outstanding naval pilots have a strong bond with their fathers. The other is by Vaillant (85) who reports the results of a 29-year study in which the family patterns of 95 men were described. One of the most striking findings is that when these men perceived their mothers to be the dominant one in their family they were more often poorly adjusted or mentally ill. These are but two research studies; literally hundreds of clinical studies and reports which link mental illness to dominant mothers and weak fathers fill professional journals.

These disturbances may appear during childhood or they may appear for the first time during adulthood. As I will describe in the chapter on child development, when the ideal family pattern is not lived out certain basic biological forces are frustrated, vital patterns of family interaction do not occur, and certain very fundamental human qualities are not formed while others are formed which should not have been.

The results are diverse, and all can be subsumed under the heading of personality disturbances. Many of these disturbances are in harmony with some of the new "norms" of society. My assertions are based on having searched, as have many others, for the roots of many kinds of personality disturbances through the process of in-depth analysis. The origins of these disturbances inevitably pointed to parents who were ill themselves and to family patterns which fell short of the ideal.

Childhood experiences within the family, and their subsequent effects, have been implicated in all of the psychiatric illnesses (psychoses and neuroses), personality disorders, perversions, homosexuality, transsexuality, transvestism, drug addiction, alcoholism, delinquency, suicide, crime, the current blurring of sex roles (which is becoming widespread at an alarming rate), child abuse, divorce, and failure to adapt to life generally or in specific instances. Those persons afflicted in one or more of the preceding ways contribute to the weakening of our society, parts of which are very sick. Conversely, healthy parents produce healthy children who can master life and avoid various forms of illness, and above all can themselves produce healthy children. The aborigines of Australia have the oldest living culture despite the harsh environment in which they live. This is based on an indestructible family unit, the fundamental elements of which (father, mother and offspring) are reinforced by relatives. There is no role confusion regarding male and female, nor homosexuality, in this culture.

The family is the unit within which the child develops courage, self-confidence, the ability to trust, autonomy, a sense of inner authority, and the capacity to be masterful. Here the biological qualities of male and female are evoked and reinforced by experiences with parents. The capacity to love blossoms; sexuality is awakened. Out of these experiences men and women learn to form a loving, intimate and cooperative relationship and to set up rules for their small organization (the family) wherein the best can be evoked in their children and in themselves as well. Learning to cooperate with others begins in the family; the process of socialization begins and is developed there. The male is, in a sense, the key in that he is ultimately responsibile, and yet the woman is equally important, for without good mothering boys and girls do not develop into men and women who can make good families. The roles of father and mother and their responsibilities are different but both are essential.

Nothing of what has been said in any way demeans the woman or exalts the man. If a man and woman wish to form an organization—a family—then there must be rules of operation by which the members of that organization shall be guided. These rules must be harmonious with the biological qualities of the male and female and the social responsibilities of each. Once the children are out of the home, social roles of male and female can change and new responsibilities can be taken on, especially by the woman.

Having a family is one of the highest callings on earth; children are our most precious and valuable resource. Their care should fall only to those who are suitable for the task. Many people who are capable of living productive lives should remain unmarried. Others are capable of marriage but should never have children. Ideally, children should be born only to those who can fulfill this highest of all callings; these are men and women who are fully male and female and who are not burdened by personality disturbances and/or psychiatric illness, and who have the time to make the family a primary career. Such individuals will then be able to organize the family structure in such a way as to evoke and reinforce in their children the finest that Nature has to give.

But the home is not a place just for children; it is important for men and women too. Even after children are in school, having a secure home to which children and husband can return and escape from the stresses of life is vital. Only a healthy woman can provide such a setting and atmosphere. To be able to regularly return to this atmosphere where one is known and loved replenishes the spirit. The marvelous quality which exists within a happy home cannot be duplicated anywhere. A family is precious, and the surest way to preserve it is for men and women to fully understand that one of the highest responsibilities to humanity is the making of a home and family.

While it is true that children can be reared in settings other than a family, there usually are serious consequences when the child is deprived of a family during his formative years. Lee Salk (71), an authority on child development, believes that those couples who prefer to place their children in day-care centers rather than take care of them should not have had children. The 50 percent divorce rate in young married couples, many of whom have had children, is cause for great alarm. These children will be deprived of life experiences which only family life can give them. Those young people who cannot succeed at marriage are burdened by immaturities in their personalities and are frequently drawn into a marital arrangement by these very immaturities. When children come neither parent is ready for parenthood and one or both will take flight from their responsibilities. Some will remarry. But the loss of a parent during early years is always a trauma for a child and will frequently cause him trouble in later life. Furthermore, several years frequently pass before the parent remarries, if ever, and vital family experiences are denied the child during that period when the foundation of personality is formed. Every day counts in a child's life.

It is always desirable for parents whose marriage is showing signs of disintegration and dissolution to seek good help before they give up and divorce. Unfortunately, good help is difficult to find. The chapter on self-help is written for those who cannot find help, and even for those who may be finding help but who want additional guidelines as well. People frequently give up too easily when faced with obstacles; nowhere on earth are the consequences more serious than when young people give up with the family they have formed.

It should always be assumed that something healthy, substantial, and genuinely meaningful brought a young man and woman together. On the basis of this assumption, much effort should be made to make the marriage work as outlined in this book before failure is admitted. It is true that some marriages are very bad from the start, that irrational reasons brought the couple together. In these instances it is better for the couple to divorce even if there are children. It is difficult to identify such marriages, however, and even in these matches which seem impossible, effort should be made to save them. If, after a period of serious and conscientious self-help and a subsequent period of professional help, there is no improvement, divorce may be the best course to take. If you have started a family, try to make it work, really work; don't just live together in a reasonably tolerable way. Remember, there is a proper way for the family to be organized. A family which is not organized in the right way is as damaging to children as a broken family. The lives of our children are in our hands; they did not ask to be born; it is our responsibility to give them a good beginning and a good life.

Just as the rising incidence of divorce is cause for alarm, so too is the rise in numbers of day-care centers for small children. While these centers are necessary for the care of children from broken homes and of those whose mothers are forced out of the home by economic need, increasing reliance upon such centers by society will, I believe, ultimately backfire. If the number of young people who are ill-prepared for parenthood increases, and if economic conditions continue to force more children into day-care centers, increasing numbers of children will grow up who are ill-prepared for life. There is no substitute for good mothering during a child's infancy, nor for good mothering *and* good fathering later on.

These remarks should not be taken to mean that a woman should never work outside of her home; indeed not. However, if a woman marries and has children then she should take care of them at least until the children are in school. Of equal importance is the man, who should give his wife his full support as a husband and as father to his children.

It would be wiser for the federal government, benevolent as its intentions may be, not to promote day-care centers but instead to spend the equivalent funds to make it possible for families to stay together or, if already disintegrated, for the mother to care for her children. Eventually it will be necessary to arrange the economy so that when a man works a reasonable work day it will be possible for his wife to stay home and care for the young and for him to have time enough to participate in family life also. Currently, pressures and time demands on men, especially those who operate their own small businesses or work in managerial capacities in large corporations, are enormous. Their families are bound to suffer. Well-intentioned as the father may be, his children will be deprived of time with him.

In addition to the enormous loss in human life, material treasure, and disruption of life generally, wars take thousands of fathers out of the family for long periods of time. Many are killed, others are wounded, and others become psychiatrically ill and can never again fully fill the father's position in the family. These men are removed from the family when the wife and children need them the most, not only in economic terms but primarily for the personality development of the children. It is impossible to estimate the cost in terms of future personality disturbances in the children of these families.

The most serious crisis facing us today is that of the family, the alterations of its internal structure, the high incidence of its dissolution, and the associated crisis of the human spirit. The fate of the family is in the hands of the man and woman who form it, and in the hands of the society which supplies its support. The family is in danger because the personalities of men and women are increasingly less mature, the distinction between male and female is less clear, and because social values which maintain or support sex role differences and the family are changing.

I believe all responsible people should oppose the blurring of values which distinguish male from female. I decry those social groups which advocate unisex life styles and which impose their values on young children in schools and nurseries through their efforts to obscure the differences between male and female. While freedom of the printed word is essential to a free society, it is unfortunate that so much favorably tilted publicity is given to those who have failed in their roles as adults and parents and who advocate, for instance, homosexual marriages as a suitable way to rear children, or who abdicate their responsibilities to home and young children and would have the husband care for children while the wife is working outside the home. Such nonsense is being taught in universities.

The consequences of open marriage, communal living, mate swapping, or living together and having children without serious commitment between the man and woman have never been tested and yet these ways of living are being openly advocated. The consequences of the half-hearted heterosexual commitments many people make might not be so serious if children were never born out of such arrangements, but they are, and these children are deprived of mature parents and good family life. When society openly endorses such lifestyles, the door is opened wider for emotionally disturbed young people to follow these life styles. Like it or not, these people have children. Who will care for them?

Society should do all it can to reverse the present trends. It should emphasize the differences between the sexes and make it possible for boys and men to be as masculine as possible and for girls and women to be as feminine as possible. Under these conditions true intimacy between the sexes can occur and the best kinds of families will form. Not only must the family be saved, it must be organized internally in such a way as to make it possible for children to become adults who can form strong heterosexual relationships, marry, and produce normal children. These changes would be preventive psychiatry at its best. What psychiatry does now as prevention is pitifully inadequate.

This is not to say that all people should marry and have children, or that those who cannot are not worthwhile citizens. Enormously good work has been done and magnificent contributions have been made to mankind by people who have not married or who have married and not had children. However, for these individuals to have had the opportunity to do their good work they needed a viable society; that very viability depends on stable institutions and those, in turn, depend on stable families.

In the Midwest and rural regions the family is faring better than in the large cities, and as might be expected the family is more highly regarded in these areas. In the large city the family is badly strained. Commuting distances for the father rob the family of his time and energy. Children are whisked into activities away from the home; barriers are erected between parent and child; economics may force fathers to work overtime or at two jobs. Mothers may have to go to work. Peer pressure which is more difficult to counteract in large cities is forcing values onto the young which are more disintegrative than constructive. These conflict with what parents believe, but the father is away so much he is tired, sapped of strength, and cannot effectively set and maintain standards for his family. The mother lacks support from her absent, fatigued, or weak husband. Increasing numbers of children are lost to the forces which destroy them as potentially strong men and women. The personal stability which derives from clear gender and sex-role definition is being eroded by the aimless, self-centered way of life so many young people are living today. Families are failing by the hundreds of thousands. Popenoe (67) notes that a strong monogamous family and the highest culture go together. If one deteriorates, so does the other. The signs of decay abound; it is a diseased society, and the trend is downward.

If all goes well, the effects of family life can evoke the best that Nature has to give; if not, family life can have disastrous consequences. Since the family provides the foundation for personality and for civilization, it is imperative that its structure and functioning be so arranged as to bring out the best in children. Children become the adults society and civilization depend on. It is essential that the effects of family life be clearly understood by those who produce children. The solution lies in salvaging the family and the way of family life which produces healthy children.

Doing anything in life halfway is not as good as doing it well. The relevance of this principle is nowhere greater than for the family. Our goal should be to reserve the high responsibility and privilege of rearing children to those who are themselves most mature, and this means masculine males and feminine females. Couples should very carefully consider, after applying the criteria of this book, whether they have the personalities which would enable them to raise children properly. If not, they should decide not to.

CHAPTER TWO

Infancy and Childhood:

Awakening and

Development

Personality development is the result of the interaction of environmental factors and constitutional (hereditary) factors. Not much can be done about heredity; but when parents understand and are guided by the principles of human development the rewards to the child, to the parents, and to society are enormous.

CONSTITUTIONAL FACTORS

Just as there are genetically determined differences in physical characteristics—body build, color of eyes and hair, etc.—so, too, are there wide variations in psychological and behavioral characteristics which are inborn. At birth some infants are placid and quiet, while others are restless and active. These qualities are traceable, or so it seems, into adulthood. Some persons are quiet by nature, tend to desire solitude; as they grow older they tend to restrict their social contacts. Others are just the opposite; they enjoy socialization, and need more contact with the external environment. These differences are normal. Some people show mixtures of both kinds of these opposite tendencies. It is an unsettled question as to what extent and which traits of personality have their origin in constitution and to what extent these traits are acquired through life experience. In some persons talents and skills seem to be inborn. "Basic" intelligence is constitutionally determined but its successful application is largely due to environmental influences.

It is crucial for the happy outcome of the child's early development that parents and other adults (teachers, relatives, etc.) recognize the constitutional uniqueness of the child (particularly those qualities which are typically male or female) and not force him to become the kind of person which is contrary to his basic nature. An aspect of the art of parenthood is to be able to recognize these qualities of a child's personality and adapt to them in a way that leads to a harmonious interaction between parent and child. Parents who place a high value on intellectual pursuits will create undue strain in a child who is not as intelligent as they, or who at a certain phase in his or her life is more interested in other pursuits, if they force the child to spend too much time studying. Some children have no musical talent or interest whatsoever, yet parents frequently insist the child learn to play an instrument. To persist in forcing the child along lines which interest the parents and not the child can lead to breakdowns in the parent-child relationship.

Certain basic qualities of personality fit with certain vocations, professions, and avocations in later life. Parents should provide the kind of exposures to situations so that the child can eventually discover where he fits best and where his native potentialities can best be evoked and developed.

A boy who is well suited temperamentally and intellectually to follow his father's footsteps vocationally should be encouraged but not forced to do so. Conversely, he might choose some other field because of his (open or hidden) hostility toward his father. A youngster who is not suited intellectually and temperamentally for a certain field might, out of hidden guilt feelings or dependent attachment toward a parent, choose his parent's field and find himself miserable, and probably not very successful, the rest of his life. Parents should try to be sensitive to the basic trait differences of their offspring and not try to change these traits to suit their own wishes or needs. Instead, parents should respect them and above all not stand in the way as the child finds a style of life which will permit the free and fullest living out and development of these basic traits. For instance, child and parent alike are placed under great strain when a muscular, action-oriented father, who must have physical activity in the form of sports for his own peace of mind, tries to impose such activities onto a son who may be small-boned, slight in build, and more inclined to intellectual pursuits. Such a father can develop a fine relationship with his son, nonetheless, provided he respects his son's differences and both discover ways to interact. It is the father's responsibility, not the son's, to take the lead in making these discoveries and to provide the best possible opportunities for his son to fulfill himself.

The most fundamental constitutional factor of all has to do with the qualities of maleness and femaleness. Much has been written about gender, and various theories have been proposed. Some believe they have strong evidence for a biologic force, male as distinct from female, which shines through despite a host of unnatural, gender-confusing, environmental influences. I believe this is correct. That gender identity is also determined by environmental factors (this refers mainly to the parental attitudes toward the child very early in life) is unmistakably clear. A careful review of the concepts of what factors influence gender identity leads me to conclude that man is not biologically bisexual—that he is not both male and female. It appears that the embryo is bipotential very early but that certain hormonal events occur within the embryo which cause it to develop into male or female and not a mixture of both. These hormonal effects not only determine the obvious sexual anatomical differences but bring about brain changes and behavioral differences in boys and girls. I am repeatedly struck by how some of my fellow professionals stoutly defend the biologic bisexuality theory. These professionals, when they are men, tend to lack maleness to some degree and some are effeminate; and if they are women there is almost always a strikingly masculine quality to their personalities. By holding to this belief, they can explain the traits of the opposite sex within themselves and delude themselves into believing they are psychologically normal when, in fact, they are not. Their effectiveness as doctors with certain patients is limited, as one might expect.

Of all the traits which deserve the clearest understanding and the respect of parents and society at large, the traits of maleness and femaleness are the most important, for when parental influence, lifestyles, roles, and social values which are not in harmony with basic maleness and femaleness are forced upon the child great harm with far-reaching consequences to the child, and later to his children, results. The paternal and maternal instincts are a function of and expression of biologic maleness and femaleness.

It bears repeating that powerful forces within the family and society are complicating the development of children by forcing values and lifestyles upon them which do not permit the fullest development and expression of maleness and femaleness. For example, some teachers in nursery and elementary schools are introducing play techniques which blur sex differences rather than distinguish them. Clothing styles make it difficult to tell a male from a female at a distance—and in some cases even up close. Hair styles reflect this blurring. The unisex movement and aspects of the women's liberation movement contribute to this blurring. The trend is to erase sex differences, not to accentuate them. These social trends run counter to natural law; Nature designed male and female as distinct and different. The environment, parents in particular, should evoke and reinforce these differences, not blur them or—worse—attempt to reverse them. When a child begins to manifest the qualities of the opposite sex, positive evidence is at hand that improper *psychological* development is taking place and *not* that his biologic nature is the basis for these changes. These qualities can be changed and this should be done as quickly as possible.

There are, of course, human qualities common to both sexes which have nothing to do with gender identity and their appearance in the child is no cause for alarm. Both sexes should be able to express a wide range of human qualities such as tenderness, gentleness, love, anger, compassion, sensitivity, creativeness, etc. It is quite natural for a little boy to pick up certain traits or mannerisms from his mother, and the little girl from her father, and in no way be destined for a disturbance of their identity. However, when this occurs excessively it is likely that the child's identification process is not proceeding properly. The terms "boy" and "girl" have powerful meanings and should unequivocally be the guiding principles for the child's upbringing once the sex of the child has been established at birth. No little boy or girl should ever be treated as if he were of the opposite sex. When a boy starts acting like a girl the fault lies in his upbringing and not in his genes. When a small boy starts to use his mother's makeup, wants to dress in her clothing, desires to play only with girls, the signs are clear that his personality is developing in the wrong direction. Steps should be taken to search out the basis for the faulty development and corrective steps should be taken immediately and decisively. Parents will find they are the cause of the trouble. Usually the mother is too possessive of the child and the father too remote or hostile or rejecting. There are, unfortunately, far too many parents who behave in such a way as to force their children to develop in a direction which is contrary to nature. Men are just as guilty as women, although the effects of women disturb gender development more profoundly because their effects on the child come much earlier in the child's life. Men often try very hard to convert their daughters into sons.

ENVIRONMENTAL FACTORS

The environmental factors which influence childhood development refer primarily to influences within the family. How a child is reared will, to a large extent, determine the final form his personality will take and how successfully and effectively he lives his life, including whether or not he will become mentally ill. It bears repeating that those parents who are unmixed in their sexual identity—that is, the father is fully masculine and normal and the mother, similarly, is fully feminine and normal—produce the healthiest children. Suffice it to say that "normal" implies the absence of unconscious conflicts which can produce neurotic or psychotic symptoms or certain malformations of character and prevent a successful adaptation to life. Some persons can be outwardly normal (no symptoms are present) under certain conditions only to become ill under others. Why people fail and/or become overtly psychiatrically ill will be discussed in the next chapter.

Normal parents are persons who remain free of symptoms within the context of a good marriage and who can live out their sexual identity and skills and abilities in appropriate social roles. Good parents love each other and can experience full sexual pleasure with each other. Neither will find it necessary or desirable to have lovers or isolated sexual experiences with others. They will be able to cooperate with each other; competitiveness with each other will be absent. Each will feel that his or her own gender is equally valuable as the other. Each will respect the other and neither will demean the opposite sex.

THE GOOD MOTHER

A normal woman is one whose own development was such as to permit her to achieve a full flowering of her femininity. Such a woman cannot completely fulfill herself unless she marries and has children—at least one child—and, ideally, only such women should have children. To exclude men and children from her life would be a heavy burden. She would be forced to find substitute gratifications for her maternal urges and her natural tendency to experience loving and being loved by a man as well as sexual pleasure with him.

A normal woman will want to nurse her infant and unless there are extenuating circumstances which prevent her, or a physiologic insufficiency, she will and should do so. Breasts are not ornaments for men to admire; they are there for a purpose—to suckle the young. Much good can be done by physicians and the relatives of young and somewhat immature mothers when they help the new mother overcome her anxiety about nursing. These early life experiences are critical in their importance, especially for the baby but also for the mother. A strong bond develops between the mother and infant through this experience. Nursing her baby, consistently responding to its needs, and the other features of infant care, are experiences which have a maturing effect on the mother.

Through the nursing experience and other experiences with the mother the infant receives the gentleness and nurture which form the core of personality. A baby should be nursed when it is hungry, regardless of the interval of time between feedings. Forcing a baby into a rigid feeding schedule is pure nonsense when its own inner rhythm causes it to be hungry at its own schedule. Allowing a baby to cry for food for long periods of time does harm to the baby. It is very important for a mother to hold her child, to rock it while nursing, and to rock it to sleep. A rocking chair is the most important piece of furniture in her home.

These good mothering experiences "fill" the child and all through life this fortunate individual will silently experience the calm and gentle reassurance of his good mother inside of him. The foundations of personality will have been formed, and if subsequent developmental phases progress well the likelihood of mental illness for the child is nil and the chances of a full and rewarding life are great, assuming the existence of opportunities in society. Some of the finest adult characteristics can be attributed to good, bountiful, and loving mothering. These include an inner sense of goodness and strength, security, generosity, courage, trust, the capacity to love, an ability to form meaningful, intimate, cooperative, and enduring relationships with both sexes, and the ability to experience sexual pleasure in a mature form with the opposite sex. Success in work and play is dependent to a large degree on having had a good mother.

This mother will, above all, experience her child as a separate individual and not a possession from which she dreads to part. As the child begins to explore his environment, the mature and feminine mother will always give reassurance, never hold the child back but will always be there should the child become afraid and need to retreat to a more secure position. Such encouragement to venture into the environment, and the reassurance when fear and insecurity strike, provide the basis for the child's capacity for mastery during subsequent developmental periods, and on through all of life. By means of a series of separations and safe returns to his mother the child develops a sense of separateness and inner security without forming excessive separation anxiety, and the discovery will have been made that the environment can be mastered.

As a consequence of this good mothering the child does not have to cling constantly to his mother or a substitute. Such childhood experiences make it possible for the individual to undergo separations later in life and stand alone without experiencing anxiety. Losses in later life will be mastered without undue anguish and depression.

Some of the most crippled people, in a psychiatric sense, are those who have missed out on good mothering during infancy and early childhood. So many women do not realize what a great service they are doing mankind when they provide good mothering for their babies and small children. Good mothers provide the foundation within their children, boys and girls alike, upon which all else is built. Unfortunately the woman's rewards, in terms of seeing the final result of her goodness and her care, often come much later in life when her children become healthy and competent young men and women. But unselfishness is a characteristic of the good mother; she can wait for the final realization of her rewards. Her immediate reward, which only women can have, is participating in this most vital of all human experiences—the evoking of the human spirit in the new life she has brought into the world and permeating it with her own love and goodness. Doing this will transcend in importance all else a woman can do in her lifetime. Never underestimate the vital importance of good mothering.

THE HOSTILE AND REJECTING MOTHER

The impact on an infant and small child of an immature, hostile, rejecting and therefore probably somewhat unfeminine mother or, if feminine, inhibited by psychiatric disturbance, is very great. Such a mother usually will not have had a completely good mother herself. A rejecting, insecure, anxious or hostile mother finds ways to avoid her baby. She will tend to not respond to the demands of her child.

Women who fit this pattern commonly let their infants cry for extended periods of time, hungry, soiled, too hot or too cold. They may be unable to nurse their infants and do not find satisfaction in holding or rocking them. They often are rough in the way they handle their children, sometimes strike them and, tragically, even beat them. Very young infants can sense the stiffness and muscular tension in their mothers which is caused by the mother's insecurity and/or hostility. Infants usually react with a variety of disturbances. Unfortunately these bad experiences are internalized by the infant and young child. Instead of having internalized loving experiences with a good mother, they become burdened by an enemy within. The succeeding developmental periods of childhood will necessarily be difficult, as will be later life, for these individuals lack courage and confidence in themselves and a sense of trust in others. They tend to be vulnerable to separations and responsibilities later in life and experience excessive anxiety in such circumstances. They expect attack and injury or hostility from friendly people and in non-threatening situations. It is hard for them to love or believe they are loved, and they commonly have disturbed sexual functioning.

THE OVERPROTECTIVE MOTHER

Another form of mothering which is, perhaps, not as devastating in its impact on the child as the hostile and rejecting mother but which, nonetheless, has its harmful effects is the overprotective mother. Such mothers have had the kind of infant care themselves which made them vulnerable to separations, that is, to excessive anxiety when separated from other persons or familiar surroundings. They are often beset by fears that injury or death will come to their child if they are not always close by, or they may cling to their child without a conscious reason for doing so. The overprotective attitude may be a reaction-formation (converting a feeling or a thought into its opposite) to a hostile attitude toward the child; that is, overprotectiveness masks hate. Women who envy and hate men are frequently overly protective of their male child, ostensibly for the purpose of protecting the boy. The overprotectiveness actually is a means by which they manage to fulfill their unconscious desire to diminish or destroy the male. Such mothers often treat their infants as if they were a part of their body. When a male child is overprotected he is denied encouragement and the opportunity to explore and become masterful, experiences which enhance his sense of maleness and capacity for mastery in later life.

It will be shown later how women may treat a child as a substitute for the penis they wish to possess. When a woman views a child in this way there is inevitably an associated hostility toward the child. There will be a constant struggle between mother and child. The child will try to free himself and the mother will cling to him. Some women are so successful in their ability to cling to their child, particularly if male, that an excessive internalization by the child of the anxious and insecure mother occurs. Not only does the child fail to develop courage and a sense of trust but effeminacy (in the male) is also the result, in some cases so extreme as to lead to homosexuality and even the wish, in severe cases, to undergo surgical alteration of the sexual organs. Mothers of transsexuals (those who believe they are of the opposite sex) are said to have held their babies against their own bodies excessively, and when standing the baby on their laps often positioned the child's feet over their own pubic area. The handling of the infant thus takes on the quality of fondling a large penis. Overly protective mothers who cannot experience their infant and child as a separate being use their child as a means for compensating for their inner emptiness which resulted from their own inadequate mothering, and for their sense of imperfection which is derived from their belief that they are anatomically lacking or deficient because they have female genitals instead of male ones. You may find this hard to believe, but it is quite true. If such mothers had had good mothers they would have gotten over their envy of the males. Their good (feminine) mothers would have made it possible for them to realize that females are as valuable and worthwhile as males. The effects of overprotection are serious; the child's courage is less and the full expression of gender and other potentialities tends to be diminished, in all likelihood throughout the remainder of life.

In short, the effects of the mother who is not fully satisfied with herself as a woman and who is, therefore, unable to completely live out her maternal instincts and functions will be such that her child will experience some kind of difficulty achieving a fully developed manhood or womanhood. As can be seen, the effects of undesirable mothering are passed on from generation to generation.

Circumstances sometimes force such a way of life on women, but a childless or husbandless woman is usually so because of her unconscious conflicts, and their characterologic consequences, have prevented her from marrying and having children. One must not, however, assume that all married parents are healthy! A high percentage are not. Later I will discuss why some people marry for the wrong reason.

Many women should not marry, and some choose not to. Such women have had the good sense not to do that for which they are unsuited, for which they do not have sufficient interest or time to do the task well. Such women often make fine contributions to mankind in other ways, and they should never be deprecated for not marrying and having a family. Many are quite normal in the sense of not showing signs of psychiatric illness; for others it is probably the fact that they have not married and attempted to make a family that has saved them from becoming psychiatrically ill.

It is remarkable how often one sees women who devote their energies to the children of others, usually as teachers, child psychologists, child psychiatrists, social workers and the like but who cannot have children of their own or, if they have children, cannot spend much time with them. Women who find outlets for their maternalism by working with or caring for the children of others deserve our respect and gratitude, provided they do a good job. It is far better for them to live a life like this and succeed than to try to be a full-time, natural mother and fail. Not only would their life be an unhappy one, but the child they might have had is spared the effects of bad mothering and bad family life. It would be much better for those women who elect to work to face the hard fact of their limitations and forgo having children of their own.

THE ROLE OF FATHERING

When the feminine woman has a new baby the father must stand by her in a helpful and supportive way. A mature man will not be jealous of his wife's attentiveness to the new child; he will freely share her with the new child, and will transmit his pleasure and gratitude to his wife in many ways. Thus the child and the mothering experience are not the sole rewards to the new mother. A baby enriches a marriage, if the couple is healthy, for both husband and wife will discover new dimensions in each other as a consequence of their increased growth with the coming of their child. Both can now discover further what maturity means in relation to the child and to each other.

It is appropriate for fathers to give some assistance in the care of the infant, however most of the baby's care will fall to the mother. Those who think men can stay at home and care for babies and young children while the mother works outside the home are misguided. To expect a man to be able to do what Nature has designed a woman for is absurd in the extreme.

During the infant's first few months of life the man's chief responsibility is to make his wife secure. The man cannot do for the infant what the mother can do; however, she cannot do her best for the infant without a good man by her side. The strengths his own mother and father gave to him will now make it possible for the husband to provide the love and security his wife needs in order to fully discharge her responsibilities to her infant. Because the woman's energies are so highly focused on her infant, the man must attend to potentially distracting demands on her, and he must be able for the time being to forgo receiving much of what he previously enjoyed from his wife. He should be able to give her much more than he expects in return.

Good men have always helped their wives. It does not diminish their masculinity to take over some of the tasks that women ordinarily do when so much of her energy is taken up in the care of the new child. It is perfectly appropriate for men to do the dishes, wash diapers, clean the house once in a while so the wife can preserve her strength. He may have to do for older children what his wife ordinarily would do. It will not hurt him to prepare meals now and then. He must bathe his wife with security, praise, and love so she can do her very best for the child. Women become irritable if they are fatigued and it harms an infant to be exposed to an irritable mother.

The father should have direct contact with the infant too. It is very important for small babies to be in contact with their father after they have matured enough to discriminate between a mother and a father. This is especially true after the first year of life. These early experiences set the stage for both boys and girls to be able to form close relationships with the opposite sex as adults. The groundwork is laid for a heterosexual relationship. A little girl discovers intimacy with a male. The female in her is awakened, and her relationship with her mother will reinforce her femaleness. Little girls who have passed through a period of closeness with their fathers will be able to be close to their future husbands. Little boys sense something different from the mother in the father. After the boy child is a few months old the mother awakens his maleness. Being held and played with and taken along on excursions with the father reinforces the budding maleness which his mother has awakened. Remember, maleness and femaleness are biological givens. Nature designed it this way; it is imperative for you to understand this if you expect your children to become normal men and women.

PARENTS TOGETHER

It is difficult to describe the quality of the experiences the infant and child can and should have with his mother and father. The child discovers that though he is separate from his parents he is known by them. There is a marvelous something which passes between a mother and child when she cares for the child; it is conveyed in her smile, her touch, her guiding hand. Fathers transmit something too, but it is qualitatively different and its effect is different in the boy and girl. The girl senses in her father a source of power and strength which permits her to be what she is, a female. The boy senses this same power and strength but in him it evokes the urge to emulate his father. The girl is designed by nature to emulate what her mother is. These are the ideals—when nature and the environment are in harmony.

It is important, therefore, for both parents to interact with their infant from birth onward, however the mother should be the primary adult in the infant's life up to a year at least. After a baby learns to walk and begins to master the environment, the father begins to play an increasingly important part in the child's life. Development and learning proceed at a rapid pace and the older the child gets the more he should enter the world of his own sex.

Daughters, therefore, will participate increasingly in mother's activities while sons will participate more in the father's world. Because the mother will spend more actual time with small children, it is important for her to direct their energies into play which provides suitable outlets for the little female or little male in her child which will reinforce what they are biologically. No child of either sex should ever feel (or be) ignored by the parent of the opposite sex.

BODILY CONTROL AND EARLY MASTERY

Control over bodily functions is important but only one of the many challenges for mastery confronting the child as he grows. Learning to walk, to control his bladder and bowels, and to carry out tasks of increasing complexity are all triumphs for the young child. Success is insured if wisely guided by mother and father, for the child will possess the courage to explore and begin a lifelong course of mastering tasks confronting him. If treated harshly for failures or forced to attempt to succeed when he cannot (particularly in learning to control bodily functions) harshness—not encouragement and the memories of success—will be recorded within his personality. An excessively strict conscience, a loss of spontaneity, and inhibition come, in part, from excessive harshness or exactitude on the part of the parents during these early years. Under no circumstances should a child be expected to accomplish more than he is capable of achieving. Nor should a child ever be punished for failing; instead, he needs encouragement, reassurance, guidance and help. Parents should show their children how to do things; they should play with them. Above all, children should feel their loving presence. When a child accomplishes some new feat he should always receive praise. Loving praise from parents for new achievements facilitates learning and the development of skills as nothing else will.

OEDIPUS COMPLEX FOR BOY

By approximately the age of three a child begins to experience his maleness or femaleness in the form of a strongly possessive, loving, and sexual interest in the parent of the opposite sex. It is *normal* for children to experience these feelings and emotions. This period is referred to as the oedipal period. If the child does not get over these feelings but submerges them into his unconscious mind we refer to this as the "Oedipus complex."

While it is true that children can experience sexual excitation toward the parent of the same sex, while being bathed for instance, it is unlikely that the sexual and romantic interests toward the parent of the same sex ever reach a fraction of the intensity of that which is felt for the parent of the opposite sex. The outcome of the Oedipus situation is dependent upon the child's earliest experiences with its mother and, of course, the events which occur simultaneously with its budding sexuality.

If the child has courage enough (and he will if his mother is a feminine woman and cared for him in the way I described in the preceding pages, and if the personalities of his parents are healthy and both parents are present during the period from three to six years of age) the outcome of the oedipal situation will be successful. The resolution of the oedipal situation is crucial for mental health and for the successful living of life. If resolved in the proper way, life will go well; if not, much can go wrong and much disappointment, failure, mental illness, and tragedy may be the result. The effects on a person's life as a consequence of the success or failure to resolve this developmental phase can influence one's values, character structure, and sexual identity. They may determine whether one becomes heterosexual or homosexual, perverse in one's sexual behavior, a failure or a success in one's life work; they may influence the choice of a life's work, vulnerability to psychiatric illness, self-destructive life patterns, even the kind of person one chooses to marry; the consequences really are far-reaching. You may find this hard to believe but I will illustrate some of these consequences in the chapter on typical forms of illness, and in the case studies. Obviously, the influence of the parents and their personalities during and subsequent to the oedipal period bears heavily on the outcome of this phase of personality development. This period is a very crucial time of life.

For the Oedipus situation to be resolved, correct behavior must be forthcoming from the parents. First, the parents must be mature, and this implies the absence of sexual identity disturbances. The father must be a mature man and the mother a mature woman. Second, the parents must love each other and have established a strong marital bond. The parent of the opposite sex must tactfully reject the child's romantic overtures but not the child. Above all, the parent must not respond seductively.

Many women do respond seductively toward their sons; often these are women who were overly protective during the boy's earliest months of life. Mothers who reject their infants also behave seductively toward their small sons. Such behavior entices the son and often prolongs the oedipal period indefinitely. Seductive and/or possessive mothers tend to make confidants of their sons and thereby make it apparent to the boy that he enjoys a special place with his mother that his father does not. Such mothers often enter into secrets with their sons and openly exclude the father. These excessively close and clandestine arrangements whet the boy's appetite and keep his unconscious hope aflame that he may indeed someday win his mother as a love object. Abnormal mother-son relationships may extend into adulthood so that not only is there a failure to resolve the original oedipal attachment to the mother, but the excessive continual maternal input into the boy's personality profoundly affects his subsequent personality development.

A good mother will continue to interact warmly with her son during the oedipal period and will in no way make him feel guilty or ashamed because of his strong and sometimes overt expressions of love for her but she, in subtle and tactful ways, will make it increasingly clear to him that he can never reach his romantic and sexual objectives with her. Such a mother will not feel threatened or embarrassed by her little "lover." It is sometimes necessary for very small children to sleep with their parents when they are frightened or ill, but when the child enters the oedipal period it is better for him to sleep in his own bed unless, of course, he is seriously ill. A night or two in bed with mother and father does no harm under those conditions.

Mothers should not permit their little boys to watch them dress and undress or bathe, or sleep with them all night when the father is away. Warm embraces at bedtime and on other occasions are necessary and important so that the little boy can experience his male sexuality and love, but these encounters must not be too prolonged and they should never be associated with behavior on the mother's part which leads the child to conclude that he has a special place with his mother to the exclusion of his father.

The parents should not conceal their affection for each other but, at the same time, excessive displays of romance such as embracing, fondling, etc. between his mother and father can dampen a small boy's spirit. A boy's father should try to balance the boy's interest in his mother by spending time with him, teaching him how to do things, and by taking him with him whenever possible. It is also important that the boy, mother, and father do things together; this permits the boy to discover that there is a way for him to be together with his mother *and* father without the inclusion of his romantic and erotic interests in his mother occupying the forefront of his attention. During his struggles with his ''love affair'' the boy's mother and father must stand by him as tolerantly and solidly as ever; this makes it possible for the boy to eventually discover that though his romance is a lost cause he has his mother and father as solid allies forever.

Another aspect of the boy's oedipal situation is the feeling he also has for his father. He loves his good father but unconsciously (and at times consciously) hates him to the extent that he wishes his father were dead so that he (the son) might have mother all to himself. Naturally, when filled by such strong hostility there is also a fear of retribution by his father. Strong fear and guilt form as a result of his erotic love for his mother and his love and hate for his father. It is the mixture of love and hate toward his father that is the primary source of guilt, the bulk of which becomes resolved in the course of time as he gives up his erotic longings for his mother. As these wishes disappear, so does the hate for the father, and with it the guilt goes too.

Associated with the hostility toward his father, the little boy develops a special type of fear about which there has been much speculation by psychiatrists regarding its origin.

Despite the absence of any such direct threat from his parents or other adults (some parents *do* make such threats) the boy develops the notion that because of his sexual interest in his mother his father would castrate him were he to find out. An incredible belief indeed, but one which probably exists in the unconscious minds of all boys. Boys do realize some people do *not* have a penis and testicles (women) and it is probable that their immature minds cause them to reason that someone removed them, possibly as a punishment. The castration fear can become quite intense in unfavorable family circumstances and, if not overcome, adds a powerful and harsh component to the child's developing conscience. His sense of fear and guilt may be quite profound and have serious consequences for his further development, as will be explained momentarily.

Having normal parents who are a regular part of his life, the boy gradually overcomes his oedipal wishes, guilt and fears, including his castration fear. Feeling secure (because his good mother from his earliest period of life lives on inside him) he will grapple with his feelings within himself and about his parents. By means of continuous interactions with his parents he will eventually discover that the only way out of his dilemma is to give up his mother as a romantic and sexual object. Good memories of the mother of the oedipal period are formed which reinforce earlier ones. Simultaneous with this realization the boy will have been strengthening his relationship with his father and overcoming his fears. The process of identification with his father now goes into full swing; the son will eventually become fully identified with his father and the world of men.

Coincidental with these realizations, he will have made new discoveries having to do with his father which are a source of deep satisfaction. His father will not have been standing idly by during this period. His father will have been forming a solid, enduring, and guiding relationship with him. The daily exposure to a man provides a powerful reinforcement to the boy's own sense of maleness, and through these experiences he acquires another loyal and ever present ally both within and outside himself. Eventually the good father will take his place by the good mother's side within the mind (personality) of the boy. The experiences between father and son can be magnificent indeed. It is difficult to put into words and adequately describe the process by which the father fills his little son's personality; that is, how the process of identification with the father takes place. There is a natural affinity between father and son which is loving but not romantic or erotic. In addition to the many times the boy observes his father from a distance and during his daily experiences with him by means of which he acquires some of his father's traits, values, and so on, there are special and exquisite moments (I am recalling experiences with my own three boys) which occur when father and son are alone together. During these fine moments good feeling passes between them, but much more occurs; the one personality—spirit if you will—passes into the other. The father fills his son with his spirit. A stillness comes for a moment or two; the transcience of life may be apparent, but at the same time there is a sense of permanence. The father is taking his place within the personality of the son; he will remain there forever. This process by which the father is incorporated into the personality of the son is a continuous process, but when father and son share special experiences, such as working together, good conversation, climbing a mountain together, etc., the process is rapid and intense. As you can see, it is imperative that father and son know each other. This cannot happen unless they spend time together, and a lot of it. Physically, the father will someday be gone, but he will live on indefinitely in the personality of his son and stand by him solidly like a rock.

The boy is willing to pay a price for such experiences with his father, the price being the giving up of his romantic interests in his mother. Son and father are no longer divided by the woman. All three are now together in ongoing life and father and mother exist side by side within the personality of the son. He has now acquired two strong and faithful internal allies who will stand by him the remainder of his life. He has set sexuality aside for the time being. When he is older, and physically and psychologically mature, he will find a woman of his own. With the firm backing of both of his parents (within him) he will succeed in forming a loving, sexual, and fully committed relationship with a woman.

During the processes of giving up his romantic and sexual attachment to his mother and identifying with his father the boy's castration fears will gradually die out. With his sexual interest in his mother rapidly disappearing, the basis for his castration fear has been removed. As a consequence of such a fortunate resolution of his oedipal situation the boy does not form a severe conscience.

His behavior will be more in keeping with his own conscious wishes and needs and the expectations of the environment rather than the demands of a tyrannical conscience.

It can be clearly seen what a vital influence the father is during the early years of a boy's life. There is no adequate substitute for a good father during this period. Good fathering requires effort and time. A quick hello, a few minutes or an hour a day with the son is woefully inadequate. Father and son need to *know* each other and discover the rewards of being together, and particularly of cooperation with each other. A father should take his son with him when running errands, etc., with, and at times without, the mother being along. Father should teach son elemental skills required for life, thus increasing his capacity for mastery. They should play together as well as work together. They should be close friends, but the father-son distinction should never be lost.

Father will, by necessity, be an authority figure who establishes rules and sets limits. The boy will discover that it is to his advantage to live by these, and he will realize that his father's rules are not unreasonable and that his own effectiveness in society will be greater if he lives by his parents' rules. These remarks should be understood in the context of each person's uniqueness, that is, the degree of parental authority offered by healthy parents leaves ample room for the son to find ways for fully expressing his own personality.

In those circumstances where the son may have been endowed with talents or intelligence greater than the father's (or mother's) or where the environment offers opportunities which were unavailable to the parents, both parents should encourage their child to go on to greater heights. A good father (or mother) will never be jealous or envious of the son's greater abilities or opportunities; rather, he will take pride in them and help his son reach these greater heights.

During the oedipal period when the boy will be experiencing intense competitiveness toward him, the father should never fall into the trap of responding in kind. Instead he will show the boy that he wants him to go as far as he can and that he, the father, will help him get there. There is no basis for competition between them. In short, a successful resolution of the oedipal situation, which includes the boy's identification with his father (father's masculinity), does *not* mean the boy will limit his level of achievement in adult life to that of his father. Quite the opposite is true. Because the father and son are not competitors, since there is no (or very little) guilt and fear in the boy toward his father, the boy is free to progress as far as his natural and acquired abilities can take him; he will feel the reassuring presence of his loving father inside of him for the rest of his life.

It is one of the marvels of nature how the boy will, under proper conditions, ultimately identify with his father instead of his mother when he has been reared by normal parents. He also acquires other human qualities from his father besides a reinforcement for his biological masculinity. Courage, fairness, gentleness, strength, integrity, etc., are taken on from the father too, but there are certain other very special qualities which he should develop from his relationship with his father. From his strong father he will learn how to stand firm when it is necessary, how to be masterful. The mother encourages him on to mastery and the father teaches him how; from both he acquires the strength to stand firm, to take a position; to be committed.

From having been reared in this way, and as a result of having witnessed the daily living patterns of his parents, he will have seen his father in the rightful place of every married man—at the head of the family. He will have seen the mutual respect and love between his parents and he will recognize that father had the final responsibility for the family and that he was the final authority. Boys who have been reared in an ideal family never fear women, or other men for that matter; they can form intimate and fully satisfying heterosexual relationships and they can enter into cooperative relationships with men. They can form strong bonds with other men because they not only have no fear of men but there are no unconscious hostile, competitive, or homosexual fears they must guard against by remaining distant from other men.

ABNORMAL OEDIPUS COMPLEX SOLUTIONS IN THE BOY

It can easily be imagined that the physical absence of a good father during the years three to six (and later) can have far-reaching effects. Fathers die, are sent to war, are taken away excessively by their work responsibilities. If the boy is fortunate enough to have a good mother she will not attempt to make up for the absent father by intensifying her relationship with her son. She will, instead, attempt to find substitute fathers for her boy and manage her own needs for a man in her life in a way which is appropriate to her own life situation. Boys with mothers like this tend to do rather well if they have some exposure to good men. Often a grandfather, uncle, neighbor, teacher, etc., will be having a much greater effect on such a boy than they or others realize. Boys with absent fathers soak up the attention and interest of men who are not their fathers. Mothers without husbands should always encourage such relationships for their sons.

The worst thing that can happen to a boy (and girl, which I will discuss later) is to have a passive, effeminate, and ineffectual father who either overtly or unconsciously hates, rejects, and competes with him and who is dominated by his wife, as all such men are. It is this marital pattern which I truly believe is the primary pollutant of the human spirit of the couple themselves and particularly of the children who are born into such families. The consequences for mankind are extreme. The marvelous experiences which characterize good family life are denied the children. Instead of gradually giving up his mother as a romantic and sexual love object, the son will be driven even closer to her by his hostile and rejecting father. His mother will gladly comply with his needs, for in addition to some degree of natural protectiveness which she may have for her son, she can fulfill her own needs for closeness to another human being by means of her son. Furthermore, she may cling to him as if he were a possession, even a part of her body. Women who marry effeminate and/or passive men have never fully developed their femininity; they may be colorless and inhibited, or more often are aggressive, domineering, and often masculinized. Some may seem feminine but this is usually a sham for they may be skillful manipulators or they may be frightened little girls. These women often use their sons as a substitute husband of sorts. Their possessive and dominating behavior with their sons provides them with the opportunity to subtly emasculate the male even though they are their own sons. As was noted earlier, such women always unconsciously (and sometimes consciously) hate, envy and fear men. The boy has many strikes against him. In addition to the bad maternal influences of his infancy period, there is no way he can resolve his oedipal situation and rapidly forming oedipal complex.

The boy's castration anxiety will never be extinguished nor will his strong erotic attachment to his mother. He will sense his father's hatred for him, a perception which, along with his castration anxiety, will cause him to fear men for the rest of his life. He will form a tyrannical, harsh conscience and a warped personality. Thus the absence of a genuinely feminine mother early in life, who should have filled him with self-confidence, courage, and trust, plus his excessively close tie with his domineering and probably somewhat masculinized (phallic) mother will inhibit him further. In addition to these factors, the presence of a hostile, rejecting, passive father who fails to provide a strong male identification object forces the boy to become passive and/or feminine in his personality makeup. There is no alternative but to remain tied to his mother and thus he is forced into submissive identification with his mother. He may show some elements of her aggressive personality but more commonly he will be passive. He will also internalize his passive father, but instead of having acquired an ally who stands beside him he will have acquired a second enemy within (the first being his mother), both of whom constantly threaten him and make him a frightened, ineffectual male. Passive and/or effeminate men always have an unconscious unbroken romantic and sexual tie to their mothers. As you can see, there are vast empty places in the personalities of boys who have been reared in families like these. Lacking are the encouraging, good and bountiful mother, the good, loving and strong father with whom he eventually identifies, and the memories of happy family life wherein the father was the head of the family, and so on. These empty places have great relevance for self-help endeavors and for psychiatric treatment, as I will show. These basic deficiencies must be comprehended and dealt with in order for self-help or for treatment to be successful.

VARIATIONS IN THE CHILDHOOD DEVELOPMENT OF BOYS

I have described two opposites in child development, one ideal and the other extremely abnormal. What follows are brief descriptions of some modifications in these extremes.

The most common form of childhood development of boys is where both parents are reasonably normal but where both are also burdened by some degree of neurosis, that is, unconscious conflicts of their own. The mother may not have become masculinized but is only unsure of her feminine identity, her role as a new mother, and her responsibilities. The father may have some residual castration anxiety and oedipal conflicts in his unconscious mind. He may be only mildly passive, or he may be quite masculine but may tend to avoid his family responsibilities, in particular his relationship to his son. Sometimes the father is quite normal but circumstances may take him away excessively, as is frequently the case with hard-working and successful professionals, businessmen, and military personnel. In family constellations like these the child may resolve his oedipal situation to some degree; however, there will remain some attachment to the mother. Castration anxiety is never completely extinguished, guilt is somewhat excessive, and identification with the father is never fully achieved. An inhibited masculinity is frequently the result. Efforts at mastery are always attended by anxiety. Success may be achieved in life but with greater effort and more anxiety than necessary.

Boys who never fully resolve their oedipal situation and who do not overcome the associated castration anxiety experience difficulty cooperating with others. For them cooperation means personal submission, an experience which (in their view) confirms their passivity and violates their sense of maleness. They resent, and find it difficult to accept, suggestions, advice, or help from their fathers or other men. To do so is to admit weakness, smallness, and accept submission. Such boys are constantly at war with themselves. They continue to strive for the full expression of their masculinity and potentialities and abilities but they cannot do so because of their unconscious conflicts.

The effects on the development of a boy when the mother is

remote or absent vary, depending on the time in the child's life when the influence of the mother is removed. If the mother dies or deserts the boy in his first few years of life he will suffer from lowered courage and self-confidence. Others, including the boy's father, can make up the deficit to some degree but these influences can never equal what the natural and feminine mother can provide. These boys will find it difficult to love a woman and may suffer sexual disturbances. To be able to experience intimacy as an adult depends upon having experienced closeness to a feminine mother.

If the mother disappears during the height of the oedipal period of the child's life, resolution of this conflict becomes impaired or impossible. The child retains his unconscious ties to his mother. There invariably is a depressive cast to his personality resulting from the loss which he usually fails to mourn. If he is fortunate enough to have continued to have a loving masculine father in his life, his male identification will take place but he will not be fully prepared to form a heterosexual relationship when he reaches manhood. Substitute mothers provide some opportunity for such a boy to work out his oedipal conflicts but I doubt is this is ever done fully. The consequences on a boy's life of the loss of a mother who dies during the oedipal period (if she was a feminine woman) are different from those if the mother deserted him. Mothers who desert their children by simply walking off, or through divorce, have invariably had a negative impact on their children from birth on. In some instances the boy is better off if such a mother does disappear; to continue to fall under her influence does more harm than having a substitute mother who may be more feminine and loving. The point here is that women who do not succeed at marriage have usually failed as mothers to some degree.

There is a difference in women and their effects on their sons (and daughters) between those who are forced by circumstances to work outside the home soon after the birth of their child and women who voluntarily go to work. The latter group uses work as an escape from their maternal responsibilities. Ideally, such women should be helped so that they can stay at home and be mothers. When this is not possible, it is probable that the child is better off with a surrogate mother than to be exposed all day to a mother who neglects it or is anxious, irritable, or depressed while attempting to carry out her maternal responsibilities.

SOME CONSEQUENCES OF ABNORMAL DEVELOPMENT IN BOYS

It is a marvel that boys who grow up in seriously disturbed family circumstances ever succeed in life upon reaching adulthood. Those who do usually have had parents who were not extreme in their own character pathology. Many do fail in one way or another, as will be described in the section on why people fail. One thing is certain, such men make poor husbands and fathers; many should not be fathers. This may seem like a harsh statement but after having seen, over the course of twenty-five years, the effects of such men (and the women they marry) on their children I am completely committed to the view that they should not be parents. There will come a day when parenthood will become a privilege and not a right.

Men who have had childhoods of the kind I have just described nearly always marry dominant and aggressive women if they marry at all, or they may become homosexual. It would matter less what kind of woman they married if they did not have children. I have known couples who were not mature men and women as I have defined them who worked out a satisfactory marital arrangement and who had the sense to recognize their inability to ever be good parents. I admire such people who have the strength of will to avoid bringing children into the world. They choose a variety of occupations; some are ballet dancers, others become hairdressers, designers of clothing (and they defeminize the clothing of women and feminize the clothing of men), often they work with food. If well endowed intellectually, and if they are exposed to an intellectual environment, they tend to choose the humanities, the social sciences, psychology, philosophy, art, and so on instead of the hard sciences and professions where they must be precise, committed, authoritative, and responsible to a high degree. There are exceptions, of course.

After having chosen these professions or vocations, some of

these individuals do mature as a result of their exposure to the responsibilities associated with work, and with family life if they marry. This can happen if the family patterns in which they were reared were not too pathological and if in the course of their lives they were fortunate enough to be associated with friends and associates who matured them; that is, from whom they received part of what they missed out on as children.

One cannot infer with certainty the nature of a person's early childhood by the kind of life's work chosen; however, the trend I described is there, and quite definitely so. As an example, pilots, whose responsibilities are great, who must be precise, committed and courageous, have different personalities, as far as I have been able to tell, from many of the men who choose psychiatry, psychoanalysis, psychology and social work where there is ample room for tentativeness, less demand for accountability for their actions, and a high degree of personal safety. Weak men cannot survive as pilots or in other exacting professions and occupations.

THE GIRL'S OEDIPAL PERIOD

Good mothering is as essential for the girl as for the boy. Having had good mothering during the first three years of her life, the little girl can, like the boy, face subsequent developmental stages and later life with courage, trust, and self-confidence. The obvious should be stated: a fully feminine mother values a little girl as highly as she values a boy. This estimation of femininity will be transmitted from mother to child in a number of overt and subtle ways from birth on. The little girl will gradually achieve a psychological separation from her mother but will continue to internalize her good mother just as the boy does. Both boy and girl may resent weaning but the other gratifications mother provides and her tactful, nontraumatic (gradual) method of weaning will prevent it from being a trauma in the life of the child.

Like the boy, the girl will experience certain sexual excitations in relation to her mother as a consequence of the care she receives, but these experiences are of minor importance if the mother is a good feminine mother. As her oedipal period approaches she will become increasingly aware of her lack of a penis. This will cause her to turn away from her mother angrily, for she will blame her mother for her *presumed* defect. These thoughts are mostly unconscious but the effects of the little girl's awareness of her lack of a penis and the associated resentment can be far-reaching as I will explain in the chapter on career women. This fact may seem farfetched to you and, of course, masculinized women and the more militant members of the women's liberation movement hotly contest this phenomenon in girls. But the fact remains. For a time the little girl believes her father may give her what she is missing. This expectation, too, is sooner or later doomed to disappointment.

At about the same time the little girl's femininity causes her to become erotically and romantically attracted toward her father, for whom she develops a deep attachment. She is now confronted with complicated developmental challenges during the period from age two-and-one-half or three to six. During this period her hostility toward her mother has two roots; she blames her for her lack of male genitals, and she is her rival for father's affections. Recall how little girls play mother with dolls and how ardently they become mother's little helper when a new baby arrives. What is not so obvious is the wish in their unconscious minds to have a baby by their father; the wish for a baby from her father replaces her wish for a penis. This progression is normal and is evidence of the blossoming female in the little girl. It is important for the father to ignite these wishes in the little girl but he should never be seductive toward his daughter so as to fan these fires too much. Just as a seductive mother who forms too intimate a relationship with her son has a bad effect on him, so too does a seductive father have a bad effect on his daughter. Such fathers usually do not have a fully satisfying marital relationship with their wife. Eventually the little girl must face many disappointments; she is denied a penis, a baby, and her father's romantic love. These are bitter disappointments for her to overcome. A happy outcome for her depends on both a feminine mother and a masculine father who have a solid marriage.

Mother and father will stand by her reassuringly if they are mature. Mother's appreciation of her own femininity and the world of women begins to have its effect on the girl. Father's respect for the mother, his love for her, and his high estimation of females in general reinforces the little girl's appreciation of her own gender. The girl realizes she cannot drive a wedge between her parents and finally she no longer wishes to do so. Her identification with her mother proceeds smoothly and she will become a feminine woman. She will internalize good memories of her strong father, who loved her and regarded her so highly and protected her, but she will not identify with him, just as a normally developing boy will not identify with his mother although he retains loving and reassuring memories of her within him. The girl unconsciously will come to realize that she will have to delay finding a male and that her baby will come from her relationship with him. A girl who develops normally will be able to love a man, experience intimacy with him, cooperate with him, and experience orgasm as a consequence of sexual intercourse. She will be a fine wife and mother when her time comes.

THE EFFECTS OF POOR MOTHERING AND POOR FATHERING ON THE GIRL

The little girl whose mother is absent or who rejects her or deprecates her, overtly or covertly, must find security somewhere. Such mothers are usually domineering, aggressive women, or may be neurotically inhibited. The girl may be fortunate enough to have another woman near her, or if her father is present she will inevitably turn to him for the nurture she should be receiving from her mother.

The husbands of such women inevitably take over some of the mothering of the child out of a sense of compassion for their child. This usually begins when the little girl is quite small. Sometimes men do this because of their identification with their own mother. They find a part-time maternal role more comfortable than paternal responsibilities. Finding most of her security from the father early in life instead of from the mother introduces a serious complication into the development of the girl. Instead of being filled with a good mother who forms the basis for her courage and self-confidence, the small child takes in a poor substitute (the father) and one which, along with the influence of the imperfect family in which she will grow up, will prevent her from developing a self-confident feminine personality. Instead of having a good mother inside, which forms the foundation upon which all else in her personality and life will be built, there is a male there—and usually a weak one at that.

Later, during the oedipal phase when the little girl's romantic and erotic sexual interests for her father appear, this early attachment and internalization of her father is powerfully reinforced (the mechanism of which I will soon describe), the combined effects of which lead to a very profound "father complex" and frequently a masculine identification which is extremely difficult for the girl to overcome. The resolution of her very early and her oedipal attachment to her father is virtually impossible because of the personality of her mother—that is, her rejection of her own feminine identity (or inability to fully express it) and of her maternal responsibilities. Mothers like this who are inhibited or domineering and aggressive and/or withdrawn and remote, do not draw the little girl into the world of women, and they provide a very unsuitable model for the child as a person with whom she can identify. Some identification does take place, and this complicates matters even more; the little girl now adds unfeminine or aggressive and domineering qualities to her personality.

It can be said with complete certainty that when a girl does not overcome her penis envy, her oedipal attachment to her father, and her identification with him, she lacked the courage to do so because she failed to receive adequate mothering from the beginning of life onward. Persistent penis envy and masculine identification of any significance is always associated with an unbroken erotic tie with the father and some degree of identification with him. Had the girl been filled with more courage, and had her parents been mature (fully feminine and masculine) and fully committed to each other in a satisfying relationship, she would have discovered that her best solution lay in becoming fully female. It may come as a surprise to you, but it can be said with absolute certainty that women who do not overcome their penis envy and their identification with their father are basically afraid to be female and are, therefore, afraid of an intimate relationship with men. Guilt, too, plays a role in their turning away from femininity. Their guilt derives from the oedipal period when mother was a hated and feared rival and competitor.

Women whose childhood development followed the line I have just described are always divided within themselves. They are biologically female, they have gotten just enough from their environment to develop some degree of femininity but they did not get the adequate mothering that makes it possible for them to become fully feminine and mature women. Some girls retreat entirely from the challenges of the oedipal period and revert into a dependent tie with their mother and remain infantile and sexless adult women; others, of course, become very masculinized.

Women whose childhood development did not proceed along reasonably normal lines are destined for much trouble in their later lives. Psychiatric problems may appear during childhood; however, the most common times of disturbances are at puberty and when they attempt to marry, and especially when they become mothers. Some become homosexual. Frigidity is a common problem, orgasm sometimes being possible by some form of genital stimulation other than through sexual intercourse. They have difficulty getting along with other women. Their marriages often fail because they compete with and diminish their husbands and cannot experience closeness with them. Some never do marry, avoiding men altogether; others have repeated affairs and may eventually marry only to have the marriage fail. They choose men who are weak, passive and ineffectual when they are able to relate to men. Some who do marry and have children fail miserably as mothers; they tend to feel well until their baby is born and suffer depression or some other form of illness after its birth. The sense of loss is great after the baby's birth, as is the guilt about their rejection of the baby, or their effort to be a mother. For them the baby is a forbidden product of ''incest.''

Many women choose careers, often selecting those usually filled by men. I think it is quite probable that the so-called ''liberation'' so many women are seeking actually reflects a flight from the responsibilities only a woman can discharge, hence women's liberation attracts many of these women. Worst of all, if they do marry and have children they perpetuate their illness onto the next generation. It is tragic that such women ever become mothers. Life begins with the mother and its ultimate outcome for men and women alike rests to a large extent squarely upon that foundation of courage and confidence, of real solidity which *only* a good mother can provide. The evidence for this assertion is overwhelming.

THE EFFECTS OF ABSENT FATHERS ON LITTLE GIRLS

When a little girl has a good, feminine mother but loses her father during her oedipal years her future growth is complicated. Unless there is an older brother or some other adult male in or around the family she will be denied the impact of a powerful growth-promoting stimulus. Her sexual instincts will not have been evoked by a male and as a consequence she will not be fully prepared for a close heterosexual relationship as an adult. In families where there was a father but one whose work responsibilities took him away excessively, the maturation of a girl is somewhat impaired. The presence of a strong father provides the security for the girl to develop her femininity.

SIBLINGS

I do not intend to discuss the effects siblings have upon one another in much detail. The term "sibling rivalry" is well known and derives in part from the competition between siblings for the attention of their parents. Siblings compete with each other in terms of who can outdo the other. On the other hand, strong bonds between siblings add to the family spirit and family unity. It is especially important that girls are made to realize that they are just as important as their brothers but that they are different.

Play among sibs and other children often provides a proving or testing ground for some of the emotions which children feel toward their parents but cannot express. Sex explorations between brother and sister are harmless if not excessive. Little girls often play out their maternal instinct with a new baby in the family. Such an arrival provides a convenient substitute for the baby the little girl would like to have gotten from her father. Wise and feminine mothers will permit a little girl to help with the new baby but will, at the same time, respond to the girl in such a way as not to impair her further growth. It is a crushing blow to a little girl to be reared in a family where males are more highly valued than females. Fathers and mothers should pay equal attention to boys and girls.

ADOLESCENCE

During adolescence parents have an opportunity to undo some of the damage that was done during the child's first six years of life. Some parents mature as time passes; these are the ones who can take corrective steps. Those parents who have not improved will merely reinforce the damage that was done earlier.

With the coming of adolescence, the complexes which formed in early life become activated within the unconscious mind. The parent must move quickly and skillfully for part of normal adolescence is the breaking of family ties and eventually a physical separation from the home.

Stated as concisely as possible, fathers and sons have a second chance to find each other, thereby establishing or rounding out the boy's masculine identification while at the same time breaking the remaining unconscious erotic attachment to the mother. Girls and their mothers have the same opportunity. The parents must take the lead. The children will not, for their natural tendency is to break away. The stronger must always lead the weaker in life.

CHAPTER THREE

The Causes of

Failure and Illness

The principles which explain why people fail in life and why they become psychiatrically ill relate directly to the developmental processes which were discussed in the preceding chapter. Success implies finding a way to fully express one's capabilities and potentials, to be able to live by the dictates of reality, and to contribute constructively to life. There are certain times and certain situations which are commonly related to failure and to emotional illness. If you are aware of these you will be better able to recognize the signs of impending trouble in yourself and take the necessary steps to avert failure and/or a psychiatric illness. Those who did not grow up within an "ideal" family will be more vulnerable.

STRESS

The simplest reason for a mental breakdown is that which occurs when the environment is excessively stressful. Fatigue, overwork, and the stresses of warfare are examples. The human organism can be pushed so hard that it will begin to malfunction. Adequate rest and sleep, diversion and play, and good food are necessary for everyone. Equally important for emotional health is an environment which is nonhostile in the human sense, supportive, and rewarding. It is remarkable how certain strong individuals can withstand a harsh or hostile physical and emotional environment. However, sooner or later even the strongest will begin to fail or become psychiatrically ill if the stresses are severe enough. The human being, like all living things, must not be overstressed.

SQUARE PEG IN A ROUND HOLE

A second cause for failure may occur when a person is not equipped with the necessary skills, fund of information, talents, or basic temperament for certain kinds of tasks, life roles, etc. A psychiatric illness may result, or he may begin to function poorly and fail.

Economic conditions often force people into a work situation for which they are not equipped. Parents frequently pressure their children into vocations for which they are ill-suited. Promotions within organizations can suddenly place a man at a job for which he lacks basic skills. Many times people can adjust to situations for which they are basically ill suited but, even so, there usually is more strain in such a person's life than need be. Strain eventually takes its toll in the form of physical illness or emotional breakdown or both. It is a sad fact of life that many millions of men and women spend their entire lives at jobs they do not enjoy or at jobs which do not provide an opportunity to express their best personal qualities and abilities. It is very important for people to have an avocation which allows for the expression of their most basic talents and skills when their vocation does not.

UNCONSCIOUS FACTORS

Using my clinical practice as a gauge, I think the main reason people fail and/or become psychiatrically ill is not related to either stress or ill-suitedness. Instead, forces within the unconscious mind are the causes for the failure or illness. The environment plays a part in this but cannot be said to be the primary reason for the illness or failure. This is a difficult idea for some to grasp but this principle must be understood in order for the best possible solution to be found for the person who is beginning to fail or become ill. The unconscious forces to which I refer are the product of various kinds of faulty childhood development as outlined in the previous chapter. Abnormal childhood development leads to the formation of unconscious conflicts which are termed ''core'' or ''nuclear'' conflicts or complexes because of the time of life when they are formed and the pervasiveness of their effects. Core conflicts have powerful effects on personality and behavior and much of a person's outlook on life, the values he lives by, the nature of his likes and dislikes, his choices, his character and lifestyle. The most common unconscious conflicts are excessive dependency and separation anxiety, guilt, excessive and unextinguished castration anxiety in association with unresolved romantic and sexual attachment to the parent of the opposite sex, and penis envy (in women). Related to the latter two conflicts are conflicts which cause cooperation to be confused with submission. In association with the conflicts of any stage of psychological development there is hostility based on frustration of infantile wishes and the hostility toward the parent of the same sex arising out of the sexual attraction toward the parent of the opposite sex. These conflicts or complexes, and others, lie unresolved within the unconscious mind and function like chief executives issuing commands which distort the individual's view of life and prevent him from making it what it could be.

LIVING SUCCESSFULLY WITH
ONE'S CORE CONFLICTS AND COMPLEXES

Having acquired certain kinds of character traits and values which fall short of those of mature masculinity or femininity, and by living a style of life which is harmonious with those traits, a person may escape overt mental illness. This is an extremely important point to understand. For instance, a woman who never overcame her penis envy or her childhood romantic attachment to her father may function rather well in a career as long as she avoids attempting to form an intimate and/or lasting relationship with a man. So long as she avoids men her (core) conflicts can remain dormant in her unconscious mind. She may even substitute homosexual gratifications for heterosexual ones or she may avoid sexuality altogether. A man may remain symptom free (free of psychiatric illness) as long as he strives only for a modicum of success in his work rather than trying to get to the top. Some persons who are heavily burdened by unconscious conflicts may marry and effect a reasonably harmonious adjustment provided they pick a mate whose character structure blends with their own. For instance, an aggressive and dominant woman may pair off with a passive man and as long as they do not strive for the kinds of marital adjustments which characterize a healthy marriage as outlined in the chapter on the family they may remain relatively symptom-free. In other words, persons who are bedeviled by unconscious conflicts and the products of these in their personality do manage to find a "fit" in their occupations and interpersonal relationships of a kind which does not activate the core conflicts that are stored in their unconscious minds. These persons do not live as fully or richly as men and women can, but at least they achieve an equilibrium within themselves and with their environment. Millions of people must be living constricted lives and never fulfilling themselves. If these "fits" were never disturbed there would be far fewer mentally ill and obvious life failures.

For most people, however, life does not remain static; the "fits" they find in the environment become disturbed. There is an inner push, a physiological trend toward maturation in the first few decades of life. Such physiological changes can be seen most clearly in childhood, at puberty, and early adulthood. Social pressures of many kinds are brought to bear upon the individual which push him on to maturity. The most common of these pressures are those which bring the opposite sexes together. There is a natural attraction between male and female despite abnormal childhood development which may tend to keep them apart as adults and it is a social convention for the sexes to mate. There are unexpected promotions, and those which are struggled for. Men are suddenly confronted by unplanned military service which catapults them into positions of heavy responsibility. Society and Nature cause men and women to make families even when they are psychologically unsuited for such responsibilities. Some children are planned for; others are conceived because they are "supposed" to occur after marriage; some come by accident.

One way or another environmental forces eventually impinge on individuals and push them into ways of life which characterize greater maturity and a deeper involvement with and commitment to life. There usually is enough "health" within individuals to make them want and attempt to mature and live a more involved and committed life. The degree of health and strength within the individual determines how far he can advance without failing or becoming psychiatrically ill. However, this very process of deepening one's commitment to life in the direction of greater responsibility and maturity activates unconscious core conflicts which, in turn, cause people to fall ill or to fail. This is a fundamental principle.

THE ENVIRONMENT AS A TRIGGER OF
UNCONSCIOUS CONFLICTS: AN OVERVIEW

Adolescence and early adulthood have long been recognized as times in life when illness breaks out and personality begins to malfunction. The emotional strain causing this has several sources. There are hormonal changes which awaken sexuality. In addition to this source of pressure from within, the youth must begin to break his ties with his parents and, perhaps most significant of all, he begins his efforts at establishing a relationship with the opposite sex. There are usually new work responsibilities as well. The confluence of these pressures demands that the youth change in many ways. Close inspection will show that the new responsibilities and opportunities are not themselves overwhelming, that is, stressful. A new job usually is not so complex; a lovely girl friend is not a source of actual threat. Giving up one's childhood relationship to one's parents and anticipating leaving home or actually leaving home is cause for grief; however, this detachment is usually gradual.

The true sources of the young person's anxiety, depression, or more serious illness are the core conflicts within his unconscious mind; his efforts to involve himself more deeply with his environment trigger and activate these. The presence of the member of the opposite sex toward whom there is a romantic and sexual interest mobilizes or activates the repressed unconscious conflicts which are a residue of the unextinguished romantic and sexual interest once experienced by the child toward the parent of the opposite sex. Those romantic and sexual interests were forbidden and were associated with castration anxiety and guilt in relation to the father or, in girls, guilt in relation to the mother. The girl who is the object of the young man's interest is not, therefore, experienced as just a young woman. There may be an excessive awe felt for her, love far out of proportion to the situation, that is, inconsistent with the boy's knowledge of the girl's actual qualities. These are feelings which betray, along with his anxiety and/or other symptoms, the presence of unconscious conflicts.

Once having had their unconscious core conflicts awakened through their efforts to establish a heterosexual relationship, some young people retreat from such involvements permanently, some for long periods of time, and some persist in their efforts only to become seriously ill. Those young people who resolved their childhood romantic and sexual ties to their parents do not form core conflicts; they are successful in these efforts as young adults.

Those who are fortunate enough not to be too heavily burdened by unconscious conflicts and who possess greater strength of personality will persist in their efforts to form a heterosexual relationship and achieve success. Some persons level off at this point and live a pattern of repeated love affairs but are never able to take the next step into marriage. They may experience love for the opposite sex but promptly drive the other person away when marriage becomes a real possibility. Those persons who live such a life pattern choose lovers who themselves are not psychologically ready for a marital commitment. Frequently men and women who make a great public display of their romantic prowess do so for self-assurance but can never go further. The Don Juan (the man who continually searches for a new love affair), while perhaps momentarily fulfilling some woman's dream of the ideal lover, is incapable of going all the way into a permanent commitment to a woman. Unconscious conflicts are the primary cause of these life patterns.

The reader will note that life situations are described in an order which shows an increasing involvement with or commitment to some aspect of the environment. Such is the case when an individual progresses from a pattern of courtships to a marital commitment. Some people are not sufficiently burdened by unconscious conflicts to prevent them from having courtships and marrying or, if so burdened, their defense mechanisms are sufficiently strong to hold unconscious forces in place so as not to disturb their ability to function reasonably maturely.

Once marriage has occurred, many kinds of maladjustments and overt psychiatric illnesses may appear for the first time. Since persons who are burdened by unconscious conflicts tend to pick persons for mates who are also so burdened, the conflicts in the unconscious minds of both may get activated and mobilized by the intensification of their relationship which follows marriage. The point is that maladjustment, and certainly illness, is not caused by a lack of compatibility of interests but caused by the effort being made to live intimately (lovingly and sexually) with a person of the opposite sex. The unconscious conflicts and their representative character traits are the bases of the trouble. Couples in trouble often try to explain their marital disharmony as incompatibility. Actually, they may have a great deal in common, and love each other.

Many marriages fail at this point if the balance in one or both persons is greater toward sickness than health; that is, if the unconscious forces are great and get out of control. The troubled person does not realize that the true sources of his unhappiness, provocative ways, symptoms, etc., lie within himself. There are secondary factors that contribute to the failure of marriage. Provocative behavior, the roots of which are in the unconscious mind, evokes destructive reactions from the marital partner. This person, too, often shows provocative behavior of his own which evokes destructive reactions from the spouse. Whereas the couple was able to love each other freely before marriage, after marriage they will grow cold, unresponsive and aggravating toward each other. The marriage is then imperiled.

It sometimes happens that the awakened unconscious conflicts become silently resolved during these turbulent times. Once awakened and mobilized, mature forces within personality can have a neutralizing or resolving effect on them. This, of course, is the happy and desired outcome. Young married couples should never divorce immediately when trouble begins. They may resolve their unconscious conflicts through the process of living together. Unfortunately, many marriages end in divorce at this point.

A less favorable outcome, short of divorce, is one which leads to an empty life. Many married couples establish a safe emotional distance from each other, thus permitting their unconscious conflicts to recede further into the unconscious mind. They may rarely express love for each other; sex will be rare or perfunctory; each will cultivate his own interests, and so on. Any effort to reintensify and deepen their relationship will promptly awaken unconscious conflicts; symptoms may appear or, more commonly, the couple will begin to do battle again. Fighting creates emotional distance between them once more.

Some married couples achieve a happy relationship before their first child or subsequent children are born. The balance of health is generally greater in persons who have been able to reach this level of marital commitment without becoming ill or "incompatible." A new baby serves as a powerful maturational stimulus for both the woman and the man, more at first for the woman, or if the unconscious conflicts are mobilized, illness may result.

In the woman, unconscious conflicts which resulted from insufficient nurture by her own mother may be awakened by her attempts to nurture her infant. The new baby may awaken her early (oedipal) wishes to have received a child from her father; her difficulty caring for her child is caused by her unconscious belief that the child is the product of incest. Stated more precisely, her own child awakens her repressed wish to have had a child by her father. The guilt associated with this repressed (the process by which thoughts and feelings are kept in the unconscious mind) childhood wish prevents her from adequately caring for her baby. Regardless of the nature of the unconscious conflicts which are triggered by the birth of the child, it is these and not the child itself which are the bases for the illness and malfunctioning in the mother.

The young mother's efforts to live out her more feminine responsibilities will also trigger those early conflicts from her infantile and childhood period. In short, with the formation of a family a triangular situation (two parents and a child) will have been created; this constellation awakens the conflicts associated with the original childhood triangle. A woman with a new baby often pushes her husband away as if he were the forbidden (father) male, and the husband reacts with hurt and anger. Some women feel complete at last when they possess a child, particularly a boy child (the child makes up for her penisless state), and they may exclude their husbands from their lives.

Men react symptomatically to the coming of children too. Many cannot accept the responsibilities of parenthood. To do so means unconsciously taking the father's place; that is, the unconscious wish to destroy the father and take his place with mother has been reawakened by having become a parent. There are men whose unconscious sense of guilt associated with these conflicts is so great that they dissociate themselves nearly completely from their families. Some withdraw angrily from their wives because they receive less "mothering" when a child is born.

There is a sharp rise in the incidence of divorce after the coming of children. Breakdowns in family life are tragic, the consequences are far-reaching.

Work is another trigger which awakens unconscious conflicts. Interestingly, work outside the home is less a conflict trigger for women than for men. Work for women provides a means for escaping from the feminine responsibilities of homemaking, motherhood, and being in an intimate love and sex relationship with a man. These are the predominant conflict triggers for women. By working the woman creates environmental conditions which permit her unconscious to lie dormant (83). She will be successful unless her feminine and maternal urges are too strong. When this is so, work becomes less satisfying and she will seek a heterosexual relationship and try marriage and at this point begin showing signs of psychic distress. Sometimes the work situation will awaken unconscious conflicts too, particularly if she must work with other women. Unconscious conflicts formed in early life with the mother can be awakened by a female supervisor. Or a male supervisor may evoke a woman's competitiveness towards males.

Working recreates the role of the breadwinner for the male. Some men can work well provided they do not attempt to follow their father's vocation or profession. To attempt to do so recreates, symbolically, the early wish to take the father's place within the family by destroying father and possessing mother. This unconscious conflict may be so profound and pervasive that success of any kind is impossible. To succeed at anything amounts to doing something forbidden. It is remarkable how intensely anxious or disturbed some men become when they are on the brink of success or have succeeded. Some men may achieve minor successes but become increasingly disturbed as their promotions increase, even though they are perfectly competent and well-prepared for their new responsibilities. Many highly gifted, well-trained, and experienced men cannot function well when their level of success becomes too great, especially when their success threatens to push them into a top executive position.

Persons whose core conflicts have not been resolved often cannot remain symptom free in the presence of their parents. Young people usually try to avoid their parents as a means by which to permit their unconscious conflicts to recede more deeply into their unconscious. Some young people may place geographical distance between themselves and their parents, believing that to do so will lead to a greater degree of personal comfort. Some children never achieve a friendly adult relationship with their parents. For example, a man's unresolved attachment to his mother creates excessive discomfort within him when in her presence, and his hostility, fear of, and guilt toward his father precludes a friendly adult relationship with either of his parents. Furthermore, sons sometimes believe they are subjugating themselves and losing their individuality when they enter into a friendly adult relationship with their father. The same formulations apply to adult women and their mothers.

CASE EXAMPLES

What has been written can be made more vivid by means of brief case examples. These examples may help you detect signs in yourself and in your loved ones of failure and/or psychiatric disturbances and increase the likelihood of your taking the necessary steps to ensure success and/or freedom from illness. If suffering is excessive, or if there is clear evidence of failure, then get help. Do not let the forces of sickness run rampant and ruin life when good professional help might reverse the downward trend of your life. It is important for you to clearly understand the kinds of life circumstances in which illness and failure are most likely to occur.

Preadolescent Children

Many young children develop transient symptoms or even severe illnesses. These, of course, require as great care as those of adolescents and adults but there is a first rule for disturbed young children that must always be looked into. When a child becomes disturbed, look first at the parents and into the family situation. Straightening out the trouble there frequently leads to improvement in the child and even to recovery from illness. When improvement in the child does not result, then professional help should be sought for the child. I will not discuss the various forms of psychiatric disturbances young children are known to develop but, rather, limit myself to the statement that because a disturbed child nearly always reflects a disturbed environment, first look into his environment. Start with the home, then the school and other aspects of the child's environment. When correcting these external situations fails to lead to improvement in the child, then professional help should be sought. However, as I explain in the chapter on treatment, be very careful whom you choose to treat your child and to guide you in reordering your family life.

Adolescence

This is a difficult time in life for a variety of reasons. The ties to the parents are being broken, and new challenges face the young person in the world outside the home. The developmental challenge is the transition from boyhood to manhood, from girlhood to womanhood. It is not my intention to describe all of the myriad forms of upheaval young people may show during this period.

Instead, I will focus on the main causes of failure to adjust to life. Some young people cannot do well in school or will fail in their efforts to hold down a job; however, the main reason illness occurs in adolescence is the demand (biological, personal, and social) that sexual role definition occurs and that relationships with the opposite sex be established.

When family life has not led to the kind of experiences for the child which I described in an earlier chapter, young people have difficulty crystallizing their gender and sexual role and have trouble forming meaningful (meaning close and intimate) relationships with the opposite sex. Without the internal psychological conditions which good family life during infancy and childhood lead to, the individual is ill equipped to live up to the demands of a mature adjustment with a member of the opposite sex.

Case No. 1: A young girl seemed to be quite feminine during her infancy and early childhood. Her parents obviously loved her, but her mother was a cold person who, despite her attentiveness, could not give of herself freely and thus failed to provide the kind of nurture and mothering which instills a full measure of confidence in a growing child. As the girl approached puberty she tended to do more things with her father and, although she and her mother associated with each other, she tended to behave in a very dependent, little-girl manner with her mother. Her mother seemed to be unable to draw her into the world of women and infantilized her by doing too much for her, thereby preventing the girl from doing things for herself. The parents of this young girl did not have a happy marriage.

With the coming of puberty this girl began to change rather dramatically. She made no secret of the fact that she hated boys; her appearance became rather mannish. When her identification with her mother and the world of women should have been consolidating she clearly rejected this identity and identified more with her father. She became overtly homosexual in her mid-teens and remained so. Her character style (mannishness) and her way of life were ways of avoiding a mature heterosexual adjustment. She avoided boys, although for a very brief period was interested in older men or very passive young males. When she made the effort to date men, which she did only a few times, she became intolerably anxious and took flight back into homosexuality. She became a career woman and a confirmed homosexual. In the hands of a very skilled doctor her life would have turned out differently; without such help she will never change.

Case No. 2: This young woman, one of two children, was a normal-appearing young child. Her father was a passive man and a problem drinker but successful at his work. When she was very small she seemed to derive more comfort and nurture from her father than from her mother. An aggressive woman, her mother was always active and busy with community affairs, openly demeaning her husband throughout the girl's early life. A brother was born when the girl was five years old. At the age of eleven or twelve the patient became extremely rebellious. Although promiscuous with boys, she could never form an enduring relationship with a boy. While still in her teens she entered into an overt homosexual way of life, rejected offers of help, and eventually became a confirmed homosexual. She will never change but has instead aligned herself with the gay liberation movement.

Case No. 3: This patient was described as a beautiful infant and a feminine little girl. Graceful and likable, she performed well in school and in dancing. Her outgoing personality caused her to be very popular through high school. Her father was a very weak man who lacked the capacity to be an authority figure; her mother was dissatisfied with her role as a woman. At age fourteen the patient became enamored of a much older man and went so far as to sleep with him. She could not date boys her own age. In college she had affairs with much older men but finally settled into an overt homosexual way of life. She had previously associated with a series of extremely unsuitable men, being capable of nothing more than transient and meaningless affairs, a pattern which continues despite several attempts at treatment.

The mothers of all three of these young women had had greatest difficulty fulfilling their roles as mature women, mothers, and wives. Of equal importance is the fact that the fathers were weak, passive men. Having grown up in such families, these girls could not develop in a way which permitted them to become self-confident and feminine, and capable of forming meaningful relationships with the opposite sex. Their efforts to do so triggered their unconscious conflicts, forcing them to flee from heterosexual relationships and accept a homosexual way of life. Take special note of this family pattern. Wherever it exists the children from such a marriage inevitably have some form of psychiatric disturbance.

Case No. 4: This was a young man whose father was very successful but who had little time for his son. The patient's mother was flamboyant, emotionally expressive, and a domineering woman. Although the patient admired his father he was much closer to his mother throughout his early life. Though he was a somewhat sickly child he was never seriously ill emotionally. During his late teens he became intensely interested in a young woman, and began drinking excessively. Every time he became involved with women his drinking became worse, and eventually he became severely alcoholic. He eventually found his way into treatment but the outcome was poor. He did marry but the marriage collapsed after children were born.

Case No. 5: This man grew up in a family where the father was a hard-working, conscientious and successful man, but one who was distant from his family. As a result the patient never had a close relationship with his father. He was very close to his mother, however, and spent a great deal of time with her throughout his growing up years. He observed a constant antagonism between his parents. He was popular in school, did well and achieved certain goals, being spurred on by his mother without his father's involvement. He first noticed psychiatric symptoms when he attempted to form relationships with women. The more determined his efforts became to succeed in his relationships with women, the more severe his symptoms became. These included anxiety, depression, somatic complaints, and impotence. He has never been able to form a successful heterosexual relationship despite treatment.

Case No. 6: This patient was a young man in his early twenties who complained of never being able to sustain a relationship with a girl. He became so desperate that he sought psychiatric treatment for this problem.

When he was a boy he had exhibited many signs of insecurity. His parents never got along. His father was an alcoholic and his mother was excessively possessive of the child. A bed wetter until puberty, the boy, nevertheless, had a successful school adjustment. After he left home for college he began to date but conducted himself so ineptly with girls that they all left him. He became depressed and sought psychiatric help. He has never overcome his impotence but after several years of treatment he found a woman who was willing to marry and do without sex. This man could be helped but he "chose" to settle for less in life.

Case No. 7: This patient showed signs of psychiatric disturbance from early life on; his symptoms included enuresis and nightmares. His father was successful but a remote person in the home and a man who was dominated by his wife. The patient's mother could not function as a mother to him during the first few years of his life but later developed a very close relationship with him. With the arrival of puberty the patient began drinking heavily, got into physical fights with his father, and could not successfully date girls. After several years of a marginal adjustment he began to date a woman several years older than himself and promptly began drinking heavily and deteriorated severely in his overall life adjustment. His treatment failed and he eventually committed suicide.

The case examples are of young men who had not resolved their unconscious romantic and erotic attachment to their mothers. Their mothers had been too close to them, their fathers were weak or remote, or both. Some of these mothers were seductive and possessive. When these boys entered adolescence they could not, in a figurative sense, distinguish a girl friend from their mother. The effort to find closeness with a girl awakened (triggered) the unconscious unresolved erotic ties to the mother, the associated guilt and fear of the father; thus the only thing to do was to take flight from the girl in one of several ways.

Case No. 4 forced himself to marry, but doing so triggered his conflicts even more and his marriage failed. He resorted to alcohol. Case No. 5 avoided the opposite sex forever. Case No. 6 found a young woman to marry who was willing to do without sex. Case No. 7 acted out his unconscious conflicts by physically fighting his father and dating older women. His desperation finally drove him to suicide.

Aside from the personal suffering all of these examples experienced, such individuals, and there must be hundreds of thousands just like them or worse, become somewhat of a liability to society. This is not meant to sound harsh or critical for these are sick people who need and deserve treatment. Men and women like these, who eventually marry, perpetuate their parents' family pattern by way of their own personalities and those of their spouses.

These are but a few examples of hundreds I could give where signs of psychiatric illness first became evident with the coming of puberty and the associated effort to form a close relationship with a member of the opposite sex. It is true that there are many new demands falling on the shoulders of the teen-ager, and often no single factor can be identified as the basis for the outbreak of an illness. Simply leaving home can trigger an illness; I will discuss this under the heading of "loss." Sometimes it is a combination of factors, such as having to shoulder the responsibilities associated with an independent existence; I will discuss this under the heading of "work." However, the most common precipitant for an illness in the teen-ager and young adult, in my experience, is his effort to form a relationship with the opposite sex. This effort activates his unconscious conflicts which are the true basis for his trouble.

You will have noticed, I am sure, that the family patterns of the patients referred to in the preceding vignettes were far from ideal. Had the fathers of these young people been strong men and the heads of their families, and had their mothers not been dominant and so aggressive and/or so ineffectual in the mothering role, these people would never have become patients because they would never have formed the unconscious (core) conflicts which later made them ill.

Many young people who were reared in less than ideal family circumstances do form relationships with the opposite sex. However, they tend to pick mates who blend with their own disturbances. Passive boys choose aggressive girls or, more commonly, aggressive girls pick passive males. That is, the girl takes the initiative. Those incapable of really close relationships with the opposite sex choose partners or mates who are agreeable to a distant relationship. Their conflicts continue to lie dormant under these conditions. Some make relationships with the opposite sex in a way which poses no threat. This can be seen most clearly in persons who experience sex role blurring. Relationships often remain platonic. There are relationships of love but no sex, or it is all sex but no love. In the unisex type of relationship, the relationship possesses some aspects of humanness, but it is neutered so that gender and sexuality hardly enter into the picture at all. Sexual differences and interpersonal commitments are less, and as a consequence unconscious conflicts remain untriggered, with the result that these persons experience less anxiety or other disturbing symptoms.

Some avoid the opposite sex for life. They may date but never marry, or they may be entirely celibate. Some persons take flight from heterosexual relationships and enter homosexual relationships as a consequence of their first brush with heterosexuality.

The point to be grasped is that when a young man and woman form a relationship this should be a step toward a richer and more rewarding life. When young people avoid the opposite sex, or when they develop emotional disturbances as an outcome of their efforts to form a heterosexual relationship, unconscious conflicts are present which have been triggered by the closeness to the member of the opposite sex. These conflicts produce the psychiatric symptoms. When a young person has not resolved his or her unconscious romantic and erotic attachment toward the parent of the opposite sex, he or she cannot form a successful heterosexual relationship because, in effect, that person cannot distinguish the ongoing relationship from the past. Sometimes a succession of courtships will promote a conflict-resolving process; maturational processes are set into motion thereby and the individual can eventually make a permanent heterosexual commitment.

When parents notice their children failing in their efforts to form heterosexual relationships they should intervene. To form them is normal; not to do so is abnormal. This sounds as if I am saying everyone should marry; this is not so. However, many young people can be helped if help is received soon enough.

When a young girl becomes masculine or extremely prim in her character style, or shows other signs of a rejection of femininity, this is a sure sign that she is in psychiatric trouble. If she has only girl friends and/or picks older women for her friends, especially if these women are somewhat masculine, parents should be alerted to possible trouble in their daughter. Discovering their daughter to be homosexual is cause for great alarm, for homosexuality is a major psychiatric illness which requires the most expert treatment. Do not listen to educators and mental health professionals who say homosexuality is normal. It is not; it is a manifestation of illness.

Boys who fail to date and who have only males for friends, or who have no friends at all, are usually in psychiatric trouble. It is good for boys to have strong bonds with other boys, but when they avoid relationships with girls something is wrong with them. Effeminacy in an adolescent boy is evidence that he is not developing as he should. Young men and women frequently use drugs as a means for quieting the anxieties which are aroused by their attempts to form a relationship with the opposite sex. Drug usage is, of course, cause for great alarm and immediate intervention. There are many other signs of illness young people show. When these appear, inquire into how they are progressing in their heterosexual relationships. The cause of the trouble will frequently be found there.

I think parents should oppose group living arrangements where young couples of both sexes live together. Such arrangements are compromises between no heterosexual relationship and a fully committed one. I do not think these communal living arrangements are conducive to greater maturity. Instead, the arrangement provides a way out and permits only a partial fulfillment of what life has to give. Furthermore, children are born. Who will be their parents? Society can ill afford ever larger generations of children who will become psychiatrically crippled adults.

The trend in many young people toward drugs, non-commitment, "doing their own thing" is a gigantic example of human failure. Theirs is a protest against convention; it is not a constructive alternative to the ills of society but a self-defeating and destructive one. Their movement reflects disintegration, not evolution on to higher human values. Their advocacy of the use of drugs, their music, their heterosexual relationships (which are fluid, transient, uncommitted), are clear signs of personal psychiatric illness which is offered as a social norm. But these people cannot be blamed, for they are the product of family life and a society which ill prepared them for the responsibilities and rewards of a mature life. Understanding the causes of this phenomenon does not excuse it. Parents should take the strongest possible stand when they see their children enter into these ways of living.

Parents must take more responsibility for changing present trends in young people. Chances are you are now more mature than when your children were young and their personalities were forming. It may be too late to do much for your offspring in severe cases, but I am convinced that in millions of families the young are on a downhill course which could be reversed if the parents would intervene and offer help and guidance. Talk to your children, find out what is going on in their lives, and offer them guidelines. Don't be afraid to put your foot down. Listen, understand, but offer and insist your child follow better values. Don't be afraid to ask for professional help, but before you do read the chapter on how to find the right kind of help, and read the chapter on self-help.

Marriage

Many young men and women successfully manage courtship and are able to marry. To be able to do so usually reflects a greater degree of emotional health. Males and females were meant to mate, and when they do (marry) this can be taken as a sign of greater health. This is not always true, as some of the following vignettes will illustrate; however, the very fact that a couple can marry suggests both are capable of a deeper commitment to the opposite sex than those who cannot take this step. It is interesting to note that although many couples can carry on a courtship without either party's showing signs of a psychiatric disturbance, when they marry signs of illness soon appear. It is the deeper commitment in the relationship which triggers the unconscious conflicts in one or both. These are the ultimate bases for the symptoms and much of the marital discord which appears. Many couples attribute their trouble to incompatibility. They have put the cart before the horse; incompatibility follows on the heels of the bases for their trouble. These are unconscious conflicts.

Some couples are capable of marrying and remaining free of

psychiatric disturbances even though both are heavily burdened by unconscious conflicts. This can be explained in several ways. Although they are married, the relationship may not be very intimate or intense and thus unconscious conflicts are not triggered. Both may have been strong enough to keep unconscious forces in control. What is very common are those marriages where neurotic (unconscious) factors of the couple blend, the most common example being that of the aggressive, more dominant woman who marries a passive, weak male. As long as nothing upsets the balance of healthy and sick forces in each of the partners in relation to the other, the marriage may survive and neither will become manifestly psychiatrically ill and marital harmony may endure. Sooner or later the balance usually becomes disturbed, however, by the coming of children or by a gradual building up of dissatisfaction. Those who marry very young frequently do so for neurotic (unconscious) reasons. Fifty percent of these marriages end in divorce.

Case No. 8: This man finally required psychiatric treatment after two marriages had failed; he eventually failed at his work, and he became alcoholic.

He had been reared in a family where the father had been a steady worker but he was a passive man; the mother had been the primary figure in the patient's life. The father had been away for many months during the patient's early life. Upon his return to the family the patient's mother became chronically ill and the patient's care fell to others. His mother and father never had a good marriage. His own signs of disturbance appeared soon after his first marriage. It was his excessively close relationship to his mother, and the absence of his father, which led to the formation of unconscious conflicts which eventually destroyed his marriages and caused him to fail. The patient himself was rather passive and he married an active, aggressive woman. Severe incompatibility erupted almost immediately. Two children were born but the marriage ended in divorce. The patient began an affair early in his marriage and after the divorce he married the woman of the affair. After his second marriage his behavior continued to deteriorate; he did poorly at work, drank, took drugs, had numerous somatic symptoms, and was unfaithful to his wife. He became overtly homosexual for a brief period. He behaved ineffectively in relation to two additional children who were born to his second wife. He eventually required hospitalization and later committed suicide. This was a very serious illness the outcome of which might have been different had he received treatment earlier.

Case No. 9: This young woman described the courtship phase of her life with her husband as having been exciting and full of many rewards. Her sexual pleasure was great. There were no signs of incompatibility between them. Within a few months after having taken their marriage vows severe incompatibility appeared. They could hardly agree about anything. She became frigid, could see nothing but faults in her husband although she admitted he was not behaving any differently than he had prior to marriage. Treatment helped her overcome her difficulties and her marriage eventually worked out.

Her childhood had been typical of that described earlier for the abnormal development of the girl.

Case No. 10: This woman became ill soon after her marriage. Her mother was an aggressive, domineering woman and her father was weak and passive. She met her future husband while still in high school and dated him on and off for many years before marrying him. She had a brief romance with a man twice her age shortly before marrying her boyfriend of long standing. After marrying she began having somatic complaints, was irritable, troubled by fatigue; there was marked marital discord. When her babies arrived she was unable to care for them, relegating their care to hired help. She eventually resorted to severe alcoholism, divorced and remained unmarried. Good treatment at the time of the affair with the older man, when she married or when the children arrived might have saved her.

Case No. 11: This woman was the only child of parents who never got along. Her mother exhibited chronic dissatisfaction with life and no one could please her. The father was absent much of the time and continuously so for several years when she was a preadolescent. It was later revealed that her father had had a succession of girl friends during the patient's childhood years. The patient always exhibited low self-confidence but managed to meet a young man and after a few years of courtship she married him. She was happy at first but within months began to inquire about his premarital sexual experiences. When he admitted having had some she withdrew from him and began to develop a variety of psychiatric symptoms. Her symptoms grew worse with each child and she eventually required psychiatric treatment. Life with her became so unbearable her husband finally divorced her. Treatment helped her over this blow but she could never progress enough to be able to marry again.

Case No. 12: This young man had never had a good relationship with his father. He had been much closer to his mother and always confided in her when he needed advice. He had a satisfactory courtship with a lovely young woman and married her within a few months. He began to experience anxiety around his wife, suffered some disturbance in his sexual potency and soon began having sexual affairs. He loved his wife, respected her, but could never fully express himself sexually with her. They eventually divorced. Treatment failed to resolve his unconscious conflicts.

Case No. 13: This young woman was the product of a fairly successful marriage, however her mother was a very socially active woman who was clearly made uncomfortable by having to stay in her home and be completely responsible for the care of her children. The patient carried on two courtships simultaneously. One man was stable and reliable; she loved and respected him. The other was less reliable but more sexually exciting. It seemed she could not find a man who embodied the qualities of each. She married the stable man, soon became depressed, there was much marital discord, and divorce ensued. She was later successfully treated and was able to marry again.

The parental family patterns of those who become disturbed as a consequence of marriage are much the same as those who become disturbed when they first attempt to form a heterosexual relationship. The fathers are either weak, passive, remote, or absent. The mothers are usually aggressive or more dominant than their husbands, and all have faltered or failed to some degree in the role of mother and, of course, wife.

I believe it is too easy for young people who have just married to divorce and that this solution to marital difficulties should be the last resort. This is particularly true when there are children. Marriage creates conditions which, if properly handled, can lead to greater maturity in both. Or, both can admit defeat and divorce, and run the high risk of repeating the old pattern with some other mate. Make no mistake, divorces are painful and costly; basically, divorce is a failure, although when marital discord has existed for a long time divorce can reflect a step toward maturity, as I will explain later.

When self-help, as outlined in Chapter 4, fails, married couples in trouble should always seek expert help, for working out their problems and succeeding is preferable to accepting defeat and divorcing.

Many who marry attempt to find satisfactions outside the marriage which they cannot find with their spouse. The most common form of this is infidelity. Infidelity sometimes occurs as a vindictive act against the spouse who fails to participate fully in the marriage by avoiding loving and/or sexual intimacy with the spouse. The unconscious conflicts are usually oedipal in nature; that is, the man is unable to express his sexual wishes with the woman he loves and respects. The same conflict is usually the basis for infidelity by the wife. When a man and woman cannot fully express themselves with each other there is usually something in their unconscious minds which stands in the way.

Greater affluence, greater permissiveness within the home and in society, have caused young people to view marriage as a less serious commitment than in times past. Loneliness appears to be a powerful motivation which causes people to marry prematurely. Unfortunately, many young people are not ready for these commitments. Faced with the challenge of making their marriage work, they take flight instead. Unfortunately, children are born to many of these marriages that eventually fail.

Parenthood

Of all the commitments of life which precipitate psychiatric illness, parenthood ranks near the top, especially for women, who cannot escape the responsibilities of being a parent as can the man by going to work every day. The coming of children usually reflects a deepened commitment of the man and woman to each other. In addition to this change, the child (or children) forces each into clearer sex-role definition. A family has been created. The child, the clearer sex roles, and the family constellation itself trigger unconscious conflicts which cause many people to become ill and many families to break up. This is human tragedy and the consequences can be extreme for the individual and for society. The forming of a family can be, and for many is, the happiest time of life; for others it is a time of tragedy and heartache.

Case No. 14: This young woman was one of many children. Her father was alcoholic, an unsteady worker, a remote figure in the home because of his own passivity and involvement with other women. When at home he was an emotional man who was overly affectionate with his children, particularly his daughters. At times he was covertly seductive. Despite his characteristics, his children felt closer to him than to their mother, who was a harsh disciplinarian and the dominant figure in the household. Her daughters, including the patient, never felt close to her.

The patient married and for the first few months of the marriage she was quite happy; then she became pregnant, had a child, and promptly became depressed. She developed fears (phobias) of the dark, could not stay alone because of her fear that someone would break into her home and rape her. She became frigid, found it impossible to be pleasant to her husband, and eventually became so provocative that divorce was becoming a probability. This woman's unconscious conflicts were resolved by treatment. Her health was restored, and her marriage was saved. She subsequently had a second child without a return of her illness, a happy outcome indeed.

Case No. 15: This woman was the mother of two preadolescent children. Her mother had been extremely domineering and her father a remote and weak man. The patient was symptom-free until after her marriage to a hard-working man who was successful in his profession but with whom she never developed a close and satisfying relationship. She managed to care for her first child with help but broke down completely not many months after the birth of the second child. She eventually developed a severe depression, drank excessively, and finally had to be hospitalized. Despite efforts to treat her, her illness improved only when she was removed from her home setting, a process which permitted her unconscious conflicts to recede into the depths of her mind. She eventually divorced her husband, gave up her children, and married a much younger man. Though she experienced fewer symptoms in these circumstances, she would become ill again were she to return to her old way of life.

Case No. 16: The father of this woman had been quite close to her. Her mother was kind and devoted but the patient felt a closer bond to her father. She was a tomboy during puberty and aspired to be a physician. Her growing-up period was uneventful, and she was married in her twenties to a man whom she believed to be strong and reliable.

She became pregnant almost immediately and developed considerable anxiety during the pregnancy. After the birth of the child the marriage began to deteriorate. Her husband proved to be unreliable and weak, but seemed to overcome this as the baby grew older. A few years later she became pregnant again but this time she became overtly ill, showing severe depression and episodes of intense anxiety. Without stating his reasons her husband left her. The patient had to return to her parents, eventually overcame her manifest illness but never married again.

Case No. 17: This woman's parents had a bad marriage; her father was a harsh man, alcoholic, and never close to his wife or children. The patient never liked her mother although she sided with her during her parents' frequent arguments. Her father frequently walked around in the nude, and her parents were not careful about concealing their sexual activities. The patient witnessed them several times.

Dating had been very difficult for her; she experienced severe anxiety when boys attempted to have sex with her. She eventually married but was frigid and could not become pregnant. The man she married was a meek, passive person who demanded little from her. Delayed menses induced severe anxiety; she recognized her dread of pregnancy. This couple finally adopted a child but the patient became so anxious and agitated the child had to be given up and the patient was hospitalized briefly. After lengthy psychiatric treatment she finally managed to adopt a child but doing so caused her great agitation and anxiety; obviously, her unconscious conflicts had not been resolved by her treatment. Women who dread pregnancy should not adopt children.

Case No. 18: This patient's father died when she was a very small child and her mother had followed a professional life which is usually exclusively a male profession. The mother and grandmother were dominant, aggressive women. The patient had much difficulty forming heterosexual relationships but finally managed to marry. The marriage promptly dissolved after she insisted upon an abortion. Many years later she married a fatherly man but could not become pregnant. They adopted a child but she became acutely anxious and could not care for it. After a few years she left her husband, lived a very unconventional life and finally, after several years, rejoined her husband at his insistence. She promptly became severely ill and required hospitalization. The marriage ended in divorce. This woman's life course could only have been constructively influenced by the most expert doctor. Such a woman should never attempt motherhood.

Case No. 19: The parents of this patient never had a good marriage. The father was a very harsh man and the mother was cold and rejecting. She had never been able to be close to her daughter.

The patient was able to marry and have children but she became progressively more anxious with each pregnancy and more depressed after each delivery. Finally she became so ill she could no longer function and had to be hospitalized. She was poorly treated and she managed to provoke her husband into a divorce during her treatment. This outcome should never have happened. The doctor should have intervened more decisively and prohibited the divorce while she was in treatment. Many such couples eventually save their marriages with good treatment.

Case No. 20: This man was the product of a marriage where the mother was volatile, emotional, and overly anxious about her child. The father was a successful businessman but he was completely dominated by his wife. The patient was mildly depressed most of his life but he managed to marry and have several children, though he had little to do with them. Furthermore, to be successful as a provider for his family proved to be difficult for him. His is a very common pattern. Many such men can (and do) become good husbands, providers and fathers if successfully treated.

Fewer men seem to become ill after becoming a parent, probably because a good portion of their day is spent outside the home. Some, however, become acutely ill, others withdraw from their families, and others become unreasonable in their behavior toward their offspring and spouse. I am referring to jealousy toward the child, overt hostility, competitiveness or withdrawal. Fathers can withdraw from their families and thereby avoid acute psychiatric illness. To withdraw from their families permits their unconscious conflicts to recede more deeply into their unconscious minds and they are no longer manifestly ill. Women cannot escape their children as readily and as a consequence they become mentally ill; their unconscious conflicts are constantly triggered and mobilized and illness results.

In Case No. 14, the coming of the child triggered a variety of unconscious conflicts. Absurd as it may sound to you, the patient revealed in her treatment that she had always wished for a penis and that she hoped the growing fetus would turn out to be a penis instead of a baby. Her depression was caused partly by anger for having gotten a baby instead. She was now having to be nurturing instead of nurtured as she wished. The overriding basis for her depression was that she had given birth to what was for her the product of incest. This unconscious meaning produced enormous guilt. For her, any man in her life was a father figure. The birth of the child had broken down her psychological defenses and the contents of her unconscious mind poured out in disguised form. The rapist whom she feared was father. Her fear of being alone was an expression of the separation anxiety she had experienced as a young infant. She was treated successfully; she quickly gained insight into the unconscious meanings which marriage, pregnancy, and the child had had for her.

The unconscious dynamics of the rest of the women were essentially the same, with minor variations. Some managed to maintain their health longer and broke down only after several children had been born. For some the mere presence of the baby, as in cases where a child was adopted, triggered their unconscious so severely that they promptly decompensated. The tragedy of cases like these is that expert psychiatric care was not available to them. Some received treatment but without good effect.

Thousands of women like the few examples given do just what these women did—they give up part or all of their family. By breaking up the family they escape the conflict-triggering situation which had mobilized their unconscious conflicts. Divorces and/or abandonment of children are acts of desperation on the part of the sick person. They are frantically attempting to ease their anguish, anxiety, depression—their suffering—and to regain their health.

Some women promptly relegate the care of their child or the children of their growing family to others and go to work in order to get away from the responsibilities of being a full-time mother. When they are less exposed to these responsibilities their unconscious conflicts can recede more deeply into their unconscious, their psychological defenses get put back together, and they may be relatively symptom free. I have known many women who are relatively symptom free when they are away from their children, but when they try to be full-time mothers they become ill again.

The signs of impending failure of the marriage are easy to detect. Instead of pulling together, the husband and wife begin to provoke each other and fights ensue. The man often withdraws from his growing family. He may become jealous of the attention his wife gives his children. Such a man never received enough mothering as a child; as an adult he wants it from his wife and feels cheated when his children get her care. Presently the wife finds herself having to shoulder many of her withdrawn husband's responsibilities. Then the children are deprived of her care. She becomes more resentful, and complains and criticizes. The husband withdraws more. He may start to drink, find a mistress, or spend more time at work than necessary. The wife is overworked, lonely, and she begins to expect too much from her children in the way of gratification and attention. Finally comes the divorce.

Many, perhaps even most, divorces could be averted if proper help were available. Unfortunately, professional people often are so inexpert that they get sold a bill of goods by their patients or clients and believe the couple actually *is* incompatible, taking the outward manifestations of their troubled lives as evidence of incompatibility and a justification for the divorce. These usually are just the outward manifestations of deeper unconscious problems. It is a marvelous experience to participate (as a doctor) in the process of helping a married couple work out the residues of the past which lives on in their unconscious minds and save their marriage.

The coming of a family can serve as a tremendous stimulus to the maturational processes of men and women. I gave an example of how the adoption of a child precipitated a severe psychiatric illness. When the childless woman is less ill but just sufficiently troubled by unconscious conflicts to be unable to become pregnant (psychic infertility), the adoption of a child may promote maturation in her. In such cases a woman who for years has been unable to become pregnant can have children of her own after she has adopted a child. I believe what happens is that since the child is not her own there is less unconscious meaning attached to it and she can become a mother. Actually caring for the child mobilizes her unconscious conflicts so that the healthy aspects of her personality can resolve them. Furthermore, she has mastered the new situation and matured as a consequence. Some women, strangely, can keep their families intact and remain symptom free so long as there is no man in their life. Many such women wrongly assume the man himself is causing the trouble when they find that they are less troubled when he is away. It may not be the specific man to whom they are married at all, but the presence of a male who triggers the woman's unconscious attachment to her father and her competitiveness toward men.

Work

While parenthood appears to be more of an illness-producing life situation for women, work is more so for men. Men may be miserable at work if circumstances have forced them to work at jobs which they hate or for which they are ill suited. Being ill suited for a vocation can produce chronic strain and in severe cases a mental breakdown, and certainly will often produce poor performance on the job. Work is usually illness-producing and/or the cause for maladjustment because of unconscious conflicts. The individual may be well suited for his life's work and may like what he is doing and yet fail to function well enough even though he has all of the skills necessary to succeed. The practical significance of this fact is that one should not immediately change jobs when signs of distress appear. To do so might be a serious mistake and one based on the false assumption that one is not suited for a particular job. The real basis for the difficulty often will be found in the person's unconscious mind.

Case No. 21: This young man admired his father while growing up, but his father was unable to form a close relationship with him. There was an undercurrent of jealousy in the father toward his son because of the son's very close relationship to his mother. The father was an exacting man, stern and yet devoted to his family, but from a distance. The marriage of this patient's parents was not a good one; there were long periods of coolness between them. The family could rarely be together on an outing without tensions arising. The patient never broke his strong infantile ties to his possessive but somewhat cold mother, and later he clearly remained too deeply attached to her.

He married young, having picked a very aggressive and competitive woman, and soon this couple had a child. The patient exhibited extreme jealousy toward his son, thus driving the boy excessively close to his mother. This fact made the patient all the more jealous and hostile toward his wife and son. The marriage survived, however, but life took a marked turn for the worse when he attempted to succeed at a life's work for which he had prepared himself. At this point frank signs of mental illness appeared which severely complicated his chronic maladjustment with his family. He went progressively downhill in his overall life adjustment, failed at the work for which he was extremely well suited, and had to be hospitalized. The marriage ended in divorce. This tragic outcome might have been averted had a good doctor treated him.

Case No. 22: This patient was symptom free and had been able to marry and have a family without apparent difficulty. He supported his family, saw military service, but then joined his father's firm. He soon began to show signs of anxiety, to use alcohol, and began to conduct himself at work in such a way as to cause his superiors alarm. When he was informed he was being groomed to take his father's place as president of the company his behavior took a sharp turn for the worse. He had to be hospitalized. This man had many strengths and had it been recognized that taking his father's position would trigger off his unconscious conflicts, and had he received good treatment, his life could have turned out well. He later committed suicide.

Case No. 23: This patient was the product of a very successful father, but because of the father's heavy work commitments he had missed out on a great deal of fathering as a small boy growing up. He worked successfully in a company until he was promoted to a position of high authority. He began making bad decisions, delegated authority and responsibility to individuals of low competence, and eventually had to give up his own position. Treatment could easily have averted this downhill life course.

Case No. 24: This patient was the son of a very successful businessman. In his home, however, his wife was the supreme ruler; she formed an excessively close bond with her son, the patient. The patient prepared himself to join his father's firm and eventually did so. Soon after joining the firm he began to conduct himself in such a way as to discredit the firm. He secretly drained the finances but fortunately his dealings were discovered before he put the business into bankruptcy. He abused his wife who eventually divorced him. Although this was a very unreflective man, a skilled doctor with a strong and masculine personality could have helped him.

Case No. 25: This young man began to show signs of disturbance when he entered into relationships with women. He eventually managed to marry, but he failed twice, his marriages ending in divorce. As a student he had shown great promise and his professors predicted he would become a fine physician. When he began his practice his behavior took a sharp turn for the worse. He provoked other physicians, sought escape through alcohol and drugs, and finally had to be hospitalized. He returned to work only to fail again. He soon ended his own life. Had he realized that both women and work were triggers of his illness and had he promptly received treatment, his life might have turned out well.

Case No. 26: This young man was brilliant and his parents had great expectations of him. His mother doted on him, and his father was proud of him but he was secretly competitive and jealous. The patient's life turned into a long series of near-successes and downright failures. In school he never made the grades he could easily have made, usually by making obvious mistakes on his examinations. Each time success at work was within his grasp he made bad decisions and failed. Had the first failure alerted him to his illness and had he received help, his life could have turned out well.

Case No. 27: This man came from the typical family which leads to the formation of unconscious conflicts in the children. He hardly knew his remote, harsh father, and was excessively close to his mother. He married but had a very difficult time holding his family together. It was largely through his wife's efforts and encouragement that he managed to hang on. He received a promotion and was able to purchase a nice home for his family but he kept his family isolated from the neighbors. He became increasingly anxious, and began being preoccupied about religion. He went through a series of so-called religious conversion experiences during which he believed he heard God telling him to give up his work, leave his family, and devote his life to religion and the ministry. He did devote his life to religious work, but fortunately for him his wife obtained professional help for him before he abandoned his family.

The principle to be grasped in these examples is that commitment to work (or school), the wish to master the environment, serves as a trigger of unconscious conflicts. These, in turn, cause the individual to fail, to become manifestly psychiatrically ill, or to suffer unnecessarily from anxiety, anguish, or depression.

Some men are able to achieve success but then promptly ruin their careers by behaving in self-destructive ways. They make bad decisions which force their superiors to replace them; they bankrupt their businesses; they disgrace themselves; and some become severely ill with typical psychiatric illnesses. Others fail before even achieving much success.

While work alone frequently serves as a mobilizer of unconscious conflicts and the precipitant of illness, work is often associated in the man with being the breadwinner for his family. This combination of being successful as a family man and at work becomes a very powerful conflict trigger. It is the position as head of the home, the family, and success at work which triggers unconscious conflicts which, in turn, prevent the man from being successful in the male role.

At one time in every little boy's life, as I outlined in the chapter on childhood development, his maleness is aroused by his mother and he wishes to succeed with her in a romantic and sexual way. These wishes usually disappear in the course of normal development, but when they do not they are associated with profound guilt. The wish to possess the mother is associated with the wish to kill the father. There are other reasons guilt forms in the young child, but this oedipal source of guilt is a very powerful one. When the repressed childhood wish to succeed with the mother is never extinguished, the guilt associated with this wish can become awakened by efforts to succeed later in life. In other words, every success becomes equated with the childhood wish to succeed with the mother (in the case of boys); all success then becomes impossible, especially highly important successes. Some men can be successful so long as they do not try to succeed in the father's field of endeavor. Others cannot succeed at anything they try. These differences can be accounted for by the strength of the unconscious conflicts.

This unconscious conflict and its profound impact on life can be illustrated by the following case example.

A young man came for psychotherapy because he had never succeeded at anything he tried to achieve. His psychotherapist had made good progress with him; the patient had done well in college and was about to graduate. The night before he was to receive his degree he dreamed that he and an older man were in mortal combat on the edge of a cliff. A woman whom he could not identify but who resembled his mother was in their presence. The patient had overpowered the man and was about to push him over the side when he realized what he was about to do. He relaxed his efforts and allowed the man to push him over the cliff. The patient reported the dream in his next hour, did not attend his graduation exercises but jumped to his death from a high building.

This patient linked success in his adult life (graduating from college) with his boyhood wish to be sexually and romantically successful with his mother (the woman in the dream). His childhood wishes for his mother were associated with death wishes toward his father (the man with whom he was engaged in mortal combat in the dream). Rather than succeed (kill his father and win his mother), he "chose" death for himself. This patient was unaware of what was going on in his mind in connection with his impending success (graduation from college). Unfortunately his psychotherapist did not know either or the patient's life might have been saved. This man's guilt was so great that he committed suicide rather than succeed. Judging from his suicide note, he had experienced an acute sense of despair the night before his graduation and killed himself without the slightest inkling of why he did it.

Hundreds of thousands of people go through life destroying themselves in smaller ways. Common ways people harm themselves are provoking others on whom their success depends, making faulty decisions, accidents, alcohol and other drugs, failure to seize upon opportunities which clearly present themselves. Many go through life making partial successes but never getting as much out of life as would be possible for them to achieve.

A common time of difficulty for women is the realization of the lifelong dream of having the kind of home they always wanted. Just as receiving a long wished-for job or appointment can serve as a prime conflict trigger for men, so, too, can the house of her dreams become the prime trigger for a woman and cause her to falter when she finally obtains it. These should be times of joy, and are in healthy people, but they become illness-producing (anxiety, depression, overt psychosis, provocative behavior, etc.) in persons bedeviled by unconscious conflicts.

A young woman in treatment reported the following dream which she had after moving into a new house. Men were moving in her furniture and one carried in a long silver serving tray with a duck perched on top. The duck's bill was curved upward like an erect penis. The man, who resembled her husband, wore a blue serge suit. An angry woman appeared and burned the house down. The patient awakened in a panic. The duck she associated with the many Sundays during childhood that she had spent with her father feeding ducks at a nearby pond. To the blue serge suit worn by her husband in the dream she recalled that this was the only kind of suit her father ever wore; he had dozens of them. The woman in the dream was witchlike and the color of the clothing she wore was the mother's favorite color. This patient's attempt to move into her own home had awakened her childhood wish to get rid of her mother and take her place with father. Her guilt, which was represented by the witch in the dream, prevented her from being comfortable in her own home as an adult.

Not only do many women begin to fail or show signs of illness in connection with moving into their dream house, many others attend poorly to their homemaking responsibilities. The same unconscious conflicts are usually the reason for this. To do well as a homemaker has for them the unconscious meaning of competing with their mother, outdoing her, and being more pleasing to the father. Their guilt associated with the old and repressed childhood wishes prevents them from doing their best as wives, mothers, and homemakers. This is why so many women go to work soon after having a child.

Males frequently avoid overt mental illness by never grabbing hold of a life's work. Such avoidance is a mental mechanism whereby the individual protects himself from the conflict-triggering effects of commitment to life. The perpetual male student is an example. Some of these men fail to succeed when they finally leave the status of student. Women do this too; however, they do it differently from the way males do. Women may use work as a way of avoiding marriage and a family, and thereby avoid an illness. Work is much less of a conflict trigger for women than for men. The reason for this is very simple and obvious. By working the woman avoids a way of life (making a home) which would trigger her repressed childhood wishes to replace her mother in the home with her father.

The most glaring example of the mechanism of avoidance is the scores of young people who cannot make mature heterosexual and steady work commitments. They frequently live on parental subsidies or work just enough to survive. These are lost persons whose way of life can be explained by looking into the childhood period of their lives. Some social psychologists and sociologists claim social forces such as rebellion against war, society's assault on the environment, etc., are the bases for their way of life. There may be some truth to these claims, but it is overwhelmingly true that these people missed out on good family life during their childhood years. The inability to work, the self-defeating rebelliousness against *all* conventions, the blurring of sex roles, the inability to make heterosexual commitments, their reliance on drugs, their music and dress, tell a clear story.

What many of these young people are searching for can be inferred from some aspects of their dress and life style. They tend to dress like the men and women of frontier days. In doing so, I believe they are attempting to find strengths in the traditions of America which their relationships with their parents failed to provide. They are desperately lonely people; they may live in groups to compensate for this. They are so devoid of good internalized parents that they cannot make a family and they find security by living in large groups where personal commitment to a single individual is not required, and where it is unlikely they will ever be alone. The decor of their living quarters, which is reminiscent of styles in the late 1800s, reflects their need to identify with a period in America's history when the men were strong men, the women were strong women, and families were close and stable. The hippie way of life is a social phenomenon which is an aggregate of individual psychiatric illnesses.

Loss and Reversals

This is a broad subject, and loss poses a challenge for all persons many times throughout life. You will have observed that up to now I have described life situations that provoked varying degrees of illness (symptoms, behavior, feelings, etc.) and malfunctioning by virtue of the individual coming closer to his life experiences. The greater degree of commitment and involvement, the increased responsibilities, triggered the unconscious conflicts which caused failure and/or illness. Now we will discuss the opposite— separation, loss, reversal. Here the individual must give up that which was important or dear to him. Such experiences can also trigger unconscious conflicts.

It has been shown that persons who suffered sudden and/or harsh separations and losses during early life are more vulnerable to those kinds of experiences in later life. This is another reason why the continuity of the child's relationship to his family should not be interrupted during his early life and growing up years. Reactions to losses in later life can be severe and their effects extremely far-reaching. Some people become depressed and never really come out of it, and remain totally or partially incapacitated for the rest of their lives, although most depressions eventually clear up.

It is difficult for young children to mourn their losses; they frequently never do and as a result a depressive quality forms in them which persists for years, and at times for life. Later losses and separations, which in themselves would be manageable, may produce anything from low-grade to severe depressive reactions. For these reasons—not to mention the negative effects on the overall personality development—those forces in society and within the individuals themselves which cause women to abandon their very small children, usually by going to work, through divorce, or simply through neglect, must be dealt with somehow. Fathers must not neglect their children either. This is another reason why I make such a strong plea for the integrity of the family. It is our most precious social institution, yet in many ways it is the least protected and supported. A small child who has to separate from his mother every day when she has to leave for work is being traumatized and made vulnerable to the stresses of adult life, particularly loss.

The women's liberation movement, and others who advocate relegating the care of small children to others so the mothers can go to work, are giving very unsound advice to mothers. This is a very bad aspect of that social movement. The mother should be a constant and loving figure in the lives of her children when they are small. When she separates from them every day she is forming a core of separation anxiety in them and a vulnerability to later loss and separation.

Once children are in school all day the mother can then spend this time in other ways; it does not matter so much where she is when children are in school, provided she does not exhaust herself and have nothing for her family in the evening. It is important for mothers to be at home when the small children come home from school. It is a very rich experience for the child (and for the mother) to be greeted by a loving mother. It is deplorable that economic conditions have forced so many women to abandon their infants and small children. The importance of constancy of parents for infants and small children cannot be overemphasized.

There appears to be a relationship between the adult's vulnerability to loss, separation, and life reversals, and the frequency and severity of separation and the absence of object (parents) constancy. There is no doubt about the long-range effects of a major early loss, as I have just described. If these separations have been severe enough, and particularly if there has been a major loss, some people never again attempt to form meaningful relationships of any kind. Some people will enter into relationships but can never allow them to become really deep. The unconscious dread of the pain and anguish of another loss is too great for them to endure, or at least they believe this to be so.

Some physicians and researchers believe they have noted a relationship between early loss (during childhood), a subsequent loss in adulthood, and then the subsequent development of somatic disease, including cancer. I believe this is probably true although, obviously, not everyone who has suffered losses will develop cancer—there are other factors at work, too. However, losses that are not fully mourned can lead to a chronic state of resignation which probably increases vulnerability to invasion by radiation, tars, viruses, and other possible carcinogens.

Looking closely, one observes that each day involves some losses which are imperceptible. The most common one is the rapid rate at which one's children grow up. It is, of course, a source of pleasure to see them grow but it is a cause for sadness too. The years race by and all of a sudden children leave home. Some people react depressively to this event and may become severely ill and remain so for a long time. You will recall the description of the woman who viewed her children, particularly the boys, as her possessions; such women seem to be especially vulnerable to depressive reactions when their children leave home.

Parents who have turned excessively to their children for love and attention, often to the exclusion of meaningful and satisfying relationships with others, including their spouse, are subject to depressive reactions when their children leave. These are the clinging, possessive parents who have wanted to get from their children rather than being able to give to them. A transient sense of loss and depression or sadness is normal when children leave home, but such a reaction should not persist.

Death of a loved one often precipitates depression of major proportions. The relationship to the loved one may have been too exclusive; there may have been no one else the depressed person loved, or the lost person may have been unconsciously hated as well as loved. The death, then, is in part a wished for fulfillment and produces extreme guilt which accounts for the depression.

The principle to be understood is that the richer the early life, in the sense of good mothering and good fathering, and the fewer the traumatic separations and losses, the better will be the capacity to manage losses, separations and reversals in later life. This is because the later loss does not reawaken the earlier one; it is also because there are rich past experiences to fall back on during the transient period of emptiness when a loss, a reversal, or a disappointment has occurred. These are stored resources to draw upon in such times of need. Furthermore, those who have had a rich childhood not only have the capacity to mourn their losses but they also have the personal strength to form new relationships with which to replace the lost ones.

I suspect the reason very old people dwell so much on the past is not only because there are central nervous system changes which destroy recent memory but because their lives become increasingly empty as they age. To be continuously aware of the emptiness in their ongoing lives could lead to much anguish, despair, and depression. Remembering the rich past is a way of avoiding being alone, a way of replacing the inevitable heavy losses of old age. This illustrates again how important a rich childhood is.

Case No. 28: This man lost his mother when he was a boy of six. It came as a sudden shock; one day his mother was no longer there. She had been an extremely gentle and loving mother, bountiful in her capacity to give love and nurture. She had taken great pride in her boy and had encouraged him to be competent and masterful. His father was a masterful man who was equally proud of his son, and though the boy lost the continuity of the family at the age of six the foundation for his personality had been firmly set.

This boy was fortunate enough to have a number of women relatives to replace his lost mother. Despite this fact he became acutely aware of the transience of life, of his aloneness. At times he would cry uncontrollably. These experiences occurred more often when he was alone on long summer days or nights, or after parting from relatives whom he had visited. As a man he was unusually sensitive to human tragedy. Parting from friends always seemed like permanent separations; it seemed that he would never see them again. Sunsets tended to haunt him. The intense presence of life during springtime sometimes created an acute awareness of his own separateness from all living things around him, and with this awareness there was a strong longing for something. When he became a physician he was very careful with his patients for the preciousness of life was ever in his consciousness. It was not until thirty years later that he finally adequately mourned his mother's death during his own psychoanalysis. As a result, separations from loved ones became much more tolerable; the sense of mystery about life preoccupied him less. The effects of loss after the age of five or six are much more readily overcome by treatment than losses before that age. Very early loss more seriously disturbs personality development.

Case No. 29: This woman was the product of parents who were far from ideal. The mother was an inhibited, rejecting woman, yet the patient grew up very closely tied to her mother.

She had been a tomboy, and prepared herself for a professional life but married before she worked in her field. She admired her husband but was very competitive with him, too. She never got along well with her own daughter but was very close to her son. When the son left home for college she became severely depressed and had to be hospitalized. It took several years of intensive treatment before she was free of her depression. This woman viewed her son as a possession, as a part of herself, and as a means for being close to another living being in order to make up for the good mothering which was missed in her early life. Without treatment such women as this often become chronically ill with either somatic or more classical psychiatric illnesses.

Acute Physical Trauma

Physical assaults on the body, or sudden threats to life, may serve as conflict triggers while also being stressful in their own right. A very common example of this are the acute psychiatric disturbances which follow major surgery. These usually clear up rather quickly as physical health is restored. It is probable that the stimulus deprivation which is often associated with surgical after-care plays a part in these illnesses. It is well known that nonspecific stimuli from the environment play a part in maintaining normal mental functioning.

The insult to the integrity of the body can awaken unconscious castration anxiety which is the true basis for the psychiatric illness. Sometimes separation anxiety plays a part too, for in a sense the patient undergoing surgery is very much alone despite the constant and expert physical care he may be receiving.

Persons who faint when given an injection by needle do so because that needle triggers unconscious fears. Such persons may be strong-appearing and may be very effective in most or all areas of their lives. The simple penetration of their skin by a needle awakens the unconscious basis for their anxiety and they escape the threat by fainting. The unconscious conflict usually involves castration anxiety.

A successful businessman required surgery on his sinuses in order to promote draining. After leaving the hospital he became agitated and continually worried about his ears and nose, and eventually became so excited and sleepless he required heavy sedation and hospitalization. He reported dreams of having been mutilated. It was the unconscious meaning of the dream—castration fears—which explained his psychiatric symptoms.

Depressive reactions are extremely common following a major medical or surgical illness. There may be direct chemical effects on the brain from the toxic by-products of the disease, but the most probable basis for the depression is the loss aspect of the illness. Major illnesses separate the individual from his loved ones and from his usual surroundings. The temporary nature of life may become very clear, death may have been close at hand.

It is probable that anyone could be forced into an illness by extreme stress. Mental breakdowns during combat are examples. People do get worn out from overwork and begin to malfunction; some may collapse totally. However, psychiatric investigations have shown that even in many of these patients unconscious forces have been triggered by the threat to life or by the chronic exposure to harsh conditions.

Usually, however, psychiatric disturbances result from an interplay of everyday environmental factors and unconscious forces. The responsibilities associated with maturity are the triggers, the situations, which mobilize unconscious conflicts that are the true or ultimate bases for the illness. Illness-triggering events may be acute and unusual, such as surgery, but they usually are the responsibilities of everyday life. Psychiatric illness may appear when young people start dating; following or in anticipation of marriage; after marriage, the making of a home and the coming of a child or children. Attempting to be successful at work, promotions, the successful achievement of a life goal, or attempting to follow the father's footsteps may make men ill.

Losses are a major cause for psychiatric illness. Illness may vary from mild depressions to psychosomatic disorders, to severe depressions and at times to suicide. The sense of loss can be caused by changing jobs, moving from one home to another, leaving home, children growing up, children leaving home, job reversals, separation from loved ones, deaths, withdrawing love from a previously loved person or place, growing old, seeing loved ones grow old, failing physical health.

Where illness has resulted from a progressively deepened involvement with some aspect of the environment, or a greater degree of commitment, or the intention to make a new commitment, the natural reaction is to separate from the conflict-triggering, illness-producing situation. It may be necessary for certain severely ill persons to shed their responsibilities and even detach themselves from their many involvements. To do so may even be lifesaving. However, for many the degree of psychiatric illness may not be that great, though painful. For these, it is much better in most instances not to withdraw from the situation but to remain involved. Remaining involved keeps the unconscious conflicts mobilized and if the mental strain is not excessive or too prolonged, conditions are right for maturation to occur. When there are supportive elements in the environment and the opportunity to periodically retreat for brief periods, the chances for maturation to occur are increased. One should never quit unless he absolutely has to.

I hope that understanding what I have written will help you identify and better understand the principles underlying most mental illness and failures. Armed by this better understanding, many should be better able to master their environment and their inner turmoil and mature as a consequence.

CHAPTER FOUR

Guides to Maturity

Persons who are failing can achieve a more successful life adjustment without the benefit of professional help through self-help. The primary focus will be on married couples whose marriage is not bringing out the best in each and, as a consequence, is not providing the best possible home life for their children.

A basic assumption upon which the guidelines that follow are based is that men were meant to be masculine, that women were meant to be feminine, and that when this is so a harmonious heterosexual relationship is possible; these qualities reflect a central aspect of health. Therefore, despite what happened to the child during his early years which may have adversely affected his personality formation, I believe there is an inner trend toward maturity and health, and an attraction for the opposite sex. This is self-evident. Nature, then, is our greatest ally in the quest for a happy and successful life. My purpose is to describe ways for giving Nature the best possible assistance. I hope to help those who recognize the need for change to find the courage to follow the guidelines outlined in this book.

I have described the characteristics of a normal family, the consequences of normal and abnormal family life for children, and why people fail or become manifestly ill, or both, at certain points in life, but especially when the effort is made to form a heterosexual relationship, when they marry, or when they become parents.

What follows is a "do-it-yourself" manual for achieving personal change without going to a psychiatrist. It will be necessary to repeat some of what was said in earlier chapters in order to provide the understanding and guidelines for change, and for pointing the direction in which men and women should proceed.

Those professionals who follow learning theory believe that changes arrived at in the ways outlined here are basic and permanent. They believe change amounts to unlearning bad habits and learning new and better ones. Those psychiatrists and psychoanalysts who follow psychoanalytic theory view new forms of behavior arrived at in this manner as merely tacked on. In their view unconscious forces must change before new behavior can reflect fundamental change. In my opinion neither group is entirely correct.

I believe that efforts at self-help can change one's habitual ways of behaving, believing, and feeling, and even resolve unconscious conflicts. When more mature ways of behaving are achieved, unconscious conflicts are usually triggered and mobilized so that the healthier aspects of personality can resolve those conflicts which underpinned the old ways of behaving. These periods of change are often accompanied by anxiety or depression, often by a great deal of dreaming, and even a transient outbreak of symptoms.

The most effective psychotherapy deals with the outward manifestations of personality and their counterparts in the unconscious mind. That is, we try to link unconscious meanings to the manifest behavior, thoughts, and feelings that are causing the trouble in the person's life adjustment. The assumption is that it is easier for people to change if they discover why they are the way they are; that is, if they discover the irrational within themselves. However, I also believe people can change without realizing what internal changes are accompanying the external and obvious changes. Man was maturing before psychiatrists existed; he did so because life demanded he do so.

I have prescribed ways for behaving to many people without delving into the unconscious counterparts of their behavior. This method has brought about astounding changes, but I want to add that I have had increased leverage with patients when I could also reveal to them the unconscious forces within them which contributed to their behavior. I dwell on this at this point in order to encourage you. You need not have insight into the depths of your unconscious mind in order to achieve lasting personality change. I am well aware that intense and deeply probing treatment (such as psychoanalysis) may be necessary in order for change to occur in some people. Young people, however, have a remarkable capacity for change; this book should, therefore, be most helpful to the young. Although the young are usually pliable and changeable, their belief that there is always time later on for changing sometimes becomes a powerful resistance to changing. Some older people can achieve extensive change with very little help under the pressure of realizing the high cost in personal suffering and the psychological damage to their children if they do not change. Another great inducer of change for some older people who are not too ill is the realization that they are running out of time; it is a matter of now or never.

There is a natural tendency in everyone not to change. The element of the unknown contributes to this; however, the primary reason relates to the presence of unconscious forces within the personality. If there were not a barrier of resistance in the mind, the contents of the unconscious would become conscious. Behaving in a more mature way tends to force unconscious conflicts into the conscious; for many, this is frightening. Furthermore, habitual ways of behaving acquire a rigidity which resists change. Anxiety, depression, or both, and at times psychiatric syndromes, may appear as individuals change. More mature behavior requires the individual to stand alone, and to do so awakens repressed separation anxiety. Mature behavior also requires the individual to be responsible, involved, and more masterful. These shifts awaken unconscious conflicts having to do with threats and guilt which prevented the person from behaving more maturely in the first place.

Another basis for resistance to change, and one which usually leads to some degree of depression during the course of change, has to do with the internal losses within the unconscious mind. These losses are in relation to childhood attachments to the parents which have remained intact within the unconscious mind. For instance, a woman who is succeeding in her efforts to become more feminine will frequently become depressed as she gives up her unconscious attachment to her father with whom she had identified. In short, the effort to achieve an intimate, committed, and sexually pleasurable heterosexual relationship will awaken all of those unconscious conflicts which prevented her from achieving a full degree of maturity in the first place. Changing also requires the individual to give up his old way of life including, on occasion, certain ongoing environmental attachments—further cause for depression.

It is imperative that those who embark on a serious effort to improve their lives should proceed at a rate which does not bring on too severe anxiety, depression, or some form of psychic disorganization. Conversely, the various signs of psychic distress should not be feared if the person experiencing them can continue to function reasonably well. In a married couple various signs of distress are often used by one party as a means by which to intimidate the other and to cause a reduction in pressure for change. Change never comes easily; nor is it ever steady. There are times when it may seem that the project is hopeless. It is at these times *in particular* that one must remain committed to his goals and *persist*.

GUIDING PRINCIPLES FOR MAKING FAMILY LIFE SUCCESSFUL

The most important task facing a man and woman who marry is to evoke the best qualities in one another—for the man to fully awaken the woman in his wife and for the woman to fully awaken the man in her husband. When this happens, the likelihood of a deeply loving and committed relationship is great. The stage is then set for children to be reared properly. Once a family is formed it is vital that the man and woman relate to each other and to their children in a way which provides the best possible climate for the children. This means that a certain organizational pattern must be established within the family, with the man as head of the family and a clear division of the responsibilities for the father and mother, especially in relation to the children.

Those who have not achieved what is possible in marriage, and who elect to follow the guidelines previously set forth, can expect turbulence in their lives until they have sustained a new level of adjustment for some length of time, thereby giving maturational processes time to take place and become firmly established. It may take several months, or a year, or more, to achieve the desired goal. Persistent and committed effort is the key to success.

The *first principle* is for both the man and woman to realize there are two parts to the personalities of each, a healthy or mature part and an unhealthy or sick part. A strong bond must be established between the healthy parts of the husband and wife, and the sick parts in each must be seen as something to be disposed of. When the disagreeable aspect of the other's personality is seen as "sick" there is no reason to be angry at the other person. The following vignette illustrates this principle.

A very aggressive female patient said to me that she could see that I didn't like bitchiness in women. I said she was correct. "Then you don't like me," was her response. I said she was wrong. I liked the woman in her that showed through periodically, but that I did not like her bitchiness. I continued by saying that it was a good thing I did not like her bitchiness because if I did it would be unlikely that I could change her. I added that I did not like illness in any form and I considered her bitchiness to be a symptom of her illness.

The *second principle* requires the male to first look at himself and identify where and how he is not living up to the values which define the conduct of the head of the family. In conjunction with his self-inspection he should ask his wife to point out his shortcomings. He should start the process by first changing himself. As he changes he must then expect the same of his wife and point out her shortcomings. She, too, must be willing to look at herself. The point to be grasped is that the primary responsibility for initiating change and insuring that change continues *rests with the man*. Nonetheless, both should follow the guidelines spelled out throughout this book. There is no reason for the woman to wait for her husband to initiate the process of change. It works best when both parties participate wholeheartedly; however, the ultimate responsibility rests on the shoulders of the man; if he starts to change, many women (and children) will too.

The *third principle* is that criticism must be abandoned. Criticism only evokes resentment and frequently fear; it rarely brings out the best in the person being criticized. Noting someone's faults can be done in a way that is not critical. Nagging at someone is destructive, never constructive.

The *fourth principle* pertains to the expression of anger, which inevitably is evoked as both parties expect the other to change. I have rarely seen expressions of anger accomplish anything constructive except in very special instances. No one can go through life without expressing anger toward even those he loves the most; however, regularly giving vent to one's anger and criticalness toward one's spouse usually makes matters worse, especially during the process of changing the personalities of a married couple and their marital patterns. When anger is felt it can and should be expressed in any of a number of ways, but in private. Some find it useful to swear, others to engage in physical activity; it should not be directed toward the spouse. This is a very difficult principle to live by, especially when the spouse has done something provocative or destructive. At such times the behavior should be pointed out and appropriate action taken, but the associated anger should be expressed privately. To direct anger at one's spouse usually amounts to taking the other's bait, that is, reacting to the spouse's behavior in order to satisfy his or her unconscious need to create distance and disharmony and even to destroy the relationship. Remember, it is in the nature of things for male and female to live together harmoniously according to certain patterns.

The *fifth principle* requires the spouse to acknowledge and reward mature behavior in the other. Everyone needs praise and positive reinforcement for new achievements. Learning theorists make much of this, and I believe they are right. Children learn more rapidly and cheerfully if they receive rewards each time they take a step forward. The same applies to adults. Progress should be sincerely rewarded. How this is done is a matter for the couple involved to work out. Simple recognition and expressions of appreciation go a long way.

The *sixth principle* has to do with providing the ability to change. For an old way of behaving to be abandoned and a new way achieved, the strength and courage to do so must come from somewhere. Patients in psychiatric treatment receive this, in part, from their doctor. A good doctor will help point the way; he will remove the unconscious barriers blocking progress, or at least make them known, and if necessary he will provide the encouragement necessary for the patient to change. Persons not in treatment can find the strength to change from encouragement given by their spouse, and by drawing upon their own willpower.

The *seventh principle* pertains to the use of force. Force in itself is not evil or destructive. The purpose for which force is used defines its value. Force can be applied in a variety of ways. A woman can force her husband to behave more maturely by refusing to assume his responsibilities. Similarly, a man can refuse to do his wife's work and thereby force her to do it. There is another application of force which falls to the one primarily responsible for the integrity and survival of and within the family—the man. When observation, discussion, encouragement, support, and persuasion by the man fail to bring about the desired changes in his wife, he must apply force. He can prevent (force) his wife from doing certain things and by using one kind of leverage or another he must insist she begin doing that which she is not doing. It is remarkable how many good things begin to happen when the man simply "lays down the law." I have never known a woman to fail to admit (in private) that this is precisely what she wanted her husband to do when she was getting away with destructive or irresponsible ways of behaving with her husband or her family, or in general. Man is not so far removed from lower forms of animal life in some respects. Take your cues from the stallion, the bull, etc. Male and female are biologically different. It is the male's superior strength and greater aggressiveness which places the final responsibility on him for changing his own and his wife's behavior. If it takes the application of force to fulfill his responsibilities, then he must use it—wisely and in properly measured doses, but use it he must.

Couples face a difficult problem when the man cannot assume this responsibility. What final leverage does the wife have when the application of the preceding principles fail, particularly the use of encouragement? It may be necessary for her to threaten to divorce her husband if he does not change for the better. This threat may be viewed as the *eighth principle*. Such a threat often initiates the process of change, making it possible for the couple to then apply the other seven principles. The man also may threaten to divorce his wife if all else fails.

There is a serious drawback to threats of divorce, however. If the couple is sufficiently disturbed such threats play into the illness of both and may actually facilitate the destruction of the marriage rather than initiate a process of constructive change. The threat of divorce should only be used as a last resort and never as an anger-provoking threat or as a means by which to manipulate and intimidate the other party and thereby attain a selfish goal. Rather it is an admission of defeat, a fact which neither party may be willing to accept.

When the use of these principles fails to bring about change, psychiatric assistance should be sought. When such help is unavailable or proves to be ineffective, the couple will have to decide whether to remain married or to divorce.

Values and Guidelines

The values and patterns of living which lead to harmony in a childless couple may be somewhat different from those which should govern the living patterns of a married couple with children. For instance, the consequences are less serious if the woman is aggressive and domineering and the man passive. It is unlikely that either party would be truly happy and fulfilled, but if they think they are and are free from psychiatric symptoms and can remain so what difference does it make? Sooner or later such couples usually show signs of discontent or more serious strain.

However, when children arrive, it is very important that the man and woman establish certain definite patterns within their family and find harmony too. It cannot be repeated too many times that for children to grow into mature men and women their father must have been a masculine man, their mother a feminine woman, and a harmonious relationship must have existed between them. However, this harmony must be consistent with the model of the ideal family. To achieve this goal will take a great deal of effort for some couples; it is my hope to be able to help many who cannot afford psychiatric treatment achieve this goal.

The top executive of an organization should be kind, willing to listen, firm when necessary but not harsh or unreasonable. There should be no question that the final authority and responsibility rest with him. A good executive endeavors to bring out the very best in each person in his organization and to promote individual and organizational growth.

I have yet to see a woman, no matter how aggressive or domineering, who did not ultimately reveal her secret wish that her husband and her father had been the head of the family. Children, male and female alike, want it this way. The most bitter complaint I have ever heard from patients toward their parents has been, "Father didn't put Mother in her place," when she dominated her husband and the family. Every married man I have treated wanted to be the head of his family but lacked the courage to assume that responsibility.

There is nothing about these formulations which should suggest that the woman should be seen but not heard, or that femininity is weak and second-rate. A mature woman is a substantial person, capable of many things in life. Through her intellect, wisdom, and awareness of the most meaningful factors affecting the members of her family she will contribute greatly to the direction the lives of all will take. But so will the man; and the final responsibility and authority must rest with him. It is he who is most at the interface between society at large and his family. He is the primary and ultimate protector of the family.

Improving a Marriage

Many married couples eat and sleep together, have children, but rarely speak to each other; they never just sit and talk. And, worse, they rarely spend time alone with each other. Having acknowledged this mutual problem, they must make the effort to talk on topics of mutual interest. Incredible events may begin to occur. Anxiety will almost surely arise in both; irritabilities will be expressed; avoidant devices will be used; excuses and tricks of one kind or another will be employed so as to avoid the effort to increase the involvement with the spouse. These tricks must be rigorously searched out and thwarted. With continued effort this pattern will change and a new measure of intimacy will have been achieved.

Talking leads to loving and to mutual respect. Broadly based cooperativeness is the ultimate objective. I do not wish to imply that just by talking with each other couples can achieve an idyllic marriage; by no means; but talking is an important place to start.

The most frequent complaint I have heard from women about their husbands is that they can push their husbands around. They are equally resentful of their husbands' refusal (or inability) to participate in family life. They complain that they remain too aloof from the family, that they are irresponsible with money; that they fail to be an authority and establish guidelines for the family, and for the children in particular. They particularly deplore the fact that the husbands pay little attention to the children. In short, these women have to assume many of the responsibilities which should fall to the man; men like these—the passive, weak and/or remote—force the woman into the male's role. The wives of such men have to become father and mother. Some of these men may be quite masterful at work but completely and passively dominated by their wives at home. The women end up doing most of what the men should do; they complain about it, and yet they may complain even more if the man starts to take his rightful place within the family.

Since it is sometimes easier for others to make observations about an individual than for the individual to be able to observe himself, it is vital that the woman communicate her observations about her husband to him when they begin to talk more to each other. No matter how difficult the challenge may seem to her, despite hesitation, anxiety, and especially in the face of her inner tendency to maintain the status quo, the wife should communicate her observations to her husband, and in as kind and gentle a manner as is possible encourage him to change. She should never do this in a hostile or nagging way, for to do so will only reinforce his own internal "critics"—those deposits of the past which have stood in the way of his complete maturation. His anxiety and self-doubt will be unduly increased by his wife's attack and the attack from within himself. His early, and often halting, efforts to change should be rewarded by encouragement and praise. These should be communicated in such a way that the man is never made to feel like a "little boy who is doing better," but as a man who is burdened by an illness which he is progressively overcoming. The attitude in both should be, "We are working and gaining on *it*"—"it" being the illness which is not his fault but the changing of which is now being striven for. A very useful view is to look upon these troublesome traits, behaviors, and attitudes as foreign bodies, things which are really not an integral part of the essential man.

The point to be grasped is that when a partially (psychologically) crippled man begins to achieve his proper identity and take his rightful place in the family, the wife must respond to this in a womanly way. He should take charge of the finances, sit at the head of the table, attend to the repair needs of the home, pay the bills, take responsibility for the investment program, spend more time with the family, etc., all with her cooperation.

A man who is beginning to find his manliness will quickly observe behaviors in his wife which are aggressive, bossy, and avoidant of certain responsibilities, and so on. It now falls to him as the head of the home to see to it that she fulfills her role. Holding the woman to her responsibilities, preventing her from behaving in her old ways, can be done firmly and kindly. Unless the woman is extremely ill emotionally she will respond positively to her husband if the stakes are high and she has made the commitment to make a success of their relationship. The stakes are always high when there are children still in the home, and even when they have left home.

He will give her courage to blossom as a woman, but he may have to do more than that too. A formidable challenge for him will be to stand in the way of those behaviors in his wife which derive from her envy of the male, her identification with her father, and identification with a somewhat unfeminine (aggressive, phallic) mother. If she cannot change her ways through her own efforts and through his encouragement and support, the sparks may quite literally begin to fly as he begins to apply force and at the same time prevent her from "running home to mother"—or to her attorney.

As the husband insists that his wife relinquish her dominant position in the family, she will probably resent having to make these changes. These are crucial and deciding moments which may take on crisis proportions, and the fate of the family depends on their outcome. Sometimes a woman refuses to change and threatens to leave the husband if he persists in his demands on her and in his pursuit of his rightful place in the family. This threat on her part is actually self-protective in its meaning for the prospect of changing can create extreme anxiety. These are women who have very little of a loving and security-giving mother inside them. They may have internalized a harsh and rejecting "bad" mother also. Furthermore, these women seem to know intuitively that the threat of being left is a vulnerability of their husbands; that is, the threat of being left by the wife awakens the old unconscious fear of being left by the mother. The mothers of weak men often disciplined their sons by threatening (by words or attitude) to leave or abandon them if they didn't obey.

The man must stand firm and not be intimidated by his wife's threat to leave. He is now receiving his supreme test; if he yields his position the illness in his wife and in himself will have won. The spirit of cooperativeness may be lost temporarily, but the man must stand firm. While some women do leave as they threaten to do, most merely make the threat while secretly hoping the man will stand firm and not let her continue to dominate and get away with her aggressive, bossy ways. As I just indicated, the wife's threat to leave awakens the man's insecurity, which is an outgrowth of his early relationship with his mother when he was an infant and little boy. To be left as a child is disastrous, and to have this fear awakened by an angry, threatening wife has caused many men to back down when they should have stood firm. I recall a very aggressive and "castrating" woman who was seeking my advice about her marriage said, "A cow knows where she stands when she is with a bull." My reply was that the trouble in her personal life was that she had never known a bull—neither her husband nor her doctor could handle her. She acknowledged the accuracy of my remark, thanked me for my consultation, and never returned. Obviously the prospect of having to change was too threatening to her.

The nearly inevitable result when the man holds his ground is that the woman will begin to cooperate and give up her domineering ways—often to the complete surprise of the man and frequently to the woman as well. Standing firm on the man's part, without fear, is the key to success of many heterosexual relationships where it has been the woman's pattern to dominate and run roughshod over the man. Many, many women have the wish to deprive the man of his maleness, to diminish and dominate him— castrate him. When the man demonstrates by his behavior that this cannot be done, the air is cleared and the stage set for a more cooperative and rewarding relationship. This then makes it possible for family life to proceed in a way which will insure the proper development of children and the greatest happiness for the man and woman.

The woman's domination may take a great many forms. She may control the money, have her way in most or all family decisions, minor or major, be the primary authority with the children, be the aggressor in sexual relations, influence his career (positively if she wishes to be the power behind the scene and negatively if she is determined to destroy the male), openly or subtly demean him, and in severe cases behave in ways which promote disintegration in him. An example is the wife who provides her alcoholic husband with alcohol. Some women destroy their husbands financially, not because they hate the man they married but because they hate men.

Some of the signs of the woman's rejection of her feminine role and the underlying conflicts leading to this rejection, in addition to those which have already been mentioned, include: sexual or general frigidity; a messy home, including haphazard care of her own personal belongings, particularly underclothing; an unwillingness to socialize, particularly with the families of her husband's business or professional associates; absence of women friends; the belief that work in the home is demeaning to her; inability to cooperate in the spending of money; overspending for trivial and nonessential items; the need to acquire possessions of limited usefulness; many more clothes, especially shoes, than necessary; resentment of her husband's financial planning on the grounds that she and the family are being deprived (this may include resentment of his insurance planning for *her* security); chronic dissatisfaction about anything and everything.

Many of the woman's destructive ways and antifeminine personality traits will come to light as a couple who have made the commitment to improve their marriage begin to work on the task of changing. If basic change is to be the result, then the man must not permit the preceding kinds of behaviors to continue in his wife and she, in turn, must communicate her anxiety, depression, resentment, etc., to her husband *and not pull away from him*. He is her best ally, not her enemy. To pull away would only increase the distance between them. Less basic change will occur, or her behavior may change slightly, but the couple will be living at arm's length with neither finding much gratification from the other. Instead, the wife must turn to her husband and obtain comfort and courage from him and praise for having changed. It is crucial that the man who is inducing change in his wife stand by her as she changes. She has the right to expect him to stand by her, and it is his responsibility not to let her down. The project may well be scuttled by his failure to be ready to respond in a security-giving, comforting and also masculine way to his newly changed, or changing, wife. Many men want their wives to change, to be more feminine, but when the wives change they find they are not up to responding to the changed wife.

Both parties must continually remind themselves of their commitment and not lose sight of their goal. They must turn to each other for comfort and security until such time as they have increased their courage and have become more self-confident. Setbacks will be inevitable, but a good marital relationship wherein both live out their roles in ways consonant with nature's endowments is entirely possible if both cooperate and persist.

The application of force when other inducements for change have failed is one of the most loving things a man can do for his wife. He is, in effect, insisting that she give up her illness and achieve health. When a woman's resistance to change is extreme, the use of sudden expressions of anger and ironlike firmness may be necessary and are usually quite effective. It is best to rely on firmness alone if at all possible. Firmness must be followed up by love, support, and praise. These human qualities which the woman receives from her husband will quiet the anxiety which the process of change will have generated within her.

The following headings refer to a number of common battlegrounds upon which married couples reveal the presence of irrational forces within themselves. My objective in discussing these special situations is to spell out some of the unconscious meanings.

MONEY

With regard to money, there usually is just so much to go around, and ideally the husband and wife will cooperatively plan their finances. When, however, the wife refuses to cooperate the husband must take complete charge. It is quite likely that a more rational allocation of money can be arrived at if both work cooperatively on the task, but where the wife refuses she must be forced or matters must be taken out of her hands. In time, if she can commit herself to the goal of a good marriage—and both must continually remind themselves of their common goal—she will change. It is remarkable how much money can be saved when the wife cooperates with a responsible husband.

It is fascinating to observe how a woman will manage money very well when her husband is unable to do so—that is, when the power is in her hands—but will do very poorly when the husband assumes, or attempts to assume, responsibility for the finances. Her inability to cooperate is clearly an attempt to defeat her husband, to rob him of his power. He who controls the money has the power.

Unfortunately, many men are irresponsible with family finances and they force their wives to take this responsibility against their own wish to do so. This is a clear illustration of the principle of complementarity in relationships. In a marriage nonpathological behaviors tend to harmonize but so, too, do the pathological aspects of behavior and personality. The woman often protests having to take the financial responsibility, and many women would gladly turn over the management of finances to their husbands if they would, or could, assume this responsibility. When men squander money on nonessentials, fail to plan for the future, for emergencies, etc., the wife is left no choice but to take control of the money, and usually of other areas of family life as well.

Some of the fiercest marital battles are fought over money. It is in this arena that the spirit of cooperativeness toward the objective of making a real marriage is most likely to be lost. The control of money provides one of the best means for a symptomatic expression of the unconscious wish for power. This wish comes from childhood conflicts in both males and females. In the woman the need for power reflects her wish to prove herself more powerful than the male; that is, "You may be male and have a penis but I'll show you I am more powerful." The man who has not overcome his castration anxiety and his feeling of inferiority may have an excessive need to prove his own powerful status. This causes him to have an unreasonable desire for control.

By far the most common way the woman betrays her competitiveness toward the male, and her inability to enter into a cooperative heterosexual relationship, is by spending money foolishly. This is done by buying nonessentials, paying top prices instead of looking for bargains, and buying too many bargains, and so on.

A mature married couple will have no difficulty whatsoever with their finances. Both will have full knowledge of their financial situation, and both will cooperate in the spending of money. In the absence of unconscious meanings attached to money, married couples will be able to allocate their funds in accordance with the immediate and long-range needs of their family. Some women have excellent money sense. Men with wives like this are fools if they reject their wife's counsel. Some women have no interest whatsoever in financial planning.

FIDELITY AND SEX

The idea of being faithful to your spouse is considered by many to be old-fashioned and puritancial. An increasing number of self-proclaimed authorities, some of whom are professionals and many of whom are not, are propagandizing the public with claims that monogamy is dead. They advocate "swinging," loose "marital" relationships, marriage by contract, group living, mate-swapping, etc. Some even claim that infidelity is a growth-producing experience. All of this is very bad advice and destructive in its effect on the individual, the marriage, and above all on the family. None of this advice is based on solid evidence which shows that such ways of life are constructive in either the short or long run.

A mature couple who have a good marriage will have no need whatsoever for any of the above experiences and, in particular, for clandestine infidelity. A couple embarked on a project of self-help, or a couple receiving psychotherapeutic help, should never be unfaithful. The objective is to resolve unconscious conflicts and alter their behavioral consequences so that a fully committed heterosexual relationship becomes possible.

Infidelity is usually caused by the inability to express both love and sexual feelings toward the same person. The most common reason for this behavior is the failure to have overcome childhood guilt about erotic feelings towards the parent of the opposite sex. For the unfaithful man, his wife will usually represent the respected, admired mother while the mistress will be the representation of the mother of his boyhood days for whom he had strong sexual feelings. These repressed memories and associated guilt prevent the man from both loving and experiencing a full measure of sexual pleasure with his wife. The same formulation applies to the woman. She projects her unconscious wishes onto her husband; that is, she has a transference reaction toward him and does not experience him as just the man she married. Frustrated and unsatisfied because of her inability to find romantic and sexual gratification with him, she may turn to a lover.

Couples burdened by the unconscious conflicts I have just described may be cooperative in their sexual relations but because they cannot find pleasure they look elsewhere. Some couples find pleasure with each other but are unfaithful anyway. The usual pattern, however, is the one where the couple is desirous of sexual pleasure with each other but manage to provoke arguments or hard feelings so that the sexual encounter does not occur or, if it does, proves to be unsatisfactory. This is seen most frequently in women. The husband makes known his interest in having sexual relations and the wife manages to do something which provokes anger in him. Her maneuver may be extremely subtle, such as an attitude of slightly bored tolerance of the act, or she may bring up some unrelated issue and provoke her husband, or she may simply be cold and rejecting. One of the most common patterns of all is that in which the couple has spent a pleasurable day together, the logical and wished for (by both) conclusion of which would be sexual intercourse. As the time approaches for lovemaking to occur, one or both will provoke the other into an argument or become obviously uninterested, using an evasive maneuver.

When these evasions and provocations occur frequently, they provide one or both parties a ready excuse for looking elsewhere for sexual pleasure. While provocative and rejecting behavior is a secondary basis for infidelity, it is not its true basis. Provocations, rejection, and the like are the means to the end, the end being the destruction of loving and sexual intimacy.

It is remarkable how married couples will sometimes temporarily experience greater sexual pleasure with a lover. The lover may or may not be more expert than the spouse, frequently even less so, and is often much less admirable or possessive of strength of character and other fine qualities. It is the uncommitted aspect of the illicit relationship which makes greater pleasure possible. Unconscious conflicts are not so fully mobilized in the unfaithful person as when attempting to relate to the spouse to whom he is committed. This principle can be clearly illustrated by the following apparently curious phenomenon. Some married couples can feel love for each other and experience sexual delight before marriage but after the marriage vows have been made sexual difficulties (frigidity or impotence) appear. Some couples grow distant except for sexual pleasure. Sexual relations may become the only time the two are ever together in any way. They can have sex but not closeness. Some couples have closeness but little sex.

In order for a couple to overcome the barrier between them and finally resolve these unconscious conflicts, they must not cheat on each other but must, instead, try very hard to break down the barrier and experience a full range of feeling (love and sex) for each other. I think it is unwise for couples to confess their infidelities to each other; much hurt may result which may never be overcome.

As a man becomes more assertive in his relationship with his wife he may find he will be temporarily disturbed in his capacity to perform sexually. The unconscious conflicts which have been mobilized by his becoming more manly with his wife are the true bases for his impaired sexual functioning. It is of the greatest importance that the wife not react to these setbacks in functioning in a hostile fashion. Instead, she must be understanding, tolerant, and helpful. She must, above all, give her man time to change and overcome his anxiety and sexual dysfunction, just as he must for her.

In a relationship where sex has little meaning, both parties should work at achieving a richer sex life if they want to get the most out of their marriage. Here some of the most difficult resistances to change may be encountered. A domineering, aggressive woman who has never overcome her penis envy, oedipal attachments, and other unconscious conflicts may experience much difficulty in behaving in a responsive, receptive manner which evokes the best from her man. It will be difficult for her to eliminate the competitive quality in her sexual behavior, or her impatience, her disgust, or her need to demean her husband. These behaviors and attitudes are all designed to prevent the woman in her from coming out and also prevent the occurrence of an intimate experience with her husband during which both cooperate and respond to each other.

A feminine woman is not an unresponsive, passive mass during lovemaking. She is receptive and responsive. Women who retain one or more of the core conflicts outlined earlier may be very aggressive during lovemaking and will want to be in the top position. Some seem lifeless, and so on. During lovemaking the man should take the woman, and when he does this in a skillful and masterful way the woman will respond if unconscious conflicts do not block her. Men who prefer oral practices, who always like the woman on top, who like for the woman to make love to them, have resorted to passivity in the face of the sexual challenge; their unconscious conflicts prevent their normal male assertiveness from being lived out.

The couple embarked on a program of self-help (and those in treatment too) should not be embarrassed to talk about their anxiety and misgivings associated with the sex act. They should try to help each other overcome inhibitions and discard ways of behaving which deviate from mature sexual behavior. A book entitled *Human Sexual Inadequacy* by Masters and Johnson (61) and another by Katchadourian and Lunde (51) provide advice on the techniques of sexual intercourse. Many of these are helpful. First to be achieved is the recognition in both parties that trouble exists, and next to be achieved is an attitude of frank, wholehearted cooperativeness.

It is relevant to comment here on the difference between so-called clitoral and vaginal orgasm. Much is written these days about there being no difference. While it may be true that the physiologic response which accompanies the female orgasm is the same, regardless of the means by which the woman's genitals are stimulated, there are clear and distinct differences in what kinds of stimulation will bring a woman to orgasm. There are differences also with regard to what area of the woman's genitals will lead to orgasm when she is stimulated.

Some women can achieve orgasm through sexual intercourse and others cannot. Those who cannot are usually capable of achieving orgasm when they receive clitoral stimulation through some other means than intercourse by the man. Some can achieve orgasm only by means of masturbation. Furthermore, some women do report a difference in their orgastic response brought about by intercourse, being able to distinguish between clitoral and vaginal orgasm. The two distinguishing aspects to the woman's sexual response are the degree of intimacy she experiences with the man and whether or not she can be brought to orgasm by his penis.

There is no doubt in my mind that the woman who can respond to intercourse with either a clitoral or vaginal orgasm is less troubled by unconscious conflicts about sexuality than the woman who cannot. Furthermore, the woman capable of vaginal orgasm through intercourse is less troubled than the one who can only experience clitoral orgasm. The woman who can achieve orgasm by stimulation by means other than intercourse is more troubled about sex than those who can have orgasm by means of intercourse.

It should not be assumed that a direct relationship exists between the overall maturity of a woman and what it takes to bring her to orgasm. It used to be believed that such a relationship existed but this assumption has not stood the test of careful study. Similarly, men who possess a high degree of potency may be disturbed, psychiatrically speaking, in a variety of ways. There is no escaping the fact that a married couple who can both achieve orgasm during sexual intercourse have added an element of closeness and joy to their marriage. Yet it is also true that some couples can achieve these experiences but fail to find fulfillment in the other aspects of their marriage.

Despite all of these varied facts, a married couple should be able to share the pleasure of sex freely and cooperatively. Ideally this should be achieved by sexual intercourse. A couple who attempt to improve their marriage should strive for the highest goals, sexual pleasure being only one among many, but they should not be disheartened and believe their marriage to be a failure if they are unable to reach this particular goal. There are a multitude of facets to a good marriage. Sexual pleasure is only one of them. Sex tends to fall into place if the rest of the marriage is satisfying. I am quite certain that a mature married couple will find no need for infidelity.

CHILDREN AS A MATURATIONAL STIMULUS

A powerful stimulus to the maturational processes in a married couple is the coming of children. I do not recommend having a child for "therapeutic" purposes; however, when children do appear it is imperative that the parents behave in ways which favor the best possible maturation for the child as well as for themselves.

Some women who are still burdened by separation anxiety and penis envy, and who did not receive adequate mothering, will treat their infant as if it were an object to be used for the purpose of abating their loneliness and quieting their anxiety; it makes up for what is "missing." They are inclined to view the child as a part of their own body. The child becomes the penis they have long awaited, or it may serve as a kind of "security blanket." This unrealistic view of the child leads to behaviors which are severely detrimental to the child's development and contributes to the breakdown of the marriage. Such a mother will devote excessive time and energy to her child; she now feels complete and has little need for her husband. The husband will generally withdraw angrily; he may find a mistress, spew hostility onto his wife and child, and so on. The intensity of his reaction will depend to a large extent on the degree to which he is unconsciously burdened.

A young mother should nurse her child, and this is an experience she should enjoy; it will be one which will stimulate the maturational process within her. The father of the child should be able to take pride in his wife and view the nursing mother with fondness and not jealousy and envy. He will be able to do this when he has stored in him the good experiences with his own mother. In short, unless there is a physiological limitation in the mother, she should try her best to nurse her child and continue to do so until it is ready to stop nursing.

I do not think it best for young mothers to work and relegate their infant's care to others. Some men resent their wives staying at home with their child. This attitude should be overcome and pride taken in the wife who wants to make a home. She will more likely find contentment in this task if she is given the rewards of a loving and appreciative husband.

It is very common for couples who have been happy together to draw apart after the coming of a child. This fact can be accounted for by the mobilization of unconscious conflicts in addition to those just mentioned. With the coming of a child, a triangle—a family—has been created. This situation serves as a powerful trigger of unconscious oedipal conflicts formed in the couple's own childhoods. It is as if the young wife is experiencing herself in her mother's place with her father, and the husband his own father's place with the mother. In order to allow these unconscious conflicts to recede, both parties will tend to move away from each other. Both become unhappy and restless, and divorce may ensue.

The new child will also serve as a powerful maturational stimulus causing a crystallization of gender identity and sex role responsibility for both the father and mother. The wife, who may have worked, will now have to stay at home and attend to her maternal responsibilities and opportunities. More responsibilities will fall to the man. All of these changes, along with the new conflict-triggering family constellation, may produce frank psychiatric symptoms, anxiety, depression in one or both, and almost surely will cause the couple to draw apart if they are burdened by unconscious conflicts and closer together if they are mature.

In keeping with their original goal and commitment, the couple who wish to help themselves will strive to make a family in the best sense of the word. The new family will sharpen their perception of the nature of their relationship and facilitate the identification of abnormal attitudes, feelings, and behaviors.

When the man sees his wife rejecting her child, he should not take over her role unless the wife is extremely hard pressed. He should, instead, try to support and encourage her. It is remarkable how much more effective women can be in the home if they receive encouragement from their husbands. Similarly, when the husband avoids his children, the wife should point this out to him. Each should encourage the other to live up to his responsibilities as mother and father in such a way as to provide the family patterns of healthy development for their children.

Parents are, of course, absolutely essential for children. Children do a great deal for their parents. Not only do they provide joys which can be found nowhere else, but they can bring out the very best in men and women. Men who are successful as fathers will usually be successful in their life's work. Not all men who are successful at their work are successful family men. This simply points out that a special kind of maturity is necessary for a man to be a successful father.

Many women who are quite successful in a career are total failures as mothers. The emotional involvements and responsibilities of motherhood trigger their unconscious conflicts and they become ill and/or fail.

SELF-HELP FOR OTHER PROBLEMS

Establishing a Heterosexual Relationship

Unmarried people are in the position of having to pull themselves up by their own bootstraps. There are, however, social forces as well as those internal ones which propel persons toward maturity. The unmarried person does not, however, have the spouse as a source of courage, observation, and as a conflict trigger, all factors which will stimulate maturation.

A young person who avoids the opposite sex is almost certainly burdened by unconscious conflicts. Given freedom from unconscious conflicts and a social situtation where opportunities exist, males and females will come together; Nature is at work.

Unmarried persons frequently complain about insufficient opportunities for meeting a suitable person. These are mostly rationalizations; the persons in question are denying the effects of their own behavior which drive persons of the opposite sex away and can in this way justify avoiding the opposite sex. There are life situations where the opposite sex is absent or where it might be prudent to avoid such contacts; but, given the usual life circumstances, the man or woman who avoids forming a relationship with the opposite sex usually has something wrong with him or her.

These remarks are not to be understood as advocating that everyone *must* form a heterosexual relationship, or that persons cannot live productive lives without them. It is better that some persons not attempt heterosexual commitments because of the severity of their personality disturbances. A child might accidentally be born (at the worst), and/or an overt mental disturbance might erupt if they attempted to form a heterosexual relationship.

It could be argued that those persons who are inhibited in relation to the opposite sex should be left alone and not urged to overcome their difficulties. The chances are fairly high they will make a bad marriage and produce children who will develop some form of personality disturbance. There is much merit to this argument; however, even persons with marked personality disturbances seek out the opposite sex, they do marry, and children are born. The forces of nature which bring male and female together are very powerful. It is better, therefore, to help them become as emotionally healthy as possible for the sake of the children they may have. Everyone has the right to be as healthy as it is possible to be. Finally, those who can find satisfaction in a heterosexual relationship are usually happier than persons who live more isolated lives.

A good place for a young man to start is to turn to his own father or, when this is impossible, to a teacher, coach, friend, or any older man who has himself achieved a successful marriage—and has also reared healthy children. This may be very difficult for an inhibited young man to do. He may think he senses disapproval from the other man. He may have a transference reaction (project repressed feelings toward his own father onto other men) to all or most older men; if not, he may soon develop such a reaction when his intentions to establish a relationship with a female become the reason for his association with the older man.

Immense good can be done by parents or parental figures for young persons. In fact, more good may be achieved than from certain professionals. Frankly, I would be inclined to rely more on the impact of a good, strong, mature man or woman on a troubled young person than on many of the professionals I have known and know. This is a sorry state of affairs but I am afraid it is true.

The young man should speak frankly of his fears, misgivings, uncertainties, and guard against a sense of having weakened or diminished himself by having asked for advice, guidance, and encouragement. He and this father, or father substitute, should meet periodically to discuss his progress or lack thereof. The father or father figure should point out the ways the younger man is failing or stacking the cards against himself. He should guide, advise, and encourage. Once the younger man has sought out the older man, the latter should see to it that their relationship endures. The stronger must take responsibility for the weaker. Parents must remember that they never cease being parents.

The major difficulty with these guidelines is that the younger man may turn to someone who is psychiatrically troubled himself and who ascribes to a value system which is largely a function of his own unconscious conflicts. I am referring to a hypermorality manifested by an excessively strict code of behavior or, conversely, a psychiatrically disturbed man who advocates various forms of immature behavior to a younger man. Therefore, I repeat, the person to whom the younger one turns for help should be a *man* in the best sense of the word, and one who ascribes to the values referred to throughout this book. A happily married man with children, who is the head of his family, who is successful in his work, is the kind of man to use as a helper. You will be surprised to find so many people who are willing to help if they are asked; this includes one's own parents.

Unfortunately, the severely troubled young man who needs help to make a successful heterosexual adjustment may not have the kind of father who can provide the kind of assistance he needs. The worst that can happen to a young man who turns to his father is to be confronted by a father who is competitive with him, or who hates and rejects him. Such fathers can give a young man, even their son, very bad advice. Had the father been a better father the son probably would not have become psychiatrically troubled in the first place. This point requires some elaboration, however.

Many times circumstances have taken the father away when the young boy needed him; military service or vocational duties, for instance. The father may have been very neurotic himself and his marriage not a good one when the son was a child. Life events may have matured the father in the meantime. Thus, years later, after having matured, eventually having made a good marriage, etc., he might now be suitable as someone to guide his teenage or adult son in his efforts to establish a heterosexual relationship.

The key to success in such situations is for the helper to feel his responsibilities for the successful adjustment of the younger man and do whatever his wisdom and judgment point to as needing to be done. A parent is never free from all responsibility to his children. The person giving help may need to ask the young one about very specific details in his efforts with women, tell him to refrain from some actions, initiate others, and so on. The psychic significance of this enterprise is that the younger man looks to the "good father" for help. With the mother no longer the object of the son's intentions, as was the situation when the young man was a boy of three to six, success is likely to ensue. There is no longer a basis for rivalry, competition, fear, or hate except in the unconscious mind of the younger man. If the older man sees evidence of a negative reaction in the young one to the advice he is giving, he should not take this personally but realize that the younger man is reacting inappropriately on the basis of feelings which are stored in his unconscious mind. The father or father figure will be helping the young man give up his unconscious attachment to his mother and find a girl of his own. This unconscious process will be taking place silently in the young man as he makes a successful heterosexual relationship.

What has been outlined for the young man who is having difficulty associating with the opposite sex, or who cannot make a commitment to a woman, applies equally to a young woman. She should turn to an older and mature woman for help, preferably one who has married and had children. Her mother may or may not be suitable; if suitable from the standpoint of her own maturity, she is the most desirable one to turn to.

Young people frequently have difficulty talking to their parents. If they can communicate with their parents, the word of the parent generally carries more weight than that of others. Young people will usually be very surprised by how easy it is for them to talk to their parents once the parents are given a chance to help. The young person may eventually have to turn to several older persons and accept the best each has to give. *Don't give up!*

The chance for a successful outcome is increased if there is frank talk about all aspects of male-female interactions. Silent processes of change will be taking place which are vital to the young person's maturity. First, factual information will have to be obtained; next, the young person will have to master new situations. Crippling unconscious conflicts will be mobilized by the new behavior, making it possible for the healthy parts of his personality to resolve them; and finally, an identification process with an older woman (or man in the case of a male) will be taking place. This combination of a close working relationship with an older (and mature) person of the same sex while simultaneously making efforts to establish a relationship with and commitment to a person of the opposite sex of one's own age is one of the most maturing life situations. The young person and the older person who are working together cannot strive for insight deep into the unconscious; they are not trained for this task. Helping the younger one discover the most successful and mature ways for behaving generally and with the opposite sex in particular is the objective. Such a relationship makes up to some extent for the good fathering (in the male) and good mothering (in the female) the young person missed out on as a child. Such supportive relationships are extremely helpful and can markedly alter the course of a young person's life and may even be lifesaving if properly handled.

Nothing of what I have just said about the importance of making a heterosexual relationship should be understood to mean that I advocate early marriage. Fifty percent of early marriages end in divorce. This is not surprising. Young people often marry for the wrong reasons. They use marriage as a means to combat loneliness, provide an easy and ready accessibility for sexual gratification. They are driven into marriage by unconscious forces. Young people should associate with a number of different persons of the opposite sex, thereby giving themselves time to mature, before making a final commitment.

What determines the choice of a mate is a complex subject. Obviously the couple must share some common values and interests. There may be elements of the qualities of the parent of the opposite sex in the person chosen. I do not intend to go into all of this. One element in the choice of a mate is crucial and must not be ignored. This has to do with masculinity in men and femininity in women. When a young man makes the decision to marry, he should be mature enough to pick a woman who is not bossy, domineering and aggressive or ineffectual in her efforts to be a woman. If he does make such a choice he should face this fact squarely and seek professional help or continue in a program of self-help.

Even when young people do not seek help from older persons or from their parents, I firmly believe parents should keep close watch on the dating patterns of their sons and daughters. When parents see their daughters pick weak, ineffectual, or effeminate boys or men, or their sons date aggressive, domineering women, and especially if they date masculinized women, they should intervene. This can be done tactfully but in a way which may lead to a reassessment of the relationship and its consequences if a marriage were to be entered into.

Parents Must Look at Themselves

For parents to be able to make such an intervention in their son's or daughter's personal life will require them to first look at themselves and see what it was about their relationship with each other and their child which caused him to be the kind of person he is. These can be extremely hard facts to face, but face them you must if you do not wish to perpetuate a tradition of disturbed marital relationships and disturbed personalities in your family tree. In particular, the parents should look into their son's or daughter's preference toward them. If they discover that their son was always closer to his mother they will almost certainly discover that the girl he is thinking of choosing for a mate was closer to her father. The same applies for their daughter. These patterns spell trouble in the future, especially when children are born. Having made these discoveries and having possibly observed that their son is passive, weak, or ineffectual—or that their daughter is domineering, etc.—and that their choices of mates are the opposite, I believe it would be an extremely wise course to strongly urge the young people to postpone their marriage and take certain corrective steps.

I urge parents and their son or daughter to read this book and discuss it and then to look into their past lives together. It may be possible for sons to finally work out a better relationship with their fathers and mature in the process (the father may mature too). Similarly, mothers and daughters may at long last fully find each other. This will not be an easy task; many will fail, but those parents and offspring whose personalities are not too disturbed will succeed.

It is the easiest thing in the world to trace disturbed personality patterns back many generations. A female patient will report that she was much closer to her father than her mother. Upon inquiry it will be discovered that her father was deeply tied to his mother who, in turn, had been tied to her father, and so on. Psychiatrists alone cannot offset these trends—nor will this book. However, it is my hope that what I have written will at least have some effect on these family patterns which produce children who grow into disturbed adults. I cannot possibly cover all aspects of child rearing, nor did I intend to. If, however, parents will closely watch the heterosexual patterns of their offspring and not hesitate to intervene tactfully even if their children are in their twenties or older, great good can be done. If I discovered that one of my sons was going to marry an aggressive, domineering, and possibly masculinized woman I would be as alarmed as if I had discovered a cancer in him. Such a choice for a mate would say, in effect, that he was suffering from a major personality disturbance and that his mother and I had failed him when he was growing up.

Parents are their children's keepers. Never forget it. Correct the mistakes which your own personalities and your not completely successful marriage forced you to make with your children. Intervene with your children (even though they are young adults) and do it effectively. There is no greater good to be done for them or for mankind than preventing your children from making bad marriages.

Becoming Successful at Work

Another aspect of maturity is the capacity to work effectively and productively and with a sense of joy. Many people find their way into a life's work which suits them, that is, which permits the expression of their primary interests, talents, or skills, but who—because of conflicts within themselves—cannot fully realize their potential. They are not ill suited for their vocation or profession but unconscious forces prevent their becoming successful. Such persons are blocked by unconscious conflicts and these usually involve insecurity and/or guilt about being successful, or both. The effort to succeed or to carry a single task through to completion usually awakens the unconscious wish to have succeeded with mother and destroyed father in the case of a male, although other more complex conflicts may be triggered too. Men with such unconscious conflicts frequently stop short of fully completing tasks or putting all of their skills, intellect, and energy to the task of fully advancing themselves in their life's work. A harsh or infantilizing mother will also have a residual effect on both males and females. To be successful means to be able to stand alone. To do so also awakens separation anxiety in those who failed to receive good mothering as outlined previously.

The first step toward self-help with regard to one's work is the recognition that one is not achieving his potentials fully, either through avoidant behavior (missing opportunities for advancement), or by provoking rejection by one's seniors. One should watch his behavior scrupulously and push himself to seize upon opportunities whenever they present themselves. Provocative behavior toward others should be curbed by the diligent application of willpower. These efforts will lead to opportunities for broader and deeper involvement with the environment (the work situation), and increased anxiety and/or other signs of psychic distress will almost surely appear in persons whose unconscious conflicts have been standing in the way. It is now crucial that one not retreat but instead hold his newly won ground and master the new work involvements. After having mastered the new situation, anxiety will generally subside and further forward steps can be taken. One's worst enemy is self-doubt and fear. One should ask himself, "Do I have the ability and knowledge to do better or undertake a particular task?" If the answer is affirmative, one should *do it*. Not only will there be the immediate reward of the successful act, but this process will further stimulate maturation.

The situation can be considerably more complicated than that which has just been described. Sometimes unconscious conflicts have such a profound impact on the individual's choice of life work that a vocation or profession has been picked which does not permit a living out of the most predominant skills, talents, interests, etc. To follow one's truest inclinations was so forbidden and would evoke such intense anxiety and other symptoms that a choice is made which is the complete opposite of what the person would really like to do or be. These alternative choices are frequently characterized by a lower degree of demand on the person in terms of precision, level of responsibility, commitment, involvement; there is often a lower social value placed on the occupation or field.

What I describe next may be somewhat difficult to follow. Success at a life's work of one's primary choice can represent the *winning* of the forbidden mother (in the case of the boy), or of the father (in the case of a girl). In women, the most common life work to which this formulation applies is making a family. A solution (not resolution) for such burdened people is never to succeed fully or completely in that particular work. In this way they escape guilt and anxiety or worse. Some people who are severely burdened by unconscious conflicts never even get this far. They relinquish their true objectives at the outset; they never choose the field of work for which they are best suited. Instead, they pick a life's work which will be less satisfying and which may at the same time reflect the interests of the parent of the opposite sex. Their choice symbolizes an *identification* with the parent of the opposite sex. By choosing this field, the person never breaks his tie with this parent. It is as if the person has said, "I will give up what I *really* wanted to do and be like the parent of the opposite sex; I will choose a less exacting field which requires less of me and represents the parent of the opposite sex. Now I am not threatened nor do I have to stand alone; I have my mother (or father in the case of a woman) with me."

A few case examples will illustrate these several ways in which unconscious conflicts can influence the choice of a life's work and the capacity to succeed.

A son may have a father who is successful in a certain field, but because the son failed to fully resolve his childhood oedipal conflicts his own vocational choice will be affected by these unconscious forces. He will retain unconscious fear of and guilt toward his father, even though he may have identified with him to some extent. He may pick his father's field but because of his unconscious conflicts he will not do well even though he is temperamentally suited for the field. He may pick a different field which does not provide for the living out of his best talents, interests, skills, and as a result he may never be fully successful. Some pick their father's field because of unconscious guilt toward the father even though they are fundamentally better suited for some other work. In this way they never fully realize their full potential, thereby punishing themselves.

More deeply disturbed young men who failed to resolve their Oedipus complex and who are more completely identified with their mothers may choose a field in which their mother was interested; these frequently are fields other than the more exacting ones such as the hard sciences. Such a man may possess all of the mental equipment to enter one of the more exacting fields but because he failed to identify with a strong and masterful father and identified with his mother instead he will pick a less demanding field. One gains the strong impression that some social scientists, psychologists, artists, priests, ministers, etc., are deeply identified with their mothers. The same holds true for some psychiatrists and psychoanalysts although, it seems, not so predominantly. The professional base for these two fields is medicine, a field which is much more exacting than the humanities.

A program of self-help as outlined may help persons who are not living out their capabilities fully but who are in the field for which they are best suited and are partially successful. Good results are considerably less certain for persons who are failing at work where the choice reflects a deep tie with the parent of the opposite sex. Their psychopathology is much more extensive and will, in all probability, require professional help.

Choice of a career or life's work should be made only after careful reflection about the basis for the interests and one's abilities for the field. Parents should always be willing to help their children make these choices, just as they should be willing to offer assistance with regard to the choice of a mate. The entire course of life may be affected by initial commitment to a vocation, profession, or field of study. Note should be taken of the father's interests and values, and the mother's. Above all, one should recognize what his own talents and most satisfying interests are and pursue those irrespective of the interests of his parents. Just because a boy's father is a businessman does not mean he must be one too, but it could mean that following father's footsteps will bring him the most rewards from life. Assessing the nature of one's adult and ongoing, as well as earlier, relationship to one's parents will provide important clues. A son who has always been closer to his mother, including during his adulthood, who picks a life's work which reflects an interest of his mother (for instance he elects to teach English because his mother was an English major) should think long and hard about the reasons for his choice before he commits himself. His unconscious attachments may be forcing him into his mother's field of interest when his talents and truer interests would be better fulfilled in a different field.

A career other than marriage and making a family provides a common and rather ideal way for a woman to avoid differentiating her femininity fully. By working she has arranged her life circumstances in such a way that her unconscious conflicts surrounding femininity and motherhood can remain relatively dormant. Under these conditions she may be relatively free from psychic distress. Men who avoid marriage are usually troubled by the same problem.

For young working women who recognize in themselves a strong attraction to men, and some maternal strivings, I recommend efforts at self-help if they are having difficulty forming a heterosexual relationship. Professional help may be necessary. For the more severely disturbed working woman I do not recommend a program of self-help. She may falsely believe a marriage and a child will mature her, as indeed they may, but the risk is great, not only for her and her husband but for the child. Therefore, I believe (good) professional help should be sought by those career women who cannot, with a minimum of help from an older woman, marry and become mothers.

The woman who has begun her family must hold herself to her responsibilities. Unless circumstances force her to work she should not, and if she finds herself anxious, depressed, or otherwise distressed she should first attempt the self-help approach, using her husband and an older woman for the helping source and, failing to overcome her difficulties she should seek (good) professional assistance. It is better for her, her husband, and especially her children, that she become a competent, masterful, and fulfilled woman and mother than that she turn the care of the children over to a nursemaid. If she cannot effect these changes within herself by whatever means she uses, she should admit the mistake of ever having attempted motherhood and relegate the care of her children to a feminine and maternal nursemaid. If she does not, and continues to force herself into a role which she cannot fill, she will do more harm than good to herself, her children, and her husband.

PLAY

Play is an important part of life. Many people who cannot play successfully may find joy in their work. Persons who have, for justifiable reasons, had to work hard all of their lives may never have learned how to play, how to use leisure time. However, there are many whose conscience is so powerful that they are not permitted the simple pleasure of play. Without there being a reason for a particular activity, such as cultivating a business deal, these people cannot relax, play, and enjoy themselves just for the fun of it. These remarks apply to sexual pleasure as well.

The primary basis for a joyless life is unconscious guilt. A guilty orientation to life may receive powerful social reinforcement in certain religious sects but for the most part the inability to enjoy life, including play, is personal and derives from unconscious roots. To be sure, a person recently or continuously exposed to suffering mankind or heavy responsibilities or other stress may not feel like playing, but for the average person forces in his unconscious are the bases for his lackluster life. Unconscious forces may directly bar pleasure or they may act more indirectly by having caused an inhibited personality, a chronic depression, a slavelike devotion to work and duty.

When such a pattern is recognized, a determined effort should be made to play. Time should be set aside for leisure activities and no matter how strong the inner resistance, anxiety, or other reactions, play should be undertaken. An annual vacation should be a part of every life; an event looked forward to and planned and enjoyed. It is incredible how many people cannot enjoy a vacation, not to mention the daily exposure to the beauty of nature around them. It has been said that the family that plays together stays together. I believe there is truth in this saying.

Some people do nothing but play. In such cases play serves as a means for avoiding the responsibilities of maturity. Close inspection into the lives of those who only "play" will reveal that they do not really play. These are miserable people who remain active, often to the point of near-frenzy, as a means by which to avoid the agony of their existence.

CARE OF THE BODY

A sure sign of the presence of illness-producing unconscious forces is failure to care for one's body. While some of the reasons for the misuse of the body may derive from the simple lack of knowledge, many people who know better don't do better. Some of the forms of bodily abuse are failure to care for the teeth, insufficient rest, failure to relax sufficiently and use leisure time well, insufficient exercise, overeating and improper diet, obesity, failure to follow a physician's instructions when physically ill (the diabetic who doesn't stay on his diet), smoking, excessive use of alcohol and other drugs, ignoring obvious signs of physical disease, unnecessary risk taking, etc. Persons who have enough self-awareness to recognize these and other forms of self-neglect or self-assault should confront themselves and, either on their own strength or on the strength from others, they should change their behavior.

It is remarkable how much anxiety or depression or other frank psychiatric symptomatology will sometimes appear when persons attempt to take better care of their bodies. It is as if their conscience says they do not deserve to be physically healthy, to minimize risks to their well-being or life. Guilt is a prime source for the preceding and other behaviors. Physical health is a precious gift but thousands of persons abuse their bodies, not because of ignorance or poverty but because of forces within their unconscious minds. Some who cannot commit outright suicide do so piecemeal through neglect of their bodies.

FRIENDSHIP BETWEEN PARENTS
AND THEIR ADULT CHILDREN

A serious form of psychopathology, and one which brings heartache to all parties, is the cruel manner in which some young people relate to their parents, and vice versa. While emancipation from parents is a necessary part of the maturational process, many young people rudely cut their parents out of their lives and often, in the process, discard some fine values which their parents have upheld. These reactions reflect any or all of the following: excessive unconscious dependence, hostility, strong incestuous attraction toward the parent of the opposite sex, the misbelief that identification with the parent of the same sex constitutes a submission or subjugation. Other reasons may exist, deriving from impressions and misbeliefs formed very early in life. Girls often turn away from their mothers out of revenge for not having nurtured them sufficiently, for having deprived them of a penis, for standing in their way with their father. The boy's primary reason is unresolved oedipal hostility toward his father. He often believes that if he accepts his father's values and identifies with him and becomes friends with him he will be cheapening or demeaning himself. He may harbor so much childhood hostility in his unconscious mind that it is impossible to be friendly with his father.

When such attitudes exist toward the parents, the parents should take the initiative and make a sustained effort to break down the wall and establish a good adult relationship with their children. Since the parents are older, hopefully more mature, and still the parents, it is primarily their responsibility to effect the changes.

Many parents and offspring have found each other by both having recognized the distance between them and finding out the reason. I am, in general, opposed to encounter groups and the like because of poor leadership and the tendency for psychological forces to get out of hand. Considerable good, however, can result if the entire family (excluding the very young children) will meet together and explore the basis for their emotional distance. Tempers should remain cool and irrational attitudes should be rigorously searched for. Children of all ages often change their attitudes dramatically when they better understand their parents and the basis for prior behavior. While these clarifications are occurring at a conscious level, and the focus is upon current or past issues not directly linked to repressed childhood conflicts, more will be going on than any of the participants will realize. Unconscious conflicts will be mobilized through these family interactions and the process of conflict resolution and maturation will proceed. I make no claim that such efforts as these will lead to a complete resolution of the unconscious conflicts in any or all, but much can and often will change, enough so that the younger ones may well live a more successful life, and congenial family relations will be established.

Frankly oedipal intentions should probably not be discussed, but the father may point out that his son was always so close to his mother that he rejected efforts on the father's part to invite him to participate in his life. The son may point out that the father was away too much, or that father seemed cool or competitive toward him and he may discover that he rejected his father's invitations to be closer to him. The parents may discover they have clung to their children out of loneliness caused by their own inability to find adequate fulfillment with each other, thereby forcing the children to break loose from their clutches. The daughter will almost surely recognize that her coolness toward her mother is based on resentment, jealousy, and hostility. She will be distressed to discover how she provoked her father unjustly, particularly with the coming of puberty. Parents and offspring should be able to become good friends; when this does not happen something is wrong.

Unfortunately, emotional distance between parents and minor children is frequently associated with destructive behavior on the child's part, such as drug usage, sexual promiscuity, goallessness; in short, the afflictions which are destroying so many of our young people. When talk sessions, as just described, do not suffice then the parents must apply force in the form of very firm control. Punishment will not bring about the desired changes because the destructive behavior in all probability is motivated by an unconscious need for punishment. Parents may have to place the child on house arrest, deprive him of privileges, deny him access to friends who are sick and destructive. Periodic search of the child's quarters in order to find drugs may be necessary. A careful accounting of the child's financial expenditures should be implemented. If the child reacts violently or threatens to run away, call the police. A show of force has a very sobering effect on the young. Above all, parents, the father in particular, should never fear having a showdown with their offspring and calling a complete halt to the objectionable behavior. Once the tide has turned, the follow-through is an absolute must. After the showdown children will usually be willing to talk. Great effort must then be expended to hold them to a constructive way of life. The show of force is an act of love; children realize that and want it to happen. Turning around a bad situation may take a few weeks or may take months. Persist and never give up. The child is yours to save. Never excuse your child's delinquent or asocial behavior. Doing so is a way of getting yourself off the hook.

The key is to draw upon the good will of all; let the children emancipate but at the same time all should ferret out and discard irrational attitudes and thus lay the groundwork for an adult relationship for the children. The bonds within the family are priceless; they should extend into adulthood and never weaken.

HOMOSEXUALITY AND MARRIAGE

At this point I wish to state categorically that I do not think homosexuals should ever attempt marriage as a self-help method in hope that doing so will make them heterosexual. Homosexuals are very sick people; they should attempt marriage only after successful psychiatric treatment, and then they should have children only after having given marriage an adequate test of several years. Homosexuals sometimes marry and have children as a cover for their illness.

Homosexuality is as much a public health problem as any of the major diseases which have concerned public officials and the medical profession. It is contrary to nature and represents displacement behavior; the individual displaces onto the same sex what his unconscious conflicts prevent him from expressing with a person of the opposite sex.

I believe it would be better if homosexuals would simply accept the fact that life dealt cruel blows during childhood and that whatever parental urges may exist within them should be sublimated; that is, they should fulfill these urges in other ways and not have children. Little good can come to children from exposure to adults who are so disturbed as to have become overtly homosexual. There are ample means for society to absorb homosexuals without children being involved. For society to permit homosexuals to "marry" homosexuals and adopt children is utter madness.

What I have said about homosexuals applies equally to many others who marry; I refer to persons with psychiatric disturbances of considerable severity. The maladies of many badly disturbed people are not always as easily identified, nor is their natural history or solution as certain. With homosexuals the picture is clear. Find good psychiatric help. Unfortunately, good help is difficult to find. Therefore, the best advice I can give homosexuals who cannot find good treatment or whose efforts to be treated have failed is to accept and learn to live with their illness. Hard facts are hard to face; the fact is that homosexuals can never be good parents. Society owes the confirmed homosexual a place so he can live as full a life as possible, but society must not uphold this way of life to the young as a variant of normality.

LOST YOUTH

Every generation has had its nonconformists among young people. Some mistakenly believe the hippie, unisex, commune, back-to-nature, Jesus, the drug cult, and other movements are or were nothing more than expressions of nonconformity. Nonconformists they were and are but they are much more too. In no social phenomenon does a clearer relationship exist than between the ill effects of family life and alienated, drug-using youth. Bratter (15) reports that these young people referred to their fathers as passive, uninvolved, disinterested, remote, compliant, ineffectual, and often emasculated by their assertive, dominant, intrusive and overprotective wives. Family life was described as barren.

Dr. Bruno Bettelheim (9) is quoted as defining their life style as "fundamentally an emotional illness." He attributes this illness to the family and notes that "permissive parents produce highly perishable children."

The ones I have known were very sick people; they were lost and were groping for a way of life which would give them at least a modicum of security. Parents who see their children identifying themselves with any movement which is characterized by extreme non-conformity and non-commitment to a productive way of life should take immediate and decisive steps to prevent further deterioration in the life of their child.

At the first sign of the interest of their child (usually the adolescent) in any aspect of these sick ways of life the parents should confront the child with what they see happening. Nipping the process in the bud is the key. Parents should absolutely prohibit their offspring from associating with persons in these movements. They should not allow their children to don the symbols of these movements. Throw out the posters, search for drugs, and be relentless. I am well aware of how difficult this can or will be, but do it you must. But more than that must be done.

Parents must face themselves squarely and ask how they failed their child in the past so that the child now is inclined to identify himself with a way of life which in nonproductive and/or destructive. They must then more actively involve themselves in the life of their child. Fathers especially must take time to supply the fathering that it is almost certain was lacking during the child's formative years. When this effort is made parents will be appalled by the discovery of how little time they have devoted to their child or children. The years of neglect or uninvolvement in their child's life will become painfully apparent. It will take great effort on the part of the parents to change their pattern of living with their children. A nondefeatist attitude is absolutely vital. Changing the trend in the young person's life will not happen overnight.

Saving the very young ones from the "cop-out" way of life is the easiest, of course. Alternatives must be provided. These alternatives include increasing family time and time spent individually with the child. Young people respond well to genuine expressions of interest from their parents. In the case of a boy, his father must make more time available for him. The same principle applies to a girl and her mother.

In addition to changing daily living patterns, the entire family should periodically have "family therapy" sessions. Father, mother and child (or children) should openly discuss what it was in their past lives together that caused the young person to adopt an uncommitted, nonproductive, and usually a destructive way of life. Parents must not be timid about their intrusion into their offspring's way of life.

Should discussion fail (that is, the rational approach), parents must and should prohibit the child from associating with those who embrace these movements. These movements represent some of the worst social influences in existence today. It is inconceivable to me that parents who love their children could stand "helplessly" by and watch their young fall prey to their influence. The key is decisive, forthright intervention on the parents' part. Having intervened, parents must then correct those conditions within the family which caused the child to develop in such a way as to be interested in these movements in the first place.

Parents who do not intervene must question the depth of their love for their child. Unconscious hate in parents toward children can be expressed in a variety of ways. One of the most common is for parents to stand idly by while their child destroys himself. The stance of noninvolvement on the parents' part is explained by them to be a reflection of their respect for the child's individuality, the right to free choice, and other such absurdities. If you really love someone, you don't stand idly by and watch him destroy himself.

It is a mistake to believe parents can improve their relationship with their children by joining their ("cop-out") way of life—by dressing somewhat like they do, trying to become interested in their music, their language—in short, their values. This is the quickest way possible to lose what little may be left of the child's respect for his parent. Remember, the parent, like the doctor, must be committed to the healthy part of the other person, offspring or patient, but must ultimately reject the sick part. It is necessary to try to understand why the sick part developed—in this instance the "cop-out" way of life—but to understand does not mean to accept or endorse what is understood. Understanding sickness is the first step toward removing the condition.

Not long ago a national figure attempted to bridge the gulf between his son and himself by entering into the son's sick way of life. He began taking drugs along with his son in an effort to "enter his world," hoping the two of them might find each other. This effort failed completely. The son committed suicide, and the father began doing strange things which defied reason and ultimately led to his own death. His was probably an unconscious suicide brought about by his guilt for having failed his son, and his realization that he himself had failed as a man. Instead of having tried to join his son's sick way of life he should have intervened and, if necessary, had his son hospitalized.

Where decisive intervention and a program of self-help— sessions of "family therapy" and new ways of relating to the child—do not work, then psychiatric treatment must be obtained. Do not hesitate to hospitalize your child if necessary. Arrange for psychotherapy. If you do, look very closely at the personality of the prospective therapist. First have an interview with him to find out what he thinks about the way of life your child has adopted. I know of several professionals who believe present day youth are merely experimenting with new lifestyles. Experimenting they are—with ways for destroying themselves outright or with ways to limit their chances for living a full and constructive life.

CHAPTER FIVE

Psychotherapy

I will now discuss various types of psychiatric treatment, with special emphasis being placed on the psychotherapeutic process.

Psychotherapy refers to all forms of treatment which rely on interpersonal interactions, including psychoanalysis. It can do much good or it can do great harm. The results of treatment depend upon the personality of the treating person, his grasp of the nature of mental life and human existence, and treatment techniques. Also of immense importance are the life circumstances of the patient, the nature of the patient's problems, and his basic personality organization.

Those of you who need or who are in treatment may require help to determine whether you are being treated effectively or are being harmed. An understanding of what is written here will also be of help to those who never enter formal treatment, particularly those of you who are trying to help yourselves.

I will now focus on those principles which make psychotherapy successful. Psychotherapy is most effective when the physician takes responsibility for inducing change in his patient. This may seem to you like a perfectly obvious and necessary orientation to the treatment process, but it is not a guiding principle for many who practice psychotherapy.

It is around this point that I feel most critical toward so many psychotherapists. Most seem to want sincerely to help their patients but they do not fully grasp the absolutely vital importance of taking responsibility for the patient and his treatment. The implications of this principle are far-reaching as I will illustrate. So many psychotherapists leave the responsibility for changing to the patient, failing to realize, apparently, that had the patient been able to change he would never have come to them in the first place.

During the treatment process the doctor's responsibilities to his patient are four in number: (1) He must induce change in his patient. To do this wisely and effectively the doctor must understand the human condition and he must have mastered techniques for bringing about constructive changes in his patient. (2) He must protect the patient from the irrational forces within himself which are unleashed during the treatment process. (3) He must protect others from these same forces within his patient. (4) He must help the patient develop his potentials and find ways for their expression.

Effective psychotherapy depends upon the patient's cooperation, of course, but bringing about change is the doctor's responsibility. As patients change (that is, resolve their unconscious conflicts and get over their symptoms and change their personality and behavior), responsibility gradually shifts from doctor to patient. By the end of treatment the patient becomes truly independent and can take full responsibility for himself, and that is as it should be. But even to the very last day of treatment the guiding orientation for the doctor should be one of responsibility. I believe psychotherapists should take responsibility for their patient twenty-four hours a day, seven days a week, just as other physicians do, and not limit their responsibility to the period of time when doctor and patient are meeting. The specifics of this guiding principle will be explained and illustrated as the treatment process is described. Meeting with a patient a specified number of times per week is a matter of practical convenience. The therapeutic process is set in motion at the outset of treatment and goes on continuously. Hence the doctor's responsibility is continuous; many doctors do not understand this fundamental point, at least they seem not to.

Many doctors do not fully understand the powerful impact they may be having on their patient or, conversely, how little; nor do they understand the power of the forces in the patient's unconscious mind which the treatment process releases. In either case, the element of the doctor's responsibility is a crucial factor in the proper conduct and outcome of the treatment.

THE MEDICAL MODEL OF TREATMENT

The working model of the mind which I have found most useful for psychotherapy combines some aspects of several theories of personality. The concept of the unconscious is centermost in my understanding of people. There is the conscious part of the mind and the unconscious part. The unconscious is the storehouse of the past; it contains much that works for us and much (in sicker people) that works against us. The misperceptions of childhood, old wishes, conflicts, complexes, the irrational, exist mostly in the unconscious region of the mind. The good past which gives personality strength, creative energies, and capacities "resides" in the unconscious too. There are also empty places in the unconscious which should have been filled by the events of family life. The forces within the unconscious (conflicts, complexes, etc.) and the empty places, have a great bearing on how a person thinks and feels, what he believes, how he behaves; in short, what he is and the direction his life takes.

I believe that personality is also a product of what is learned, and of events which condition individuals to be what they are.

Treatment, then, which is based on these theoretical views of personality must (1) clarify and remove unconscious forces which produce illness; (2) fill the empty places within the patient's personality; and (3) eliminate destructive and promote constructive behavior—a process which is based on relearning.

The model upon which my understanding of the therapeutic process is based is, therefore, largely psychoanalytic, but it is more accurately a synthesis of what I have come to believe to be the best principles of various theoretical points of view. This combination of principles works provided the doctor understands that it is he who is responsible for making treatment work. The human being is a complex organization. All well-functioning and productive organizations have a responsible chief executive. During treatment the doctor is the chief executive. After treatment the patient becomes his own chief executive.

EXPRESSIVE PSYCHOTHERAPIES

The most fundamental element in expressive or "uncovering" psychotherapy is that psychiatrically disturbed people suffer from unconscious irrational forces (these are conflicts, fears, beliefs, attachments, etc., which formed as a consequence of childhood experiences), and that these forces produce disturbances in feeling, thought, or behavior, or all three. Should the doctor try to rebuild the repressive and defensive part of the mind, put things back together as they were, or should he bring these irrational unconscious forces fully into consciousness and resolve them, thereby bringing about personality change?

If the doctor is skilled in working in a way which brings unconscious forces into consciousness, and if the patient is strong enough to come to grips with his inner life, I believe it is nearly always desirable to employ "uncovering" therapy in a careful and orderly way which does not overwhelm the patient. Removing these forces from a patient relieves him of heavy burdens. It is like draining an abscess. This process should always proceed at a rate which does not overstrain the patient. Unfortunately, this can be very difficult to do with some patients. It is common for patients to become very anxious or depressed or develop other symptoms as this process is set into motion. New and at times troublesome behaviors usually appear during treatment when unconscious contents are being brought into consciousness. Some patients may develop a frank psychosis. It is not uncommon for a person's values, interests, and even his entire view of life, to change rather dramatically—at times permanently—as a result of the mobilization of his unconscious conflicts, thoughts, and feelings. Mobilization of unconscious conflicts does not always mean their removal or resolution. Put another way, insight into one's inner life does not necessarily bring about change, that is, abolition of the irrational feelings, beliefs, behavior, or more pervasive personality change. What is even more troublesome is that conflicts, etc., that have lain completely dormant can become partially mobilized toward consciousness and have a powerful effect on the patient's life without either the patient or doctor knowing why these changes in the patient are happening. These points will be discussed in detail.

This kind of treatment, which is sometimes called expressive or exploratory psychotherapy, insight therapy or psychoanalysis, depends upon strict confidentiality, some degree of regularity of appointments (usually for forty-five to fifty minutes per session) at a frequency of several appointments per week (usually three to five). It is possible, however, to do very effective expressive treatment when seeing the patient only once a week. The point is that expressive or uncovering treatment should be conducted in such a way as to bring into consciousness that which was unconscious with the objective of getting rid of irrational forces, thereby liberating the patient from the bondages of his past existence.

FREE ASSOCIATION

As the patient talks freely, the doctor discovers new facts about his patient and also identifies the ways in which the patient resists the treatment process. Resistance to treatment has two aspects. There is resistance to making self-discoveries and there is resistance to changing. The doctor's first responsibility is to help the patient overcome resistance to self-discovery. It sometimes takes hard work to overcome resistances. There are many ways for going about this, one of which is continued silence on the doctor's part for a while, but not for too long. When a patient is blocked in his progress by his resistance, the doctor must figure out a way to help him. For the doctor just to silently sit there hour after hour is wasteful of time and presupposes a kind of pulling-oneself-up-by-bootstraps type of strength in the patient. I would soon find another doctor if mine remained silent most of the time. There are times when remaining silent (on the doctor's part) is very necessary, but an excessive use of silence is generally a reflection of a lazy, passive, irresponsible, or stumped doctor (possibly all four) trying to appear wise. If you are making progress with a doctor who rarely says anything, fine; but if you are not, and he remains silent hour after hour, I doubt if you will make much progress.

As the patient talks from hour to hour, unconscious meanings will become progressively mobilized and patients often make ''spontaneous'' self-discoveries. More often, however, the doctor discovers deeper meanings in what the patient is talking about and offers these to the patient in the form of interpretations. Insight can be very superficial, such as recognizing a pattern in one's behavior; for example, provoking an argument with one's spouse when the occasion calls for affection; or the insight may go deep, far into the past, and reveal some of the basic roots of personality.

Obviously there is much room for error in the interpretative process; therefore the doctor who fires off ill-considered or hasty interpretations (sometimes called wild interpretations) is doing no good whatsoever and will, in fact, be impeding the treatment process. An interpretation is at best an assumption or a hypothesis yet to be confirmed. Confirmatory evidence for the accuracy of an interpretation (by the doctor) or self-insight (achieved spontaneously) can take several forms. Symptoms may disappear, feelings may change, behavior may change, dreams may appear which are confirmatory in nature. The point is, interpretations must be made with the care, precision, and incisiveness of the surgeon. A diseased organ cannot be removed by cutting in the wrong place; a house cannot be built by hammering at the nails timidly, tentatively, or wildly. One must be on target, the mark must be hit. Good treatment cannot be done by the doctor constantly wondering, supposing, tentatively suggesting, and so on. He must collect his evidence and then make his interpretative statement with conviction but also with an open-mindedness which will permit further testing of the validity of his interpretation in case he was wrong. Doctors who jump the gun and fire off interpretations without sufficient evidence, or who remain silent most of the time and hardly ever say anything (thereby missing many opportunities for good work), are equally worthless. Keep an eye on what is happening to you; you should have faith in your doctor but don't be blind. I realize how difficult it may be for you to make these judgments; however, interpretations which are valid tend to ring true when you hear them; they should improve your life. Give your doctor a chance, but if he never says much or is off the mark with what he says, I would look for another doctor.

THE THERAPEUTIC ALLIANCE

As a patient continues to come to his appointments, a therapeutic alliance or, as it is sometimes called, a working relationship must develop between him and his doctor. There must be a basic good feeling in the doctor for his patient and vice versa. Without this foundation little is likely to come of the treatment effort. If the patient is really convinced that the doctor does not have some degree of liking for him, and if the patient does not like his doctor, treatment should end. The doctor should have the integrity to take the initiative and discharge his patient if, after a reasonable period of time (within a few months) he has not developed a sense of compassion and/or liking for his patient. A patient must eventually form a positive feeling for his doctor, a liking for him, a sense of common purpose toward the treatment goals.

Patients should be very circumspect about quitting treatment because they openly dislike their doctor. Such feelings are often unconsciously transferred from their parents and others and may mask a basically sound therapeutic alliance. When, however, a neutral feeling or dislike persists from the beginning, I think it is doubtful that much success can come of the treatment. Sometimes a strong sense of dislike at the outset is a resistance to treatment and serves to mask the subconscious awareness on the patient's part that the doctor really knows his stuff and is, in all probability, going to succeed. One must, therefore, take time to assess whether or not a therapeutic alliance is forming. If not, it is better to find another doctor. If such a relationship never forms, regardless of who the doctor is, the patient better face up to the fact that he is in a high state of resistance to treatment with any doctor. Such patients should seek the services of a reputable doctor regardless of their feelings and if there is evidence that the doctor has some liking for them they should persist.

A negative response to any doctor, or a rather immediate worsening of the patient's clinical condition during the course of treatment, is sometimes referred to as a negative therapeutic reaction. This very difficult development during treatment can usually be dealt with effectively by a competent doctor who knows how and is able to take responsibility for his patient.

The therapeutic alliance has two functions. The most obvious is that the sick person now has an ally; he is no longer alone with his illness, he can gain strength and courage from someone else. I suspect the doctor becomes for the patient what a good mother is to a small child—a source of courage and security. A second, less obvious effect the doctor has is that he awakens in the memory (the unconscious storehouse) the "good" past—mother, father, relatives and friends who were good in the broadest sense of the word—and mobilizes these good experiences. It is as if the current helping hand reminds the patient of those of the past; there are elements of fathering in this too. He thereby gains courage and strength from two sources—from within himself and from the person from whom he seeks help. In a sense the doctor becomes the good mother and good father the patient may never have had, or not had enough of. At the same time he serves as a trigger of the repressed memories of good experiences with the parents. More will be said about this as the technique of good treatment is described in greater detail.

THE TRANSFERENCE

Transference is a phenomenon that can exist in relation to any person or situation in life; no one is ever immune to it. When one becomes involved with the environment—that is, with a person, persons, or situations—these external environmental factors trigger and mobilize unconscious forces. These unconscious forces are feelings, attitudes, wishes, instinctual energies, complexes, and conflicts. The presence of these unconscious "forces" color one's perception and feelings about ongoing experiences and persons. This is transference. The art of successful living is to be able to recognize transference distortions when they exist and not let them influence one's view of life, one's decisions, and one's actions.

When a patient meets regularly with his doctor, talks very frankly about himself, his life adjustment and his past, transference reactions toward the doctor form alongside the working relationship with the doctor. One of the main therapeutic tools of the doctor is the analysis of transference; that is, revealing to the patient what his feelings and perceptions really mean. This amounts to transforming the transference reaction into its original form, to the memories and associated feelings which belong to the past. Transference is memory in experiential form. Transference tends to ameliorate or disappear entirely as the past is remembered. When the past is remembered, the present can be distinguished from the past.

Some doctors make the mistake of assuming that a patient's entire past, or at least that part which is causing his illness, can be experienced in transference form in relation to him (the doctor). This can never happen. What should happen in successful treatment is that the patient discovers that he is making transference distortions not only toward his doctor but toward many people and situations in his life. In successful treatment the patient will find that he has transference reactions toward his spouse, children, boss, work situation, friends, etc. Thorough treatment requires an analysis of all of these transference reactions, not just those in relation to the doctor. Therefore, the doctor who focuses only on the patient's transference in relation to himself is doing an incomplete job. No doctor can ever trigger the forces in the patient's unconscious mind as effectively as can real-life experiences. The reason for this is easily explained. In life one is actually interacting with the environment and this greater degree of intensity more completely triggers unconscious forces. For example, a woman patient will have her unconscious conflicts triggered by her husband or lover with whom she has an ongoing relationship much more effectively than can the doctor whom she visits for a few hours per week.

Doctors who fail to analyze the patient's distorted (transference) beliefs and feelings in relation to persons and situations other than themselves and the treatment situation miss opportunities for much constructive work. Doctors make a serious mistake when they try to refer all transference distortions outside the treatment situation (which they have properly picked up) onto themselves. They make the assumption that these are displacements of feelings and thoughts which belong in the treatment situation. Patients frequently complain that their doctor tried to convince them that most of their feelings towards others were really displacement onto others of their transference toward him. Doctors who make this error fail to understand how widespread transference can be. I previously said that effective psychotherapy depends as much on precision and incisiveness as surgery. This is an example of what I mean. A doctor who always believes his patient is, in reality, talking about him (the doctor) when he is telling of his feelings about someone else (boss, spouse, children, or friends) is not being precise. In short, if you have a doctor who only analyzes transference in relation to himself you probably are not getting as much out of your treatment as would be possible if the doctor had a clearer understanding of the widespread nature of transference and its proper use in treatment.

The point to be grasped is that transference is the past felt and expressed in the present in experiential form. It is transformed memory and is, therefore, a form of resistance to insight and to change. Doctors who can work effectively with a patient's diverse and dispersed transference reactions will usually be of great help.

The ability to recognize transference and then knowing how to get the patient to recognize and really grasp its true meaning requires considerable skill. This is no job for amateurs or self-styled "therapists." The successful outcome of treatment depends to a large extent on how skillfully the patient's transferences were handled. When left untouched, or if poorly worked with, the patient's life can be done great damage.

As the patient progresses in his treatment he will discover that there are two aspects to his relationship with his doctor and others. His relationships have their real aspects; they are based on reality but they also have transference meanings. The ultimate objective of treatment is to help the patient resolve his unconscious conflicts so that his transference reactions disappear, so that he experiences life more in terms of what it really is.

Transference reactions can be just as troublesome as they can be helpful. Perhaps the most troublesome is when the patient cannot understand the true basis for transference beliefs and feelings. This kind of difficulty is quite common and seriously complicates treatment; treatment may fail because of the patient's inability to recognize, analyze and resolve transference. Some patients are especially unable to see into their transference reactions and never can despite the best efforts of their doctor. These same patients often are so convincing in the way they express their transferences that the doctor may lose his objectivity and react nontherapeutically to his patient. This is a sorry state of affairs and can lead to much trouble.

One of the most common instances where the meaning of transference is not recognized is the woman patient who cannot see that her beliefs and feelings are inappropriate and believes she has fallen in love with her doctor. Patients like this are generally unpsychologically minded; they have difficulty reflecting on their inner problems and therefore cannot grasp the true nature of their transference reactions. When this happens treatment gets bogged down and progress ceases. Some women believe their doctor should marry them, that they have at long last found their true love. Needless to say, they have not and were they to enter into a nontherapeutic relationship with their doctor they would, in all probability, soon discover that their expectations would not come true, that their doctor was not in reality the way they thought he was.

Transference resistance (this means when the patient cannot see the meaning of his transference reactions) can take the form of excessive hostility, distrust, competitiveness, dependency, idealization, etc., as well as excessive sexual and loving feelings. When these reactions are not successfully analyzed and resolved the results of treatment will be jeopardized to a considerable degree. In short, it is very important for patients to clear up their transference reactions before they terminate treatment. Transference is probably never resolved entirely, but the bulk of it should be. Many inexperienced therapists do not recognize transference when they see it, and they know even less how to handle these reactions.

Some doctors develop transference reactions toward their patients. These reactions are antitherapeutic in their effect simply because the doctor cannot accurately assess his patient nor can he behave appropriately toward him because of his own distorted picture of and feelings toward his patient.

There are several types of unconscious conflicts which lead to a form of transference resistance which is often ruinous to treatment. The transference reaction prevents the patient from accepting help from the doctor and he becomes stubborn, resists changing, appears not to comprehend what the doctor says, has doubts about the doctor's interpretations, etc. The common denominator in these attitudes is a refusal to cooperate with the doctor. The patient believes that to cooperate and to change as a result of treatment reflects a personal diminishment; that is, he feels subjugated, demeaned, made small, when he accepts the doctor's help. Of course nothing could be further from the truth. In patients where this transference resistance is not severe the progress of treatment is merely slowed, but where the belief is very strong treatment may fail, and frequently does. Every patient exhibits this kind of resistance to some degree.

A woman patient who is troubled by these unconscious conflicts will resist cooperating with her doctor and resist changing because to do so means for her to give up the penis she believes she possesses or wished to possess. More precisely, it means giving up those traits which originally formed because of her envy of the male and his genital. To give up her wish for a penis leads directly to her acceptance of her femininity, a state which, in her mind, is a depreciated one and one which she lacks the courage to accept. Thus, changing becomes a process of being devalued (castrated) and subjugated (by cooperating in treatment) to the doctor.

A second basis for resistance to treatment and to changing follows on the heels of the preceding when a woman patient begins to resolve this irrational belief and transference feeling. She will discover intense loving and sexual feelings within her toward her male doctor; these feelings are a function of her femininity. These feelings are "real" in that they are felt for the good male doctor who is, in fact, helping her, but they have transference (oedipal) meaning too. The doctor is the forbidden love object—the father—and she must now resist changing further lest she be overwhelmed by her strong feelings and surrender herself to him. Guilt and the sense of forbiddenness block her.

At the deepest level are the anxieties associated with closeness which are a function of the infant's early experiences and misperceptions in the early days of life. These refer to impressions of the mother as hostile or dangerous and therefore someone not to be too close to. Some mothers do hate and do reject their infants.

Mothers who hate and reject their babies are often "phallic" (they envy males); they have not fully accepted their own femininity, cannot be freely giving, and unconsciously (and at times even consciously) aspire to be men, or they have not overcome their penis envy and the characterologic consequences of all of these unconscious complexes. A common feature of their personality is an aggressiveness and a tendency to be domineering. Patients who had mothers like this can experience their doctor as dangerous; furthermore, they don't want to be like their mother. They resist cooperating because of these conflicts. This particular transference resistance is more prominent in women patients who have women doctors.

To recapitulate, women patients resist cooperating with their doctor and resist changing because they are made anxious by the sense of closeness to their doctor. This derives from deep conflicts which formed very early in life as a consequence of some degree of breakdown in their relationship with their mother. Next, to feel close to their doctor and cooperate with him brings out femininity in women. This trend toward femininity conflicts with those aspects of their personality which derive from penis envy; therefore, cooperation amounts to castration and subjugation. Finally, guilt blocks cooperation when feminine urges toward the male doctor are contaminated by oedipal feelings, that is, unconscious romantic feelings for their father which were formed in childhood. When the doctor is a woman all of these conflicts can be experienced; however, the castration and submission conflicts to the mother are more prominent.

The basis for this form of transference resistance (resistance to cooperation and to changing) in the male has the same source at its earliest level as described for the female—conflicts arising from a breakdown of the early mother-infant relationship. Not filled with a basic sense of security, and limited in his ability to trust, the boy will have trouble in his oedipal period. Depending on his family constellation and the personalities of his mother and father and their relationship with each other, he will be left with various residues from his oedipal period. Some degree of failure to overcome his conflicts surrounding masculinity will be the result. At the extreme, he may have become feminine as a result of his unresolved dependent and sexual and romantic ties with his mother, and his distant (or absent) relationship with his father, or he may have failed to overcome some degree of fear of and hostility for his father and may have retained some passivity in his personality.

Where the conflicts just described exist, and they are nearly always there to some degree in every male patient, the patient will experience help from the doctor as a subjugation. The male's pride suffers when help is offered, and he resists being helped. In extreme cases the patient may experience treatment as sexual seduction in which he will lose his masculinity. In every male, no matter what his outward appearances are, there is a powerful urge to be male; no male really wants it otherwise. When unconscious conflicts are overcome and treatment is successful, cooperating with the doctor and identifying with the world of men will no longer be experienced by the patient as a subjugation and an indignity.

If the male patient overcomes the conflicts which cause him to view treatment as a submission or subjugation, he will be faced with a new set of transference experiences which may also assume resistance proportions. These are hostility toward and fear of the doctor (father). He will experience the doctor as a rival, a competitor whom he hates and has reason to fear. He will find it hard to believe the doctor really wants him to succeed in life.

When treatment bogs down, each patient must be honest with himself and consider the possibility that he is contributing to the failure of treatment because of his lack of cooperation with his doctor. He should look for signs within himself of stubbornness, argumentativeness, rebelliousness, excessive preoccupation with ideas of "self-fulfillment" and "autonomy," excessively long periods of silence, coming late to appointments, paucity of new material to be worked on, frank feelings of competitiveness, a sense of being demeaned, a pervasively negative attitude toward treatment, and a feeling of being forced into a mold by treatment. The doctor must be given a chance and unless the patient cooperates with him treatment is doomed.

I wish to make it perfectly clear that patients with the kinds of conflicts just described that lead to transference resistance, upon which many treatments founder, can only cooperate so far. To expect them to be able to overcome this resistance to treatment on their own is unreasonable and amounts to asking the patient to cure himself. Similarly, young people frequently refuse to accept very sound and wise advice from their parents or other adults because of these same unconscious conflicts. The primary barrier is the unconscious subjugation conflict. This conflict (in children) causes many parents to fail (just as doctors can be made to fail) in their responsibilities as parents.

These remarks lead directly back to the issue of the doctor's responsibility for his patient and for the successful carrying out of treatment. In short, it is the doctor's responsibility to overcome these most difficult resistances in his patient. If he fails to do so, he has failed his patient. The patient's illness will have triumphed. When the doctor succeeds, the patient succeeds.

There is no better test of the doctor's skill and maturity, and his ability to take responsibility for the successful conduct of the treatment and for his patient, than his ability to overcome these transference resistances and resolve the patient's conflicts which led to their formation. It is this particular challenge which separates the men from the boys.

After having decided that he is cooperating to the best of his ability, the patient should decide whether or not his doctor is actively trying to help him overcome his resistance to changing. If he detects an attitude on his doctor's part which, in effect, is saying, "It's the patient's problem" (that treatment does not progress), he should seriously consider finding another doctor. If progress does not resume after the doctor has interpreted this resistance, the doctor should modify his technique so that progress will resume. I cannot go into details here on how one goes about this. One thing that the doctor should not do is lapse into a state of silent indifference and expect the patient to overcome his impasse.

This most troublesome of all of the forms of transference resistance does not appear at any particular phase of the treatment. It usually crops up whenever the patient is on the brink of taking a major step forward in his treatment. It frequently appears in especially clear form at the very end of treatment when a few very important changes are yet to be made. Rather than go all the way to a successful termination, this resistance will appear and often precludes a really good treatment result.

Patients in the grip of this transference resistance are generally helpless. They often want very much to cooperate but have the greatest difficulty doing so. Many patients manage to provoke the doctor to anger, or convince him of his failure. When this happens, treatment ends short of reasonable goals. The doctor who throws up his hands in disgust, anger or resignation has been defeated. Both the doctor and patient are the losers. The same applies to parents who are trying to change their preadolescent or adolescent children through a program of self-help.

ACTING OUT

I will now return to the theme of the doctor's responsibility. The first, you may recall, is the induction of change in the patient through the process of working out unconscious conflicts and their personality and behavioral consequences. Another kind of responsibility has to do with the patient's safety during the treatment process. Treatment which aims to bring unconscious forces into consciousness often proceeds at anything but an optimal rate. Ideally, patients should be able to resolve or at least control the conflicts and other unconscious forces which are mobilized by treatment. Often they cannot control these forces and it takes time, sometimes months, to resolve that which treatment mobilizes. In the meantime it is very important for the patient *not* to make irrevocable decisions during treatment. Patients often are forced into action by the unconscious forces which treatment mobilizes. These actions, hereafter termed "acting out," can be harmful to the patient and to others. Unrealistic decisions can be made, relationships can be formed which have little real meaning, affairs entered into, divorces and marriages frequently occur, some patients become suicidal. Great harm can come to patients (and to others) who are not protected from themselves during treatment. New behaviors, feelings, attitudes, and beliefs which emerge during treatment must always be fully understood for they may be largely expressions of the patient's unconscious mental life and not based on rational factors at all. One of the most common forms of acting out is the forming of a relationship with the opposite sex which is not based on genuine interest for the other person but is, instead, the result of unconscious forces.

Treatment cannot be conducted in a vacuum and it is, therefore, important for patients to remain involved in life and increase this involvement during treatment. However, new relationships and interests that are formed early in treatment should not be taken too seriously. Certain types of relationships should be actively discouraged by the doctor, and prohibited in some instances. The doctor should consider himself responsible for what the patient does during treatment—and what he does not do. It is the height of irresponsibility on the doctor's part to mobilize the patient's unconscious conflicts and then stand idly by as the patient is pushed by newly mobilized unconscious conflicts within himself into various kinds of activities and commitments, or out of them, without knowing why, frequently to his disadvantage or detriment and possibly that of others.

Early in treatment a young man may choose a girlfriend on the basis of his unresolved, unconscious, erotic attraction to his mother; that is, on the basis of his unconscious Oedipus complex. Not having resolved his conflicts, his character may be disturbed by excessive passivity, for example. If the doctor is unaware of the unconscious basis for the patient's attraction to the girl, or if he fails to understand his responsibilities to his patient, the patient may marry this girl during treatment only to discover he has picked an unsuitable, and usually somewhat unfeminine, girl who is just as disturbed as he is. These marriages run a high risk of failing and ending in divorce. As can be quickly seen, such events are bad mistakes and the consequences are tragic when children are born into such a relationship. Even if no children are born there is much heartache in a bad marriage.

The doctor often finds himself in a difficult situation when confronted with this kind of problem. This is especially so when his patient came for brief psychotherapy only, or can afford no more than a few sessions, and may be seeking help in overcoming his fears surrounding marriage. In such instances the doctor should probably help the patient go ahead with his commitment unless he has clear evidence that the girlfriend is an unsuitable prospective mate.

A much wiser and more responsible course is for the doctor to advise against, and if necessary prohibit, marriage early in treatment, and at times during the entirety of treatment. By doing so he will be blocking the expression of unconscious forces in the acting out. The unconscious forces will be redirected into the treatment situation where they belong and can be resolved. The principle to comprehend is that the doctor must not let the patient's unconscious forces run rampant and harm or ruin the patient's life or that of others during treatment. This principle is the same one which guides parents with their children as they are growing up or during a program of self-help.

Later in treatment, when most of the patient's illness has been resolved, forming relationships is less likely to have symptomatic meaning and they are, therefore, less likely to fail. It may even be appropriate, and in some instances necessary, for the doctor to actively encourage the patient in his quest for a mate or in his efforts to make mature commitments. Ideally the patient should have terminated treatment and have been on his own for a few months before choosing a mate. Patients frequently continue to change (mature) after successful treatment has been terminated, and the kind of person they will choose is a function of their maturation. Furthermore, patients gain much support from their relationship with their doctor. Without such support, despite the careful therapeutic work, they may be unable to stand alone. Such persons are usually weak because of early life experiences. The doctor must be careful not to get his patient overly involved in life and then have the patient's life collapse after treatment has ended.

Some patients become overtly or covertly self-destructive during treatment. The work of uncovering previously adequately defended against, that is successfully repressed, unconscious guilt, sense of futility or desolation, anger or other complexes of feeling and thought may lead to an acute state wherein the patient believes he must or may be seized by the impulse to kill himself. In such instances the doctor automatically becomes completely responsible for his patient and must actively intervene and protect his patient. Interpreting, and thus making fully conscious, the reason for the patient's self-destructive urges frequently will not adequately control the situation. Not to actively intervene is the height of irresponsibility on the doctor's part. The patient will require a period of hospitalization in most instances; the doctor must protect his patient.

Some therapists let their patients do nearly anything outside the therapy situation. These therapists believe it is their responsibility to do no more than decode the patient's communications; that is, provide insight to the patient. These therapists were either poorly trained or lack the capacity to take responsibility. Usually they are passive, timid and generally unable to make deep life commitments themselves. In short, they lack the personality qualities and proper conceptual understanding for doing responsible and effective psychotherapy.

I know of a woman doctor who let a young woman patient, whom she had in psychotherapy, elope from treatment and impulsively marry a very sick patient. This doctor then tried to treat both of them, hoping no doubt to be able to help the pair make their marriage succeed; the marriage should have been annulled. This sick couple soon broke off treatment, had two children, and then divorced. This result was tragic, and one must wonder what it was in the doctor that prevented her from behaving more responsibly. One look at her provided the answer; she was a masculinized, aggressive woman.

Some patients want to make major vocational changes during treatment. The motivations behind such urges must be fully understood before permitting them to be acted upon. I recall a young physician in treatment who wanted to give up his profession and enter a field in the humanities. He was, in reality, a good physician and would have been unsuited for the field which rather suddenly began to appeal to him during the course of his treatment. To have permitted this major change would have been a terrible blunder. As it turned out, the underlying motivations for wanting to give up medicine as a career were oedipal in nature. The patient's father was a physician and his mother a social scientist. Treatment had mobilized the patient's childhood hostility for his father and his strong sexual and romantic attraction for his mother. His negative feelings toward his father (as a boy) caused him to feel negatively toward his profession and feel positively for his mother's field. That is, he wanted to break down his relationship with his father and be closer to his mother. To have permitted this major life change would, in reality, have permitted nothing more than the acting out of unconscious forces (oedipal feelings and motivations) and would have reflected a breakdown in the treatment, the doctor's irresponsibility, his stupidity, or both. The patient did not need to change professions; he needed to resolve his childhood conflicts about his mother and father which remained alive in his unconscious mind.

The question will surely have arisen in your mind as to how the doctor can tell when new interests of the patient which arise as a consequence of treatment are motivated by unconscious forces or when they reflect newly found levels of maturity and a changing and more mature system of values. The answer revolves around assessing the relative weight of irrational unconscious forces and rational ones over an extended period of time throughout treatment. Making these distinctions is not always easy and frequently these decisions must be delayed until the end of treatment when all the facts are known.

The task for the doctor boils down to one of constant assessment of the patient, his behavior, attitudes, new interests, etc. The assessment is one of deciding to what extent various features of the patient are normal (based on rational considerations) or abnormal (based on irrational unconscious factors). This is the constant task of every physician; is what he confronts normal or abnormal? Sometimes the decision is easy because of the obviousness of the normality or abnormality. Grossly psychotic behavior, drug usage, clearly self-destructive acts, are definable as abnormal at face value. Conversely, normality is often easily recognizable. A mother's newfound ability to show affection to her child, a man's newfound capacity to be successful at work, etc., are examples.

Some newly formed attitudes, interests, values, behaviors (during treatment) are not clearly normal or abnormal. The doctor must then determine their meanings by means of the patient's dreams, free associations, transferences—in short, from information gained from the patient's unconscious mind. This takes time and final judgments should never be made hastily.

A woman may feel the need to go to work outside the home during treatment. This wish may reflect a rational decision or may be an expression of unconscious motivations. In the first instance, her family may need additional funds, her children may all be at school, and her marriage not sufficiently satisfying to make her life full. She may have worked before marriage; her family may be grown enough to no longer need her as much, and so on. In the second instance, a woman may want to go to work as a way for avoiding her home responsibilities as wife and mother. The treatment may have awakened her penis envy and her competitiveness toward men, or her guilt toward her mother, and so on. By going to work such a patient may be ''defying'' her doctor, competing with him, and renouncing her own gender. To permit this woman to act out these unconscious forces amounts to playing into and reinforcing her illness. Women who are homemakers often do wish to go to work during treatment as a means by which to take flight from their responsibilities as wife and mother because of the unconscious guilt which derives from the Oedipus complex which the treatment has mobilized. For them to remain in the home amounts to taking mother's place. Since this is forbidden, they seek to spend their time elsewhere.

It is important to be very careful during treatment about major changes in one's direction in life, especially when the urge to do so appears suddenly. The doctor must at all times protect the patient from himself by making as fully conscious as possible the basis for such changes. When the patient cannot control himself the doctor must intervene in some effective way.

Direct interventions into the patient's life may demand a great deal from the doctor, and his responsibility may at times be heavy indeed. Weighty decisions may have to be made which could alter the remainder of the patient's life.

A patient of mine, well along in treatment, became interested in a new life's work and in another woman. I could never find clear, unequivocal evidence that he was acting out some unconscious motivation. As a result I let him go to work in his new vocation and I did not demand that he give up his girlfriend. For a while he did well at this new work even after terminating his treatment.

Though I could never put my finger on it directly, I felt uncomfortable about having agreed to his decision. For reasons not entirely within his control he began to fail, divorced his wife, and married the other woman. He eventually abandoned this work and slipped into an overt psychiatric illness. After having suffered much personal anguish, and sustaining further financial reverses, he returned to his original vocation for which he was well suited. He discovered he loved his work and soon became quite successful. He divorced the new wife and remarried his original wife. It had been a mistake to let him change jobs, divorce, and quit treatment. In this instance I really did not know what was the right thing for him to do. I know better now.

This example illustrates how difficult the assessment between normal and abnormal may be. Had we been able to know his decision was largely an acting out (that is, symptomatic behavior) we could have averted it and the outcome of treatment would have been successful. Success was ultimately achieved but at considerable additional expense of money, time, and anguish.

One of the most serious forms of acting out is divorce during treatment. When unconscious conflicts have not been resolved and divorce occurs during or soon after the conclusion of treatment, the divorce is usually an acting out. That is, it is a symptomatic expression of unconscious conflicts, conflicts which should have been brought into consciousness in the treatment and resolved. The consequences of divorce are serious and often downright tragic. There are several kinds of reasons a patient wants to divorce his or her spouse during treatment. One of the commonest is the patient's idealization of the therapist (usually of the opposite sex) and a corresponding temporary blindness to the fine qualities in the spouse. Such a patient is usually experiencing intense affection for the doctor and, along with that affection, is transferring old unconscious attachments to the parent of the opposite sex onto the therapist. Indeed, the spouse may seem like a dull person when the patient is in such an emotional state in relation to his or her doctor. Given time and wise handling of the situation by the doctor, this state will pass and the patient will see life in a clearer perspective.

Strong negative feelings for the spouse are often based on old grievances which become revealed by the uncovering treatment process. Intense hate may be experienced. All of this will usually pass if wisely handled by the doctor. Divorce may result if the patient is permitted to act on these feelings.

Another cause for the breakup of marriages is when the patient splits his transference reactions, attaching the positive (loving and sexual) ones onto the doctor and the hostile ones onto the spouse. The doctor gets it in the heart and the poor spouse gets it in the neck! The doctor who is stupid or irresponsible, or both, may fall into the trap of letting the patient act on these strong hostile feelings and obtain a divorce.

A frequent cause for divorce is failure on the doctor's part as well as the patient's to recognize the fact that the patient is divorcing the wrong person. Stated more precisely, the patient may be attempting to resolve his unconscious childhood attachments to his parent of the opposite sex. For instance, a man may be attempting to resolve his dependent, sexual, and romantic ties to his mother. Now, when faced with these mobilized conflicts during his treatment, he may act on them by divorcing his wife, thinking he is separating from the source of his trouble when in fact the source is within himself. To act does not resolve unconscious conflicts as he would discover were he to enter into another marital relationship. It is this very unconscious problem which causes men to see wives as mother figures and wives to see their husbands as father figures. When this unconscious state exists severe marital problems are the inevitable result, and it is frequently these very problems which forced the patient to seek treatment.

Treatment of such patients may progress very well up to a point. For instance, a woman patient may gain some insight into these old unconscious attachments and wishes toward her father and she will very sincerely want to break this childhood attachment. The proper way for her to go about this is to recognize the transference expressions of these old attachments in relation to her doctor and husband, then remember as much of the past as possible, keep working this material over and over until she gradually gets over her old attachments to her father. At the same time she should be working hard at improving her ongoing relationship with her husband. She should intensify her relationship with him, try to liven it up in bed, become more loving and cooperative.

Unfortunately, the opposite happens all too frequently. As the unconscious conflicts (the attachment to the parent of the opposite sex) become mobilized the spouse becomes repugnant. The reason for this is that the unconscious attachment (romantic and sexual) for the parent of the opposite sex and the associated guilt feelings become displaced onto the husband or wife; the patient has developed a transference reaction to the spouse. The wish to divorce the spouse represents the patient's desperate wish to "divorce" the parent of the opposite sex. The patient is divorcing the wrong person in divorcing the spouse. Acting out never resolves unconscious conflicts. By divorcing the spouse, the patient has put distance between himself and a member of the opposite sex. He may, indeed, even become more comfortable, psychologically speaking, but the unconscious conflicts will not have been resolved by the divorce.

Any doctor who lets this happen is a fool; worse than that, he is a dangerous person. He has let the patient act out instead of properly holding the patient within certain bounds or agreed upon rules of treatment and maintaining conditions which increase the probability that the patient will resolve his unconscious conflicts. A little thought will make evident the heartache, tragedy and far-reaching consequences of divorces (especially when there are children) which are the result of such a breakdown in treatment. Many divorces during and after treatment could be avoided if the doctor knew what he was doing. It is interesting that patients who divorce during treatment usually retain an *overly* fond, and at times somewhat romantic, attachment to their doctor (of the opposite sex) long after treatment has ended. This attachment reflects the unresolved transference; that is, it is a reflection of the patient's unresolved attachment to the parent of the past who lives on in his unconscious mind and whom he "sees" in the person of the doctor, and whom he did not divorce during treatment but should have.

Patients who are driven to acting out like this usually paint a rather disagreeable picture of their spouse to their doctor as a means by which to gain his endorsement of the divorce. Doctors would do well to call the spouse in to hear his or her side of the story and make a few direct observations of their own. Frankly, I think it is a very wise policy to have an appointment periodically with the mate of the married patient one is treating. It keeps everyone's perspective clearer and the patient much more "honest."

Divorce is sometimes a necessary outcome of treatment. There are patients who change a great deal during treatment. Usually the untreated spouse changes too. This is very desirable when it happens. Married patients should always be living with their spouses during treatment so that the spouses can adapt to the changing patient and change also. Actually, two are being treated for the price of one. Sometimes the patient's spouse must also enter treatment with some other doctor, or with the same doctor—I prefer the latter. Unfortunately, there are occasions when the spouse simply cannot change along with the one who is being treated. By the end of treatment such a couple will be badly out of phase with each other; they may have become virtual strangers with very little in common. Divorce is now almost inevitable because a successfully treated person will not, and should not, accept a life of misery.

I think there is hardly ever any real necessity for divorce to occur during treatment. It is true that the unchanging spouse of a changing patient can act as a roadblock or impediment to further changes in the patient. When such a situation arises the doctor has several alternatives other than recommending or allowing a divorce. He can accept a slower pace of treatment for his patient in the hope that the spouse may eventually change or, and this course is the best, he can induce the spouse to enter treatment. If I were treating a patient several times a week I would gladly assign the patient's spouse one or more of those hours in order to insure forward motion in my patient's treatment and his life as well. Divorce is bad business and should be avoided if at all possible; this is especially so when there are children. The divorce of a very young couple who married for neurotic reasons (that is, largely for unconscious, irrational reasons) may be desirable and actually can be encouraged in rare instances.

The simple truth is that treatment is (or can be) an extremely unsettling process; a great deal gets stirred up from the depths. Perceptions change, values and interests change, moodiness may occur, symptoms may appear out of nowhere and then disappear, anxiety and depression may exist for brief or prolonged periods. In short, the patient may become very difficult for the spouse to live with, provoking reactions in the spouse. Furthermore, the spouse usually gets a great deal of transference displaced onto him. Marriage can become badly strained by any or all of the preceding. When conditions like this exist, divorce should never be contemplated.

Sometimes patients discover their unconscious conflicts have prevented them from fully expressing their sexual drives with their spouse. They may love and respect their mates but cannot act romantically with them. During treatment the patient may overcome his inhibitions and become interested in a member of the opposite sex outside the marriage. This frequently turns out to be an acting out. That is, instead of directing his sexual interests onto the spouse, where they belong, so he can at last experience both love and sexual drives toward the same person, the patient continues to split these interests, expressing one toward the spouse and the other toward the lover. Such situations reflect a breakdown in treatment and not uncommonly lead to divorce. Treatment has been a failure when this happens.

It frequently happens that a successfully treated and therefore much changed patient induces great discomfort in the unchanged spouse. The latter may initiate a divorce rather than adjust to the changed patient or seek treatment himself. I believe the patient's doctor should always personally intervene in situations like these and try to dissuade his patient's spouse from obtaining a divorce but, instead, to go into treatment. The doctor who understands his responsibilities will attend to this complication.

SIGNS OF PERSONALITY CHANGE

A discussion of what change means could itself fill many pages. A great variety of changes can occur during psychotherapy. The term will be used here to refer to essential personality change. This will be the focus so that those who enter treatment with the expectation of achieving such changes will have some guidelines to follow in order to assess the progress they are or may not be making.

Fundamental changes need not come slowly, but generally they are relatively slow in coming. The rate at which a patient can change depends primarily upon the rigidity of his personality, his psychological mindedness, and to some degree on his intelligence, the kinds of early life experiences he has had, his age, the severity of his illness and, above all, upon the personality, technique, and degree of commitment of his doctor—that is, the maturity of his doctor and how hard and how effectively he works all affect treatment outcome. Some therapists believe that listening, understanding, and compassion are all that are required of them. Nothing could be further from the truth.

Sometimes changes which appear early in treatment ultimately prove to be evanescent. Such changes are sometimes referred to as transference cures.

After having had the goals of treatment explicitly defined the patient may appear or behave as if those goals had been achieved almost overnight. Such changes are never durable. Sometimes they come about because of the patient's affection for his doctor (usually in the case of women patients with male doctors), or they may be unconsciously designed to mislead the doctor and throw him off the track, thereby permitting the patient to avoid really coming to grips with his illness. Sometimes they appear because of a sense of greatly heightened encouragement the patient experiences because of his having a helping hand in the person of the doctor. When such support is removed, patients usually revert to their old patterns.

Usually patients get much worse before getting better. New symptoms may appear, they may become anxious, bitterly discouraged, and even badly depressed. That this should happen is both expected and logical. The treatment process mobilizes unconscious forces and interferes with the patient's habitual way of maintaining an internal equilibrium. As indicated earlier, their values, attitudes, and interests may change, a wide range of transference phenomena may appear. Periods of high resistance to self-discovery and to progress will inevitably appear along the way. It is of vital importance that these varying phenomena be understood and that treatment be continued to a proper conclusion.

Other factors beyond the control of the doctor cause treatment to be interrupted. Given circumstances where it is possible to continue treatment, it is imperative that some of the above developments do not deter the doctor from continuing. Inexperienced doctors, or those troubled by personality difficulties of their own, find rationalizations for deserting the patient when the going gets rough.

A common occurrence which can easily cause the doctor and patient, especially the latter, to become discouraged and believe treatment should be terminated is a newly developed and/or progressively worsening depression. Depression which arises during treatment is usually a good sign; it signals change. In my experience depression reflects intrapsychic loss, that is, the saying of goodbye to figures and ties of the past which have lived on in the unconscious mind of the patient. As the work of treatment takes its effect the patient inevitably must break his childhood ties and thus become able to form new and mature relationships. This process includes the forming of a new and qualitatively different kind of ongoing relationship with his parents—provided they can permit such changes in the quality of the relationship with their now adult offspring.

It is a truly remarkable phenomenon to observe the regular but transient sadness or episodic depression appear following a phase in the psychotherapy of patients when they are in the process of giving up their childhood attachments. Newly found feminine or masculine qualities, as the case may be, regularly appear following these phases in treatment.

SIGNS OF SUCCESSFUL TREATMENT

Patients who have been effectively treated are able to enjoy life more. They are able to play more effectively; they tend to work less compulsively but at the same time they work more efficiently. Self-destructive tendencies disappear. Where a heterosexual relationship was impossible previously, it now becomes possible. Parenthood is possible. Creative talents become freed. Behavior that was once compulsive and stereotyped gives way to a more flexible, appropriate type of behavior. Work inhibitions disappear. Frank psychiatric symptoms disappear. Free-floating anxiety and depressive feelings, episodic or constant, should disappear. Sexual pleasure should increase.

A patient who has been thoroughly treated should have overcome identity difficulties. This refers to what he is in a vocational sense and also, and especially so, in the sense of gender. The effeminate man or masculine woman can be one of the most difficult kinds of patients to treat, but unless these mixed identities are changed, treatment was not totally successful. Naturally, persistent homosexuality after treatment has been terminated is a sure sign that treatment was a failure. The treatment may have helped the patient in some respects but failed in its most significant feature.

The success or failure of treatment can also be defined in terms of the original goals. If they have been reached it is probably legitimate to say that treatment was successful. The difficulty with this is that as treatment proceeds new psychopathology is inevitably uncovered. Original treatment goals are accordingly modified.

Many attitudes, values, character traits, behaviors, and even symptoms, will not yield to exploratory psychotherapy, including psychoanalysis. I think the reason for this is not so much that "uncovering" therapy is worthless but is due largely to the doctor's failure to realize that he must do more than bring insight to the patient.

I find it most distressing to hear of people who were in psychoanalysis many years but who are really no different afterwards. No doubt they discovered much about themselves but for all practical purposes they remained unchanged. Often patients have changed to some extent but not nearly enough to justify the high expenditure of time, money, and effort.

A successfully treated person should be able to do a great many things he could not do before treatment. Above all, he should be successful in his work, and should be able to marry and become a parent. He should, in short, be able to fulfill the definition of a normal man or woman.

What is it, then, that doctors do wrong? I am referring to therapists and analysts who strive to bring about extensive personality change but fail to do so. I think there are several things. They remain too detached, aloof, or neutral. Some even claim to be indifferent to the outcome of treatment. This is absolutely incredible to me. How can a physician remain neutral in the face of illness? Actually it is impossible to be neutral toward one's patient. Even in psychoanalysis, where such a stance is said to be necessary for the proper development of transference, the analyst cannot be neutral. Whenever he points something out to a patient, confronts him, makes an interpretation, he has abandoned neutrality. Nonetheless, I think Freud's cautioning that the analyst should not moralize, but should serve as a screen or mirror, has been overdone. Experience has shown that patients develop transference toward the doctor and others in their lives when there is no semblance of neutrality in the other persons.

I believe neutrality in the conduct of psychotherapy should be abandoned and the doctor should, as I noted earlier, take a stand for health and against illness. A patient needs to know where his doctor stands.

THE PLACE OF VALUES AND THE ENVIRONMENT IN PSYCHOTHERAPY

It is a complete myth that a psychotherapist can remain neutral toward his patient or in relation to what the patient tells about himself, his life, etc. Persons who attempt to remain neutral toward their patient are either fooling themselves or they are denying their patient one of the most effective aspects of treatment, or both. The doctor must be *accepting* of the patient but *rejecting* in relation to the patient's psychopathology, regardless of its form. At first this distinction is difficult for the patient to grasp inasmuch as he usually feels that his psychopathology is an integral part of himself, especially character traits and behavioral patterns of long standing. It rarely serves a purpose for the doctor to scold a patient for behaving in a certain way; however, even this extreme form of a stand against the patient's illness may be very effective and even necessary in some instances.

The principle here is that the doctor should ally himself with the mature and healthy aspects of his patient and that the two of them (doctor and the healthy part of the patient) align themselves against the patient's illness. There should be, then, a constant pressure in the therapeutic experience—the doctor's stand against illness and for health. Naturally this pressure or alignment alone will not cure the patient, but this clear orientation is, I believe, vital to treatment; it provides an outside force on the patient to change.

This point may seem self-evident to the lay public whose doctors openly take such a position against their physical illnesses. This attitude toward illness is not as pervasive among psychiatrists and psychoanalysts, and certainly not so among many of the varied persons who claim to be psychotherapists. In fact, some claim only to seek to provide understanding for the patient but will go no further than that. Some therapists form opinions (judgments) about the patient's behavior but keep them strictly to themselves, conveying an attitude of neutral interest to the patient. Some therapists are so disturbed in their own personalities and values that they openly reinforce the patient's illness. These stances deprive the therapist of valuable leverage. Some therapists and analysts believe it is their mission to help a patient go where he wants to go and be what he wants to be regardless of whether or not that behavior or way of being is pathological. I recall a psychoanalyst telling me he helped a young patient discover her homosexual inclinations and eventually settle into an overt homosexual way of life. This, in my opinion, is a total treatment failure.

The psychotherapist should always try to help the patient fulfill himself in life—fully develop his potentials and find suitable outlets for them—but fulfillment should come in a mature way. Unfortunately, the sick side of people seeks expression and fulfillment too. To foster this is to make sick people sicker. Many therapists help patients find greater peace of mind by helping them alter the environment to suit their personalities and needs, even though these include sick elements, rather than changing the patient's personality so it will fit better with the demands of the adult world. Patients have an uncanny way of selecting doctors who will be of little real help to them and who will reinforce their sickness. Psychotherapists should never just "help patients go where they want to go" unless it is clear that where they want to go is in a healthy direction. The exception is the very sick patient who cannot change and a place has to be found for him which provokes as little psychic disorganization as possible.

The essential point in the preceding remarks is that effective psychotherapy cannot be done without a value system by which the therapist is guided. No physician could practice physical medicine without values (urinalysis, blood analyses, chemical analyses, physical symptoms and signs, etc.) to guide him, to help him distinguish abnormality from normality, nor can a psychotherapist. Some may not realize this, but all are guided by a values system of some kind.

Therefore, an integral part of good treatment is the upholding of normal values. Within the range of normal there is ample room for diversity and individuality, for uniqueness. However, some ways of thinking, feeling, and behaving are clearly abnormal. Students of the human condition know this very well, and this knowledge must be used as a guide if one person is going to treat another effectively.

As treatment proceeds, the doctor first identifies the various forms of the patient's pathology and then attempts to discover the underlying reason for them. This process amounts to an appeal to the rational forces and strengths within the patient to abandon his illness, to grow. This has been discussed to some extent; however, to recapitulate, the doctor analyzes the patient's dreams, free associations, metaphors, slips, and transferences, and thereby exposes the underlying motivations for the pathology. However, it frequently develops that these insights do not cause the psychopathology to disappear.

Many dynamically oriented therapists rework the old insight, hoping that the next time around the problem will clear up. They also search in new directions on the assumption that there are other motivations yet to be discovered which, when found, will make possible the resolution of the patient's illness. The search continues, and sometimes this approach works but many times the search goes on for years and the insights get worked over again and again and grow stale and the patient fails to change. Then what?

Some therapists and analysts rationalize their way out of such situations, thereby ducking their responsibility to the patient, by saying the patient now has all the insight there is to be found and if he *wanted to* he would change, that to change is now a matter of free choice. I believe this is incorrect. Patients would change if they could.

I believe in the importance of insight; I always start treatment by searching out meanings behind the various forms of the patient's psychopathology. However, when insight fails to bring about change I think pressure should be applied on the patient. Pressure can take several forms. The most logical form of pressure to apply is encouragement; logical because most patients are lacking to some degree in the most essential human quality—courage. Patients should be encouraged to think more maturely, to behave in new and more mature ways, ways which suit the basic fabric of the patient's personality. At the same time, patients should be encouraged to abandon their old pathological ways. For example, a man should be actively advised and encouraged to stop treating his wife in immature, hostile, or provocative ways and, in turn, substitute better ways. He should be encouraged to abstain from immature or perverse sexual practices, and so on. A value system should be upheld to him and urged upon him; for instance, take his place as the head of the family.

This combined pressure on the patient to abstain from the old sick ways on the one hand, and to behave in new and more mature ways on the other, will serve another very useful purpose besides helping him behave more maturely. It will also cause the patient's unconscious mind to pour out its contents. The reason for this is perfectly clear; since the old ways of thinking and behaving are blocked, the unconscious motivations must seek expression in some other way; they will surface somewhere since it is in the nature of things for unconscious forces to find expression, be it in symptoms, behavior, character style, dreams, or language. Furthermore, new ways of behaving will trigger those unconscious conflicts which prevented the patient from behaving maturely in the first place. The patient may begin to experience very intense transference, dreams will increase, metaphors will crop up with new frequency, and so on. In short, the supply from the patient's unconscious will be so rich that the doctor will have more than ample material to reveal to his patient. This combined process of pressure away from illness and toward health and analysis of unconscious meanings must proceed at a rate which does not overwhelm the patient and force him into a more serious illness. He needs time to work through the rapidly emerging insights and time to master his new and more mature way of being and relating to the environment.

This approach is, then, a mixture of intense analysis—it is psychodynamic in every respect—and also a form of behavior therapy. The two complement each other beautifully. I am convinced that pure analysis cannot achieve what this combined approach will bring, and I am equally certain that pure behavior therapy falls equally short in its results. Both types of therapy work to some degree for some patients, but neither works as well alone as the combined approach. I have tested these procedures repeatedly and I am absolutely convinced of this.

Severe behavioral problems, phobias, established sexual patterns—in short, long-standing patterns of living which are maladaptive (pathological)—require a behavioral therapy element in the treatment plan. Occasionally such forms of illness will yield to analysis alone, but they will more often yield to the combined approach of analysis and persistent efforts on the part of therapist and patient to draw upon the willpower of the patient to change his way of being.

If, after a reasonable period of analysis, a symptom (say frigidity in a woman) does not clear up, the doctor better pay close attention to the way she behaves in bed. He may have to instruct her how to go about it, and as she tries to change her way of behaving with her partner, anxiety or other symptoms will probably appear. Direct messages from her unconscious will appear in abundance in her treatment. I think it is vital for the doctor to decipher these messages and help the patient understand what her unresponsiveness or anxiety is really all about. A high degree of uncooperativeness or repressed hostility or guilt or penis envy or anxiety associated with closeness may be discovered. This insight needs to be thoroughly worked over at the same time the patient is practicing new and more effective ways of going about the sex act. Given enough persistent effort, good analytic work, encouragement, and advice from the doctor, the chances of success are excellent. Psychoanalysis alone can never do as much for a frigid woman as a combination of (1) treatment and (2) a good man in bed with her. Instructions from the doctor as to how to cooperate with that man may be necessary. Incidentally, that man in bed should never be the analyst! If the patient is married it should always be the husband. If the husband is troubled by some form of impotence then he too must receive professional help.

The good doctor, the one who really knows what he is doing, will never be content to make the patient's unconscious conflicts conscious and leave the rest up to the patient to change or not to change. He will see to it that the patient changes in a mature direction in the face of this insight. If, for instance, strong infantile erotic ties to the mother are uncovered in a male patient, the doctor will immediately suspect, if he has not already made this discovery, that the patient's relationship with his wife is falling short of what it might be. He will make detailed inquiry into that relationship. The doctor will point out what the patient should stop doing and will advise what he should start doing—if the patient has not already made these observations himself. The doctor will periodically reevaluate the patient's relationship with his wife to see how the patient is progressing, while at the same time analyzing the patient's conflicts. The same principle applies to all other aspects of the patient's life, his children, friends, work, etc. No part of the patient's existence should be immune to careful inspection by the doctor in a treatment endeavor that is geared to bring about maximal changes for the patient. This includes religious beliefs and practices—everything in the patient's life. It is astounding how much pathology can be uncovered by this approach. If the doctor works only with what the patient tells him spontaneously, the treatment will necessarily be limited in its outcome. Many patients are quite candid about themselves; some, however, are very guarded and may not even know they are concealing vital information about themselves from the doctor.

CHOOSING YOUR DOCTOR: HIS PERSONALITY AND VALUES

It should be fairly obvious from what has just been described that the most effective treatment requires a great deal of involvement and commitment on the doctor's part, and from the patient. The doctor must have the personality for it, obviously, or he cannot work this way. I shudder when I think of the thousands of people who call themselves psychotherapists and purport to be able to help others. So very many of these individuals are, from outward appearances, very disturbed. I have been asked many times, "Why are there so many kooks in psychiatry and psychology?" I have noticed that those professionals who advocate these so-called freer sexual lifestyles are usually social scientists or psychologists, although some psychiatrists do too. Those I have known who advocate such ways are burdened by unconscious conflicts which have prevented them from achieving the maturity necessary for a monogamous relationship. They quite naturally endorse values which make it possible for people to avoid making such a commitment.

The fact is that there *are* many very strange people in these and the allied professions who, I believe, do a great deal of harm, and there are more who do very little good. To a large extent this is so because they do not understand much about the human condition, its various forms of pathology, and even less about how to go about changing sick people into healthy ones. Some even go so far as to deny the existence of mental disturbances and yet are willing to collect fees for the time they spend with their "patients." Many of these "therapists" are very disturbed people who endorse the sick values that are creeping into our society and threatening its vitality.

I speak with some certainty, having worked in a psychiatric center where I have observed a large number of psychiatrists, psychoanalysts, psychologists and social workers. In addition, I examined the applications (which contained the life histories and psychiatric and psychological test evaluation data) of hundreds of physicians and (fewer) psychologists who applied for psychiatric and psychological training. Furthermore, I have seen what has happened to the children of many of my colleagues whose personalities fell short of the ideal—passive men with aggressive and domineering wives. A very high percentage of these children showed personality disturbances, and some became severely ill psychiatrically when they were faced with the challenges of life. I am well aware of the pitfalls in overgeneralizing, but these are my observations nonetheless. These observations parallel those of Edward Glover (39) who writes, "Taken by and large, groups of psychologists manifest rather more personal peculiarities and rather less social discipline, than the more conventional professional bodies."

These observations are cause for some pessimism with regard to the value of the mental health professions. Much good is done, of course, but until the personalities of those who enter these fields (psychiatry and psychology in particular) are mature (masculine) men and (feminine) women, and until these professions are placed in the center of the field of medicine where they belong, the impact of the mental health sciences on society will, in my opinion, be limited.

Those professionals who endorse certain trends in society seem not to understand what is happening. Having known so many mental health professionals with personal psychopathology, it is to be expected that they do not recognize the dangers of the sex role blurring which is taking place, that they cannot recognize homosexuality as an illness, that they fail to see the consequences of the "do your own thing" way of life, and that some endorse the changes that are undermining the very foundations of society. It is no surprise to me that so few of them are able (or willing) to stand up and publicly take a position on the changing values in society.

When I am asked by students how they should pick a psychotherapist, I advise them to first look at the individual, then at his wife (or husband), and then at their children. These facts may be difficult to obtain, but you will be surprised by how much you can find out if you work at it. Begin by asking the doctor about his marital status, what his children are doing, and so on. Ask him what he thinks about various matters, such as homosexuality, drugs, infidelity, the man's place in the family, etc. Frankly, I think the children of the doctor provide the best evidence of what kind of person he probably is. If the doctor's child is obviously disturbed (neurotic, mixed in gender, a drug user, a hippie, etc.), choosing that doctor should be done with care. If the doctor cannot rear normal children, chances are that personality factors within him will prevent him from being very effective as a therapist. This is not to say that he cannot do some good with certain kinds of patients, but it is unlikely that he will be able to bring about extensive change in patients. It is shocking that so many psychiatrists, psychoanalysts, and psychologists have very disturbed children. Experience has taught me to advise staying away from such professionals.

Many women who become physicians, and especially those who enter the fields of psychiatry, psychology, psychoanalysis and social work, have not been able to fully develop a feminine identity. Many of them are aggressive, domineering, masculinized, and hostile toward men, and rejecting to some degree of women and competitive with them. Just because such a woman doctor has been analyzed is no guarantee at all that she has overcome her difficulties and can help patients achieve maximum benefit from treatment. Such a woman can no more help a young woman overcome serious barriers blocking her from becoming a normal, fully feminine, woman than such a woman can raise a child into normal womanhood; nor can she help males become fully masculine and masterful. Yet such women are very prevalent in psychiatry, psychoanalysis, and clinical psychology. I have seen very few really feminine women (at least as I understand what femininity means) in the mental health fields. Take a close look and you will see what I mean.

These women can do some good for patients to be sure, but I am equally sure they often do very little good and some even do harm to patients. I know of instances where disturbed young women have received no help whatsoever and, in fact, were led to believe that their pathologic personality traits were quite acceptable. Aggressive, unfeminine and/or masculinized women do not belong in the specialities of psychiatry or psychoanalysis any more than they should be mothers. Such women professionals are of little use to those men and women who are having trouble making their marriage work and conform to the ideal pattern which was outlined in the chapter on the family. They cannot be fully effective with either men or women patients, and often give bad advice when they are in a consultant's role.

Such women can be of little help to male patients who are struggling to find their masculinity. Male patients may feel better for a time, but this is not to be taken as evidence of real help.

Distressed and troubled people often feel better for a time when they are listened to and believe they are being helped. Sooner or later their disillusionment will come when they discover that their "improvement" was temporary and they are not changed at all. About all such women therapists can do is give timid, defeated souls a false sense of security, and help with minor problems only. A truly feminine psychiatrist, analyst, or psychologist can do enormous good if she is well trained, just as can a masculine therapist who is well trained.

Equally limited in effectiveness is the passive and/or effeminate male psychiatrist, psychoanalyst, or psychologist. Such men can rarely help a male patient develop to full masculinity and find his way into his rightful place as head of the family. Psychiatry and psychoanalysis will take great strides forward when such individuals are no longer admitted to training programs. Unfortunately, aggressive and domineering women and passive and effeminate men are attracted to the fields of psychiatry, psychoanalysis, and clinical psychology.

Aggressive, unfeminine women and passive, effeminate male doctors are unable to hold up the values of normal maleness or femaleness to their patients as goals to be achieved. They do not understand the characteristics of normal family patterns. Even if they have an intellectual understanding of these values and characteristics, their personalities are ill equipped to enable them to change their patients. It is an absolute myth that when such a doctor listens sympathetically to a patient, desired changes in the patient will result automatically. It takes much more than understanding and empathy to change sick people into healthy ones.

Doctors have a wide array of other disturbances which will interfere with their ability to help certain kinds of patients. Cultural differences can make for trouble, although not always. A masculine doctor who has not overcome his competitiveness with men will find it difficult to bring his male patient to a full state of masterful maleness. Very rigid doctors will be unable to help a patient overcome his rigidity, and so on. This discussion could go on almost indefinitely. Doctors with abnormal personality traits and other kinds of psychopathology tend not to be able to help patients who are similar to themselves.

Suffice it to say that when a patient fails to progress in treatment he should, of course, ask himself if he is cooperating fully, but he should also consider the possibility that his doctor's personality, theory of personality, and treatment techniques are blocking progress. Some doctors possess the strength and flexibility to overcome the barriers they have placed in the path of the patient because of personality difficulties of their own, but when this is not so the patient should find another doctor. It bears repeating that the final responsibility for the forward motion of the treatment falls squarely on the doctor's shoulders. If, after a reasonable time (a few months) no progress is being made, you should look carefully at your doctor.

It is unfortunate but true that patients become very loyal to their doctors; they are much too kind, forgiving, and tolerant toward them; they act as if their doctor is the only one on earth who can help them. This attitude frequently is an expression of the patient's own resistance to change. That is, a patient unconsciously knows his doctor cannot be of much help to him. He clings to the doctor for dear life because of his own fear of changing; it was, in all likelihood, his awareness of personality defects in his doctor which led him to choose him in the first place.

It is important for a patient to carefully consider his reasons for selecting his psychotherapist, especially if this selection is made on the basis of a positive reaction toward the doctor which formed very quickly after having met him, or even if you have known him for a while and you have thought the matter over. The choice might be, and often is, based on the unconscious realization that the doctor will not be of much help. As much as people want to change, they also are afraid to. Find out what the facts are about the doctor in question. Look up where he trained, look at him very carefully and, if possible, find out about his family. Stay away from doctors (male or female) who have never married—unless the problem for which help is being sought is a relatively minor one. Never go to a homosexual doctor (this information is difficult to discover), and avoid passive and/or effeminate male and aggressive and masculinized female doctors. When severe family problems are the basis for the quest for help, pick a doctor who shows evidence of having made a success of his own family life. *Never* be casual about the person to whom you entrust your future.

Deciding on the doctor is a difficult decision for people to make; however, there are a few guidelines to go by. Avoid those persons who are not qualified by some form of established organization. The degree of M.D. or Ph.D. by itself does not mean much although, as a generalization, I think it is better to choose a psychiatrist than a psychologist for your psychotherapist because I believe physicians tend to have stronger personalities and understand and can assume responsibility better. Psychiatrists must be physicians while psychologists are not. Certification by the American Board of Psychiatry and Neurology is not a sure indication of competence as a psychotherapist by any means but it is a positive factor nonetheless. Membership in the American Psychoanalytic Association is evidence of good training in the technique of psychoanalysis but, again, many male psychoanalysts are passive and many female psychoanalysts are aggressive and fail to fully comprehend the responsibilities they should be shouldering. I believe it is safer to choose an M.D. psychoanalyst than a lay analyst or one with a Ph.D. in psychology.

Pick an M.D. who is trained as a psychiatrist, who looks like a man (or woman), and whose children are healthy. If he is psychoanalytically trained this is usually an additional positive factor; however, I have known of really fine young physicians who were eager to master the speciality of psychiatry, who did so, only to be chipped away at later by psychoanalytic concepts and teachers, who by the end of their psychoanalytic training (nine years on the average, which usually follows psychiatric training) had become somewhat aloof, distant, and by no means nearly as committed to curing people as they once were when they were young. Unfortunately psychoanalytic training does have this effect at times. Some physicians who acquire psychiatric and psychoanalytic training never lose their basic medical orientation toward illness. Those are the doctors to pick for psychotherapists, provided they are normal appearing—and they usually will be. Maturity and the capacity to take responsibility go together; those are the doctors who really help others.

In addition to forming an impression of the kind of personality your psychotherapist has and the training he has received, it is important for you to get some idea of the value system he lives by.

His values will have considerable effect on how he treats you. Nearly all persons who have some kind of professional qualification and who do psychotherapy believe it is bad for patients to be self-destructive, to have the various symptoms of classical psychiatric illnesses such as phobias, obsessions, depression, excessive anxiety, compulsions, frigidity, impotence, etc. They usually are not neutral about these kinds of psychopathology. In the back of their minds at least they have the objective of getting their patients over their illnesses.

There are other kinds of values which reflect psychopathology and personality disturbances about which mental health professionals differ markedly. For instance, if you want to be cured of homosexuality you should not go to a psychotherapist who is homosexual, or a nonhomosexual doctor who believes homosexuality is one of the variants of normal sexuality. If you are having problems making your marriage successful, you should not go to a psychotherapist who believes the importance of the family is grossly overrated and that spouse-swapping or infidelity are acceptable ways for working out problems, or that "open marriage" is the best solution.

Since I have placed so much emphasis on the importance of family life and the way the family should be structured, it is terribly important for you to know what your psychotherapist's views are about the family and male-female relationships, especially within the context of the family. If your psychotherapist does not have the kind of personality or value system which approximates what I have outlined you should take a good look at what you are getting into with him. That is why I said look at his family and you will get a rough idea of what effect his values and his personality will have on you. If he does not have a family, think twice about the possibility of getting the kind of help that will make your family life turn out the best possible way. For instance, I know of a childless, aggressive woman psychotherapist who helps her married women patients get over their psychiatric symptoms by giving up their homemaking responsibilities through going to work and relegating the care of their children to others. It would be much better for these women and their children and their husbands if they could get over those unconscious conflicts which prevent them from making a success of their home life. It takes the right doctor to make this happen. Sometimes a woman is too sick to change sufficiently so she can shoulder these responsibilities. In that case changing the environment to suit the very sick and unchanged patient rather than trying to change the patient so she can meet the responsibilities of mature womanhood may be a wiser course.

I know of another doctor, a man who is a tyrant with his family and whose wife and children are as disturbed as he, whose married patients always end up divorcing their spouses. While divorce is sometimes a necessary and logical solution after successful treatment, his "treatment" results show how his personality and beliefs (value system) influence those who come to him for help. In his lifetime this sick doctor will do enormous harm to others.

If your young daughter is struggling with her sexual identity, do not send her to an aggressive women's liberationist psychiatrist (or psychologist, social worker, or whatever) and expect to see your daughter emerge from her treatment as a lovely feminine woman. If your child is floundering in college, is smoking pot or using worse drugs, do not send him to a weak psychotherapist who openly or secretly embraces a way of life which reflects noncommitment, "doing your own thing," who is not opposed to pot smoking, who endorses "swinging" and similar far-out values. You can often tell whether or not he does by the way he dresses. I once asked a professional man who was sincerely trying to be of help to large numbers of young people who were clearly adrift what it was these young people were really looking for. Without a moment's hesitation he said, "Good fathering," and then added, "I guess I'm too anxious to provide it." His reply did not surprise me; he wore sandals, had long hair, and had a medallion around his neck. Nor was I surprised by his response with regard to what they were searching for. Had they had strong fathers whose presence had been a regular part of their family life as children they would never have failed to grasp life in the first place. This man could not possibly be an effective psychotherapist with hippie youth. It would be a matter of the blind leading the blind.

Obviously I believe psychotherapists should have the personalities and live by a value system which cause them to treat patients in such a way that they can make families survive and structure them in the way I have outlined. I believe the mental health professionals who do psychotherapy, counseling, guidance, or whatever, could do enormous good for society if they practiced sound principles. Unfortunately, many of those in these professions no longer know where they should stand with regard to the new values which are sweeping the country. Some endorse the unisex movement; some believe the new lifestyles which break down the traditional family structure are quite acceptable. Many have reservations about what they see but are too timid to take a stand and uphold the best in human values. Some really believe that current youth movements have found a "new freedom" and will eventually make a contribution to society. Others cannot recognize the folly of men assuming the woman's responsibilities in the home and the woman working. Some believe it is perfectly all right for babies and small children to be cared for and reared in nurseries and day-care centers while both parents work or pursue careers. These are disastrous trends which the mental health professions should vigorously oppose with their patients and by means of public opposition as well.

The values of society and those of mental health professionals are inexorably bound together. For example, the American Psychiatric Association has deleted homosexuality from its section covering sexual perversions in its official diagnostic manual! It is vital that these fields do not lose their heads about the radical changes in society and within the family. The constructive impact could be enormous if psychiatry and allied professionals would openly oppose these trends.

A TRIAL OF TREATMENT

The best way to decide on the capability of the doctor is a trial at treatment. Just because you and he "work well" together and you may be feeling much better does not mean the treatment will be successful. Patients may feel very comfortable when nothing is happening, simply because of the interest shown by the therapist.

Patients should feel a pressure from their doctor to change; new awareness should occur; the doctor's involvement and commitment should be clearly evident. Frankly, the best signs of progress are, at least in the earliest phases, a worsening of one's condition but a simultaneous realization that one has acquired a real ally. Symptoms may, and usually do, get worse for a time. New discoveries should lead to change, and if they do not the patient should sense an intensified effort on the doctor's part to make things happen.

The doctor who sits back, rarely says anything, never makes a value judgment about various aspects of his patient's personality or behavior, and limits himself to such remarks as "What do you think about that?" or "Please elaborate," "Ha," or similar noncommital remarks is, in my opinion, relatively worthless. Such remarks on the doctor's part may be appropriate early in the treatment when the doctor is getting to know the patient or when they are interspersed alongside other communications. If this is about all the doctor ever says, I suggest you drop him.

OTHER KINDS OF PSYCHOTHERAPY

Up to this point I have written mostly about expressive psychotherapy and psychoanalysis. Some patients are too ill for this kind of treatment. To "open them up" would induce a worsening of their illness with the added risk that the patient might not recover. The decision to do exploratory therapy, including psychoanalysis, instead of supportive therapy is a difficult one and requires diagnostic know-how, sensitivity, and experience. Psychological testing may or may not be helpful. I have known of instances where the psychologist advised against psychoanalysis because of the patient's "high potential for regression." The doctor doing the treatment did not agree because of his own assessment of the patient, and the analysis went beautifully. The only sure way for the doctor to know what the treatment of choice should be is to start treatment and see what works best. There are exceptions to this rule. Severely ill, psychotic patients, persons of low intellectual endowment, persons with very poor self-control, tend not to do well in expressive types of treatment. Actually, psychotherapy is often a mixture of expressive and supportive techniques.

Supportive psychotherapy can have several objectives. Some patients are so ill that the primary goal is to help them make decisions about very simple matters in their daily lives. Keeping such patients functioning is the primary objective, although goals can be elevated periodically if the patient shows evidence of being able to do better. This approach is very suitable for chronically psychotic patients who are unlikely to ever be able to regain their earlier level of life adjustment. The skilled use of drugs blends very nicely with supportive therapy. I have never nor will I ever recommend psychosurgery.

Supportive techniques are also designed to correct disturbed ego processes. For instance, a patient's projections may be worked with, with the goal of having the patient eventually give up his pathological defenses, that is, his sick ways for adapting to life and keeping his unconscious conflicts under control and out of awareness. This technique aims at getting the personality to work as it should by focusing directly on life adjustment rather than on unconscious processes which overwhelmed the person in the first place. Some doctors deal with unconscious forces in psychotics and sometimes such a technique is effective, but they also (usually) have to work very hard on other personality processes at the same time. I have little confidence in the usefulness of depth interpretations in severely ill psychotic patients; their personality is too badly disturbed to be able to make use of this kind of self-knowledge. Therefore, if you have a relative who is severely ill, and possibly also chronically so, stay away from the would-be workers of magic—with their deep interpretations—and find someone who aims his efforts at the most accessible aspect of the illness—that is, to the patient's psychotic behavior, thinking, and feeling, and his adjustment to reality.

Supportive psychotherapy is appropriate for very shaky people who are on the brink of a psychosis. Work with these patients is often like desperate efforts to keep the dike from leaking, or plugging up holes and cracks that are leaking. Usually the doctor takes a sympathetic, directive, and encouraging approach. He tends to direct the patient's attention away from his morbid preoccupations. He may become very directive about how the patient should live his life by telling him not to do certain things and to do others. Expertly done, supportive psychotherapy can do wonders with *manifest* illness but tends to leave latent illness or those unconscious forces which could produce manifest illness, were they to be sufficiently mobilized, more or less untouched.

This last remark requires some qualifications. I have seen patients mature rather nicely with nothing but supportive therapy. I said mature, and this implies that unconscious conflicts were modified, or possibly even resolved. With the constant reassurance, support, and encouragement from the doctor, patients will be able to behave in a way they previously had been unable to. These new involvements in life, the new commitments, mobilize unconscious conflicts enough for a silent process of resolution to take place. This happens in ordinary life. People manage on their own, or bolstered by friends and family and spurred on by social demands, to involve themselves in new and more mature commitments to life. They master these new situations and these, in turn, create favorable conditions for the resolution of whatever unconscious conflicts they may have.

Supportive therapy is often very appropriate for adolescents and young adults who are having trouble establishing a mature life adjustment. The art is to understand how much pressure to put on these patients and what to support and what not to support in their personality and behavior. Equally important is the necessity for recognizing when support alone is not working and when more is needed.

A moment's reflection will reveal how profound the effect of the doctor's personality and value system can be on the patient who is receiving supportive psychotherapy, or the person embarked on a program of self-help who turns to others for guidance and encouragement. A mature doctor who possesses the sensitivity to understand what unique form of lifestyle is appropriate for his patient can do an enormous amount of good for his patient by steering him in the right direction. A doctor who is psychiatrically disturbed, whose character is warped by his unconscious conflicts and whose values will necessarily be equally warped, can do enormous harm to patients he is treating by supportive psychotherapy. He will support the wrong aspects of his patients' personality and behavior. The larger cities are full of such sick people who call themselves psychotherapists. They go by various kinds of titles including, unfortunately, those which should identify real competence. As a rule of thumb, stay away from weird-looking people who call themselves professionals and who purport to do psychotherapy. Fortunately, they often do look and behave in a weird manner and can be quickly identified. Look at the therapist's office; if its decor is exotic, beware.

Patients can get into all kinds of difficulties when they are given the wrong kind of advice and "support." If there were a widely and generally accepted code of conduct which characterizes a normal man and woman the problem would be less complicated. Many who call themselves psychotherapists believe that almost anything a person wants to think or do is normal. "Do your own thing," regardless of what it is, just so long as it is satisfying you, is often a guiding principle of these people—anything goes. This is not treatment.

In addition to the bad values which may be imposed on sick people by sick or poorly informed or ill-trained therapists, transference phenomena inevitably appear in these "supportive" therapies. This adds serious difficulties to the situation. It takes sensitivity, perceptiveness, and much skill to know how to handle transference reactions in patients, particularly those in supportive psychotherapy. Many who try to help others do not know the first thing about how to recognize and use transference constructively.

The transference reactions are complicated by the ordinary human reactions people have toward each other. Thus, when feelings and fantasies begin to run high between therapist and patient, much can go very wrong. Note, I said between the two parties. Ill-trained and often "sick" therapists are just as subject to ordinary human responses (feelings, etc.) *and* to transference reactions as are those who have come for help. Some unscrupulous "therapists" exploit these reactions in their patients to their own advantage by prolonging the "therapeutic" relationship and entering into unethical associations with their "patients." I am referring mostly to sexual affairs. Even some psychiatrists and psychoanalysts, who should know better and should have better self-control, get into affairs with their patients, to everyone's disadvantage. The best trained and most ethical doctor has feelings too and can develop transference reactions toward his patient; however, his greater health, stability, and ethical code will make it possible for him to control himself and not let these reactions interfere with the treatment.

Pastoral counselors often carry heavy burdens which they are ill equipped to handle properly. People naturally turn to these "men of God" in the belief that they must surely have special wisdom from God, or possibly even a special word from God for them. Furthermore, because of the scarcity of well-trained and competent psychiatrists, and because of their high fees, people turn to their minister or priest for guidance, advice, counseling, often presenting the thorniest of personality and life problems. A few of these counselors, no doubt, have some degree of competence or have lived life long enough to be able to offer good advice. Some do counsel wisely. Unfortunately, most of the clergy, I suspect, simply do not know what they are doing or what they are getting into when they enter into a counseling relationship with a church member.

The most obvious explanation for this state of affairs is that the clergy has very little knowledge of the nature of psychiatric disturbances and knows even less about the techniques of treatment, including supportive treatment. The high frequency of sexual affairs between the clergy and the women they initially set out to help by counseling is evidence of this fact. These affairs, I am sure, are the result of transference reactions in each toward the other which were then acted upon. Transference should never be acted on, for this merely temporarily satisfies an unconscious motivation. After such satiation the motivation reappears, much like hunger which requires periodic feeding. The clergy is not trained for properly handling transference, yet I venture to suggest that they are bombarded by feelings and beliefs of their parishioners which are heavily laden with transference meanings along with actual, and at times very thorny, reality problems.

In light of the kinds of personality disturbances which exist among the clergy and considering how very little training most of them have in the understanding and treatment of psychiatric disturbances, it is not surprising that they should be relatively ineffectual as helpers of those with troubled minds.

A very knowledgeable nun, fairly high in the Catholic hierarchy, who had known many nuns and priests and who was well trained in psychology, made the observation that most of the priests she knew were tied to their mothers, and the nuns were tied to their fathers. It is my impression that such conflicts exist among non-Catholics too. It is well known how many young people first think of entering the church during puberty as a reaction to their profound guilt about sex. Guilt about sex is always associated with unresolved unconscious oedipal and preoedipal conflicts.

If a choice has to be made between a minister or priest and one of those persons on the fringe of the mental health professions who call themselves "psychotherapists," I think it is safer to seek help from the clergy. Most ministers and priests have a conscience, though excessively enlarged in many, and they are more honest. Their basic honesty, conscience, and integrity is strongly in their favor in contrast to freewheeling "therapists." Their values regarding the conduct of men and women within the context of family life are undoubtedly better than that of some of the more disturbed persons who claim to do psychotherapy.

Nothing of what I have said about the personalities and unconscious conflicts of some of the clergy should be taken as criticism of their purely spiritual functions or of the church as an institution. My remarks are aimed at the kinds of problems the clergy are likely to confront when they try to influence the lives of others as they enter into intense counseling responsibilities. This is a human, not a spiritual, matter. It is just as important for the clergy to be free of personality disturbances and have good training if they undertake the task of influencing the lives of others as anyone else. Unfortunately the church, like the mental health fields, attracts people who have some degree of personality disturbance—at least that is my clear impression.

Group therapy is a legitimate and a very effective form of treatment if it is conducted by a competent and healthy professional. Patients who require support and some insight into themselves may be helped materially by well-run group therapy. It is rarely possible for people to gain the depth of insight into themselves as in a psychoanalysis, but they can be helped and even changed to a considerable degree, nonetheless. There is strength in numbers, and people of good will who are willing to work at treatment and abide by the treatment rules will make progress if their therapist is mature and understands the human condition and the group processes. Watch out for charlatans, however. Here is where they are because of the greater moneymaking possibilities.

There are pitfalls in group treatment which need to be discussed. The group experience can induce psychic regression just as individual treatment can. Regression is induced when unconscious conflicts are mobilized by the intense relationships that are formed in the treatment setting, be that group or individual treatment. As you can quickly see, the therapist of a group of six to eight patients may have his hands full if the treatment becomes too intense. All of these patients will have developed transference reactions, not only toward the doctor but toward the other members of the group. The two dangers are (1) that patients will disorganize into some form of serious psychiatric illness, or (2) they will act on the unconscious conflicts that the treatment has mobilized, not fully realizing what they are doing and not having enough time (because of the six or seven others who want to talk) to keep the therapist adequately informed about what is happening to them during treatment and between sessions.

Patients in group treatment, like those in individual treatment, should not make major changes in their lives while in treatment (such as divorce, marriage, job changes, love affairs, etc.). Above all, the patients in group treatment should not have anything to do with each other outside the group sessions. To do so opens up opportunities for the acting out of personal unconscious conflicts and problems, nearly always to the detriment of treatment.

Other forms of group treatment are the various kinds of sensitivity groups, retreat marathons, and the like, which are led by self-proclaimed healers or prophets who claim to know the secret of success and happiness and life. It is doubtful that these experiences have any lasting therapeutic impact on people.

It is likely that these various group experiences may break down certain inhibitions in isolated, shy, and inhibited people. Any therapeutic activity that has this objective should also take the responsibility for insuring the person's safety after the inhibitions are removed. Reports on the effects of sensitivity groups clearly show that people may indeed behave differently after these intense experiences, but to say they behave more maturely is doubtful. Reports are appearing in increasing numbers in the psychiatric literature of serious mental breakdowns and suicides after exposure to various kinds of sensitivity groups. This is to be expected. As I have said several times before, intense interpersonal involvement mobilizes unconscious conflicts and often induces sick behavior. Since most who enter sensitivity groups are searching for answers to their life's problems, it is safe to assume they are psychiatrically ill to some degree. Small wonder, then, that there are frequent disastrous consequences resulting from these group experiences. Leaders of these groups all too often are lacking in training; they often are emotionally disturbed themselves and haven't the slightest comprehension of how to handle the psychic disturbances which inevitably appear during intense interpersonal interactions. I venture to guess a high percentage of the leaders of these groups are in it for the money and have little concern, let alone a sense of responsibility, for the health and welfare of their followers.

Some of these groups are little more than a disguise for sexual orgies. It is difficult to imagine lasting good effects from these activities. If married couples partake of these group activities they should be prepared for the eventual dissolution of their marriage.

Behavior therapy is a treatment technique which aims directly at the abnormal behavior. The theoretical system behind this treatment holds to the view that the behavior in question *is* the psychopathology and denies the existence of unconscious forces. Behavior therapists believe that the patient's abnormal behavior is caused by learning or conditioning. The task, then, is to unlearn or relearn or decondition the person so he will be free of his abnormal condition. There is much merit to their theory and to their treatment techniques.

I think there is little doubt that some behaviors are the result of conditioning, and that some traits or ways of acting or reacting are learned. Behaviorists go too far by throwing out the concept of the unconscious mind. Unconscious factors can produce some form of abnormal behavior and then die out over the years, leaving the surface (abnormal) behavior intact and a permanent part of personality. It is precisely in instances such as these where behavior therapy techniques are very effective in contrast to psychoanalysis.

If you have an isolated symptom, such as a fear of a specific situation or act, behavior therapy may be very helpful. Sexual disturbances, phobias, specific inhibitions, and the like often yield very well to behavior therapy techniques. Sometimes the symptoms disappear forever; at times they return or others may crop up in their place. The latter occurs when the unconscious basis for the symptom has *not* died out. When the symptom which permits partial expression of the unconscious conflicts is removed and the unconscious conflict is not simultaneously resolved, it is quite likely that a new symptom will appear.

I will not go into the details of how behavior therapy is done— there are several different techniques—but limit myself to these few remarks.

I think it is unlikely that behavior therapy can bring about thorough personality change or significantly affect the major psychiatric illnesses. I do believe it is a very worthwhile technique which can be used as an adjunct to psychotherapy which is designed to bring insight to the patient and resolve his unconscious conflicts.

If you are in psychotherapy and you have one or more symptoms or traits which will not yield to treatment, then it would be entirely appropriate for your doctor to invite the assistance of a behavior therapist to work on the resistant symptoms. Your doctor may also be skilled in behavior therapy. If so, he can add this technique to his regular psychotherapy. Do not expect to achieve major personality change as a result of behavior therapy. There are those who disagree with this statement, but I think they are wrong.

Hypnotherapy is used in two principal ways. Placing the patient under hypnosis can be used to recover repressed memories which, when recovered, should lead to the removal of symptoms. This type of therapy works rather well for the traumatic neuroses where the person sustained a severe shock and reacted by forming a symptom of some kind. Hypnotherapy is sometimes used as a shortcut for expressive therapy. Some claim good results. I doubt if the results are as durable as might be believed at first. Repressed memories which are recovered during the hypnotic state are not as squarely faced and worked through as those which are recovered during full consciousness.

The second way hypnotherapy is used is by employing suggestion during the hypnotic state. The patient is told he will no longer experience his symptom or symptoms after he is fully awake. This technique relies on what is called "post-hypnotic suggestion." I have serious doubts that symptoms, particularly those of long standing, can be permanently removed by post-hypnotic suggestion.

Some patients can be taught how to hypnotize themselves and, having achieved various levels of altered consciousness, they appear to be able to influence bodily functions and head off trouble symptoms of one kind or another.

Hypnosis is a fascinating phenomenon and it can be used alone and can unquestionably be used as an adjunct to psychotherapy just as can behavior therapy techniques. If you go to a behavior therapist or hypnotherapist, discuss your treatment objectives frankly and be very clear what you are getting into. Of course you should be equally careful with regard to *any* type of treatment.

There are a number of other therapies, such as implosive therapy, transactional analysis, guided imagery, primal therapy, etc., with which I have had no direct experience. In keeping with my rule to discuss only that about which I have direct knowledge, I will not discuss these therapies except to caution you to be very careful about what you are getting into. I suspect transactional analysis is the most beneficial of these therapies if the therapist is well experienced and personally mature.

TERMINATION OF TREATMENT

When is treatment complete? There is no single answer to this question. One answer might be, when the original goals have been reached. Unfortunately it sometimes appears that the goals have been reached and termination follows, only for the patient to discover that his old problems have returned. The improvement may have been due to the supportive aspects of the treatment or environmental changes, and with the support gone and old or new responsibilities to face once again the symptoms frequently return.

Sometimes patients go away from home to a hospital and are treated in an environmental context which is quite different from the one in which they became ill. Usually the responsibilities of work have been greatly lessened by this move, and often patients are separated from their families. Under these new conditions unconscious conflicts recede back into the depths of the unconscious, repair takes place within the personality (anxiety, depression, and other symptoms disappear) and the patient and doctor think the patient is well, and in a sense he certainly is. Treatment may seem like a tremendous success. The patient is manifestly well but the old unconscious problems are still there, ready to make trouble when and if the patient returns to his former responsibilities and commitments.

There is no magic within a psychiatric hospital. Many patients improve in a hospital for the reasons previously outlined. In addition to being removed from the conflict-triggering environment which made them ill, patients are treated kindly, there is ample time for rest (one of Nature's finest medicines!), and there may be various specific therapies added, of course. Some patients will not improve after having been removed from the conflict-triggering life situation because their illness is too great; then intense therapy is required to cure the patient. Others fail to improve in the hospital because their illness was essentially lifelong so that treatment has to be constructive rather than reconstructive in nature. Others fail to improve simply by virtue of having been hospitalized because loss was a major reason for their psychic decompensation. Patients have to come to terms with losses and the underlying conflicts awakened by the losses have to be worked through. This may take a long time. Losses usually have to be replaced and this also takes time. Some losses are irreplaceable; it takes time and much mental work to adjust to this fact.

The doctor who allows his patient to divorce and give up family responsibilities can easily fool himself and his patient about the nature of the patient's improvement. Here again, it is quite likely the improvement in the patient may be due in large part to the removal of conflict triggers. If the patient marries again he is very likely to discover his old problems and symptoms will return. It is true that a divorce follows logically, and sometimes inevitably, after a successful treatment because the patient's spouse failed to change. Such a patient will be able to marry another person and will probably get along well—if his unconscious conflicts were resolved.

The really acid tests, the surest criteria, of successful treatment are the disappearance of the symptoms, troublesome behavioral traits, etc., *and* the ability to do after treatment what had been impossible or very difficult to do before treatment, within the limits of the patient's talents and abilities, and within the context of the responsibilities of a mature life adjustment.

For instance, after successful treatment, an unmarried person should be able to marry, and the kind of person he marries should be of unmixed gender and a nonpsychiatrically ill person. If a man who has been unable to marry is able to marry after treatment but chooses an aggressive, domineering, or possibly even a masculinized, woman, proof is at hand that his treatment was not fully successful. Similarly, if a woman picks a passive or psychiatrically troubled man for a mate after treatment, treatment probably was not fully successful. Some men and women can marry after treatment but cannot have children and become parents. In the absence of physical reasons or extenuating circumstances, this is evidence of incomplete treatment.

The effectiveness of treatment, then, can be assessed from several vantage points: (1) What the doctor says has happened. This is frequently a poor test. (2) Before and after comparisons of the patient with himself. This is a fairly good test provided the environment around the patient is taken into account. (3) An assessment of the patient's environment after treatment. Successfully treated patients surround themselves with better environments. Old friendships which were originally formed as a consequence of the sick elements within the patient may be given up. The patient's spouse will either be divorced or much improved because of the impact of the successfully treated patient. Work patterns will have improved.

Psychological test data can be helpful in deciding whether treatment has been successful. However, the environmental context in which the patient is living must be taken into consideration.

Tests can look quite good if the patient has become asymptomatic in an environment which is free of conflict triggers (his usual responsibilities) only to reveal many pathologic signs when he again returns to a conflict-triggering environment. How the patient functions is much more reliable evidence for health or sickness than psychological test data.

The reasons for treatment failure, given adequate time and money, fall into several categories:

1. Personality difficulties of the doctor.

2. The doctor's failure to understand the human condition— what constitutes a normal man or woman and a mature adjustment, and that Nature is the doctor's greatest ally.

3. The doctor's training. He may not know how to induce change in the patient. The key lies in knowing how to make the unconscious conscious, how to apply pressure on the patient, how to use environmental factors to the advantage of the treatment, how and when to use prohibitions, when to give encouragement and support, and finally, the realization on the doctor's part that it is up to him—it is his responsibility—to make treatment work.

4. The severity of the patient's illness and certain core conflicts and their characterological consequences. Obviously certain forms of severe and chronic illnesses are difficult to change. Aside from these, penis envy and predisposing associated conflicts and the consequent aggressivity in women, and castration anxiety and associated predisposing conflicts and the resultant passivity and/or femininity in men are particularly difficult to resolve. Doctors with similar conflicts do not stand a chance with patients who are so burdened if they attempt to bring about basic personality change.

5. The environment of the patient. During treatment it is very important—I think essential—for the patient to be living in the context of his usual life responsibilities. Patients who are treated in a relative environmental vacuum never achieve as extensive or as durable changes as those who are surrounded by an environment that offers the opportunity for a mature adjustment. The presence of available and mature members of the opposite sex is especially important. The environmental context should be flexible enough not to inhibit the changing patient. Skillful use of the environment

is one of the most effective ways I know of for bringing about really significant changes in patients.

These are very basic truths and all should be looked at closely when planning treatment and during treatment. Take a good look at the doctor, then at your own environment, and if everything looks favorable go ahead. Remember, males want to become men and females want to become women. Nature wills it this way.

I find that treating both the husband and wife rather than just the patient who first comes for treatment is the most effective way I have yet discovered for bringing about really significant improvement in married people and in their family life.

In summary, it is appalling to think of all the harm that has been done and is being done by some psychiatrically disturbed psychoanalysts, psychiatrists, social workers, self-styled "psychotherapists," the clergy, sensitivity group leaders, and heaven knows who else, in their efforts to do "psychotherapy." Even the consequences of simple advice-giving can be far-reaching, not to mention the consequences of tampering with another person's mind when the tamperer is ill trained or psychiatrically disturbed to some degree, or both. As much care and expertise are necessary in the practice of psychotherapy as in any of the procedures used by the various specialities of medicine. Psychiatry is a relatively new field within the profession of medicine. Unfortunately, many who practice this speciality— particularly those who engage in psychotherapeutic procedures— do not yet realize that pathogenic (illness-producing) forces within the mind must be dealt with, in principle, in the same way as other physicians deal with illness-producing agents.

There are no established controls or generally accepted rules, principles, or technical guidelines governing the conduct of those who call themselves psychotherapists as there are, for instance, in the specialities of internal medicine and/or surgery. The examinations for physicians who have trained to be specialists in surgery and internal medicine and most other specialities assess the doctors' treatment capabilities in great detail prior to their certification as specialists. This is not so for physicians who specialize in psychiatry (with regard to their ability to do psychotherapy). Actually, there is no way the doctor's ability to conduct psychotherapy can be assessed other than direct supervision over a long span of time. Furthermore, there is a large number of nonpsychiatrists who practice psychotherapy. Virtually anyone who can get a patient or get a group of people together for group therapy can call himself a psychotherapist. In short, there is hardly any way for the professional community to check on the psychotherapeutic work of those who do psychotherapy— regardless of the basic profession to which they belong.

There is much room for creative work, for innovation, for uniqueness in style in which psychotherapy is conducted, but there is also much room for ineptness, bungling, and quackery; much that is called psychotherapy today is dangerous and even exploitative. Psychoanalysts have a rather good code of conduct and some good treatment principles to guide them as well as a system of controls while the analyst is in training, but even in this field much is done that is antitherapeutic, and many factors creep in which limit the effectiveness of treatment. The therapeutic work of those who aspire to be certified by the American Psychoanalytic Association is closely examined before they are certified as having passed the standards of that association; however, once the psychoanalyst has been certified there is no way for his peers to check his work as there is in other branches of medicine.

It bears repeating that the physician who practices psychotherapy and psychoanalysis is just as responsible for his patient as is any other physician. Each psychotherapist should be guided by this principle. He must protect the patient from the forces of illness within himself and he must protect others around the patient. It is the doctor's duty to remove these pathogenic forces, that is, the patient's unconscious conflicts and their effects on the personality. He is responsible for inducing change in his patient. This means getting the patient over his illness and promoting his maturation. He is especially responsible for the careful handling of those unconscious forces he mobilizes within the patient by the treatment process. He certainly is not responsible for the fact those forces are there, but he is responsible for having unleashed them and he must see to it that his patient and others are not harmed by them during the weeks, months, or years the patient is in treatment.

A patient's perception of life, his behavior, and his values can change markedly as unconscious conflicts are mobilized by treatment. The doctor must take great care that the patient does not act on the basis of these transient states. Many patients divorce, change jobs, marry, etc., during treatment only to regret these changes later. Psychotherapy is a serious matter and requires great care, skill, talent, and a mature personality on the part of the doctor in order to be able to properly manage the conflicts of people. Those who practice psychotherapy should reflect the best in human values in their personalities and should be guided by beliefs which are expressions of these same values. The personality traits of the therapist and his beliefs determine what he judges to be the focus for the therapy, how he reacts to it, and profoundly affect his capability to bring about change (both good and bad) in his patient. Be very careful whom you pick for your psychotherapist or the psychotherapist for members of your family. Great, great good can come from expertly done treatment—or your life can be wrecked. Your family may break up, you may lose your children, your personality may be influenced in the wrong way. How your children develop, what they become, and so on, will be affected by how well or how poorly you are treated. Keep a very close watch on your therapist and if your life does not go in the direction I have tried to define and describe in various places in this book, you had better seriously consider having a consultation with another doctor or changing doctors.

CHAPTER SIX

Careers
and the Family

It is in the nature of things for males and females to mate—nothing could be more obvious—but as civilization has evolved, the challenges and opportunities facing men and women have created conditions which seriously undermine family life. In contrast to former times, it is now much easier for women to go to work; higher education is as available to women as to men. These opportunities can seriously conflict with making a home and rearing a family. Similarly, work demands have become a powerful force which remove the man from his family.

Given the existing economic setup a young man must work to provide for the care of his family. His continuous presence is not as necessary for the proper rearing of *infants and very young children* as is the mother's. A man must be all the more committed to his work after he is married and has a family in order to support them, but he must *not* neglect his family as far too many men do as they become overly drawn into their jobs or careers or avoid their family responsibilities for personal reasons.

The future life course of a young woman who does not marry soon after graduating from high school or college is not as simple as it is for the man. The high value placed on an education, and the growing trend for women to work, causes many young women to prepare for a vocation or profession and to embark on a career other than that of making a family. Some expend an enormous amount of time, energy, and money preparing for a career. Sooner or later their urge to mate wins the upper hand, and many working women marry. Marriage alone does not complicate the life of a young career or working woman unless her career separates her from her husband.

How much time a young couple devote to each other or to their careers is of little concern. When children are born the situation is entirely changed, and the question of how time and energy are allocated is a matter of great importance. Whatever one does in life, one should do well; therefore, those who make families should properly discharge their responsibilities to their children. The problem with so many men and career women is that when they attempt to make a family, forces within themselves and the careers to which they have committed themselves prevent them from doing this well.

CAREER WOMEN

In the past a woman's primary career was marriage and a family. Now women constitute nearly half of the work force of the United States. Many of these are young women who have not married but eventually will; others are women whose families are grown; some are women who have not and never will marry; others are widows, or divorced as a consequence of their own choice and all too often because they were abandoned by their husbands. Unfortunately, tens of thousands of women who have families and who would prefer to make their family their career are forced by economic need to go to work. For an increasing number of women the idea that having a family is a career of the highest value has slipped from its former high position and these women go to work or develop a career rather than tend to their young family. Their children are suffering serious consequences.

With the coming of a child or children, women who have worked or have had a career in a profession or vocation are faced with a difficult decision. The decision to stay at home and care for their child or return to work soon after the birth of their child confronts all of them. It is not easy for anyone, man or woman, to stop working at something he or she has done for many years and has enjoyed. Much satisfaction comes from the exercise of skills and abilities and the earning of money. To set aside an entire way of life is not easy. Furthermore, for men, and women, money may have a special meaning aside from its necessity for daily living.

I have no doubt whatsoever that if the new mother who has been working is mature and ready for motherhood she will want to, and should, stay home and take care of her baby and should remain there at least until her child goes to school full time. When the child is at school all day it does not matter so much where the mother is, although she should be at home when her child comes home from school. In other words, it is of vital importance for a woman who has a baby to take care of it. Not to do so denies the child the most vital of all human experiences. So-called object constancy (the parent) for infants and young children is extremely important for their personality development. Babies and young children develop best when their mother is present all of the time. Of course, this statement does not apply to severely disturbed mothers; they should not have had babies in the first place.

One of the outstanding women of psychiatry and psychoanalysis, Helene Deutsch, has written a painfully frank account of her past life under the heading of *Confrontations with Myself* (22). She now freely admits that she deprived her son and herself of a rich source of happiness by not devoting herself full time to his care. She attributes her inability to have done so to her own unconscious conflicts which consisted of her deep identification with her father, her envy of the male, and her profound hostility toward her mother, and, also, to the pressures of her career. Her mother had dominated family life, including Dr. Deutsch's father, whom she describes as a passive man. She believes motherhood is a full-time occupation, and she regrets not having followed her own good judgment at the time. Though Dr. Deutsch welcomes the greater freedoms women enjoy today she notes that, "though woman is different now, she is forever the same, a servant of her biological fate, to which she has to adjust her other pursuits."

It is equally important for fathers to be constant figures in the young child's life. However, since fathers must be away part of every day, it is imperative that the mother not be away too, during the early years of life. Care in day-care centers can never equal what a mature mother can provide her child. Furthermore, day-care centers are often staffed by transient and indifferent personnel. Some women baby-sitters are quite good, but even they are no substitute for the continuous presence of a mature mother. I have no wish to make mothers feel guilty for not taking care of their children, but facts are facts, and they should be faced.

Many women who have worked find staying home and caring for their children somewhat difficult in the beginning; they miss the intellectual stimulation and human contact their work provided. They should persevere, because if they are mature enough they will discover that the joys of being a mother and making a home exceed those provided by their job or career. Mature women soon will no longer miss the satisfactions of work, for they are fulfilling their deepest natural instinct, their highest responsibility to nature and to society. I honestly believe that if all mothers ceased caring for their babies civilization would collapse.

Some women who have worked and then begun a family are unable to discover the joys of making a home; in fact, they may suffer great personal strain. Many soon return to work; others stay at home, are miserable, and do a poor job at homemaking and motherhood. Some become so disturbed they eventually require psychiatric treatment.

The career women I have treated had all grown discontented with life for a variety of reasons. Some had worked for years but longed to marry and have a family; however their unconscious conflicts forced them to behave in such a way as to avoid meeting eligible men, or if they met them, they drove them off with their provocative behavior at about the time it seemed a marriage was in sight. Others had been able to go through the ritual of marriage but were unable to make a happy marriage. Some had gotten so far, despite serious flaws in their marriage, as to have one or more children. All of these women were miserable. A few of them were contemplating suicide as the only apparent solution because the impasse they had reached in life was so unsolvable for them. They did not want to give up their career, yet it was no longer satisfying; they wanted to marry but could not, or, if they had married, it was not working out. Those who had children recognized they were failing in the care of them; these mothers were aware that they were missing out on some of the richest experiences of life. They could see that their children were not developing well and, furthermore, their career performance was no longer up to par. These women were at serious cross-purposes with themselves. Their natural instinct was pushing them toward heterosexuality, marriage, motherhood; something else within them was pushing them toward the continuance of their vocation or career. I believe this inner conflict accounts for the high suicide rate in professional women who are still in the childbearing age range (much higher than in men or the general population).

My strong impression is that a feminine young woman who has matured is unlikely to place a vocation or profession higher in her scale of values than her family. Many women do go to college or work for a few years after graduating from high school. It is not long, however, before they marry and soon abandon aspirations to work. Some very fine and mature young women do have difficulty finding a mate because of personal, physical characteristics or the short supply of men in the area where they live; or they may have taken on responsibilities which force them to continue working. The simple truth is, however, that a mature and feminine woman will usually be married by her mid-twenties, barring unusual circumstances. One cannot categorically say that all unmarried women are not mature. That all women who do marry early or by their mid-twenties are feminine and mature is not true either, of course. Young women may marry for neurotic reasons, that is, for reasons other than a genuine readiness to mate. The reasons include the wish to get away from a miserable home life, a means for finding security, undue concern about the social norm that everybody should marry, a means by which to vicariously live out the role of a male through a husband, the wish to win a "forbidden" man, the urge for a baby, and so on.

Unfortunately, many of the career women who do marry are just feminine and mature enough to be able to marry but not mature enough or feminine enough to make their marriage a complete success, and of course, they tend to choose men who are also short on maturity. This fact accounts in part for the high divorce rate and the fact that many of these women work rather than care for their babies and young children. Some of these women remain at home and live miserable lives and rear their children poorly, thereby contributing to another generation of disturbed individuals. They, and everyone else, would be better off if they did go to work and turn over the care of their children to a more mature woman. Some mothers who continue working would become overtly psychiatrically ill if they gave up working and stayed at home to care for their children. However, everyone would be even better off if these women could receive good psychiatric treatment so they could make a success of their family life.

The woman who embarks on a vocational career must be aware that a significant aspect of her basic nature will go unsatisfied if she never has a family. She should be aware of what she is getting into as she sets her life course. This is no small consideration. Heterosexual commitments and maternalism are powerful needs; to find substitute satisfactions for these biological imperatives can be very difficult and, even if found, a deep sense of bitterness and futility often appears in career women when the opportunity for a family has passed them by. Take a long view and try to imagine what life will be like when you are thirty, forty, and older.

While I have no proof or evidence based on a large-scale and exhaustive in-depth study of career women, I have treated a sizable number of them, and I have supervised the treatment of many others which was being done by other doctors. These women all share certain obvious characteristics which any observant person can detect. All were dominated by unconscious conflicts which were remarkably similar and which the treatment process exposed.

When I first began to treat career women I was astounded by the profound change in their view of life following the resolution of those unconscious conflicts which had prevented them from marrying and becoming mothers, or being happily married and effective mothers if they had been able to marry. As my experiences increased, my amazement increased even more because of the regularity with which certain unconscious conflicts were found to be the bases for their difficulties and because of the equal regularity in the extreme changes in their view of life and their values which were brought about as a result of treatment.

It could be argued that the career women I have known and treated were a special group, that they did not constitute a fair sample of all career women, simply because they came for treatment while many career women do not, and that those unconscious forces which I discovered in them had led only to their psychiatric disturbances and had nothing to do with their earlier life course which had led to choosing a career. You will have to accept on faith my observations that direct links existed between their unconscious conflicts and having chosen a career. Their need for treatment resulted from their inability to overcome the effects of their unconscious conflicts which prevented them from making a heterosexual commitment and having a family.

No one knows what motivates all career and working women, nor have I observed career women in sufficient numbers to claim absolute validity for what I believe about them; however, it is striking how many of them share certain visible characteristics. I am referring to career women with whom I have been acquainted and others of whose treatment I have had knowledge. Their personalities are very similar to those I have known in depth as a result of having treated them. Having made these observations over many years, I believe my inferences about career women are valid. Women who go to work or make a career after their children are in school or their family is grown, and those who are forced to work because of economic need, are strikingly different from many women who have pursued a career without interruption during their adult life.

The one single fact that stands out among all others with regard to the early life of these women and, therefore, with regard to the unconscious conflicts in them, is that some degree of breakdown existed in their relationship with their mothers when they were infants and young girls. During their very early life their mothers either rejected them to some degree or they were excessively anxious with their new responsibilities as a mother. These mothers were themselves not ready to be mothers. Some turned much of the care of their infants over to others; some seemed devoted to their girl babies, but were crippled either by inhibition and other personality difficulties, or followed guidelines which they were taught so as to make it hard for them to fully respond to the needs of their infants.

Furthermore, the mothers of these little girls who never marry and who follow a career instead usually have bad marriages because of their own partial rejection of femininity and their inability to form a deep and meaningful relationship with a man. Their husbands are frequently not strong men within the family; they may be passive or remote; they may be powerful men in their work but remote or passive in their family. Some were too close to their daughters and may even have been seductive, at times overtly so.

When a poor relationship exists between a man and his wife, children inevitably have difficulty during the oedipal period. Nature eventually propels the little girl toward her father; he is the first male in her life and he evokes the female in her. The career women whom I have treated in depth without exception had not broken their oedipal (romantic and erotic) ties with their fathers, nor have they overcome the envy of the male genital. This is so because of the kinds of personalities their parents had and the imperfections in their marital relationships. When the mother is not close to her husband, the little daughter gets too close to her father and has difficulty breaking her tie to him, or the opposite occurs. The father is distant and the little girl continually needs warmth from father figures. This unresolved romantic attachment to her father is inevitably associated with penis envy and envy of the male's way of life. The little girl eventually identifies with her father to one degree or another. The more she identifies with her father, the more she ultimately rejects her mother as a model. Furthermore, her mother never provided a picture of satisfied femininity to her, a fact which caused the little girl to reject a feminine identification all the more.

I once heard a sportswoman of national prominence (whose personality exhibited many of these qualities) remark at a luncheon where she gave a brief speech that she was so deeply engrossed in her sport because it was "visible and measurable." This metaphoric phrase expressed (in my opinion) much more than she or the audience realized. In one brief instant she had delivered a message from her unconscious mind which revealed that her deep devotion to her sport was related to her envy of the male and his genitals. It is my hunch that when she was a young girl she never overcame her envy of that which is "visible and measurable" and, as a consequence, she compensated for the absence of male genitals by becoming "masculine" in her character formation and fiercely competitive—traits for which she found expression in her sport. Metaphoric phrases often occur during moments of strain and tension, conditions which permit unconscious meanings to surface. Metaphors, like dreams and slips of the tongue, are extremely useful during psychiatric treatment for the purpose of revealing the contents of the unconscious mind to the patient. This woman deprecates homemaking and motherhood and actually attempts to discourage young women from following such a life course.

I again recommend Helene Deutsch's book, *Confrontations With Myself* (22), to young women who are career oriented. Dr. Deutsch discusses with unusual frankness how the personalities of her parents and her life with them led to the development of her own neurosis and profoundly influenced her own personality development. She hated her mother and apparently her mother lacked affection for her. Dr. Deutsch was cared for by nine different nurses, but she was always her father's little darling.

She was painfully aware of her father's passivity in relation to her mother who ruled the household in a tyrannical manner. She attributes her inability to be a full-time mother to her unconscious oedipal conflicts and her dedication to a career, to her envy of males, and her deep identification with her father. A dream, in which she possessed both female and male genitals, eventually led her to the realization of how her wish to simultaneously be her father's prettiest daughter and his cleverest son determined the whole of her personality.

The conflicts within herself which Dr. Deutsch describes and which determined the entire course of her life are identical to those which I have observed in the career women I have treated or have known in depth. Disclosures such as are recorded in Dr. Deutsch's book are immensely valuable; we are deeply in the debt of such courageous professionals.

When young girls who are destined to choose a career for life reach puberty, a single fact emerges; they cannot establish a meaningful and enduring relationship with a young man. Some avoid boys altogether. Some date for a while but eventually give up. Others become homosexual immediately. Some try heterosexuality for a while but either eventually suppress all interest in sexuality or become homosexual. Some carry on in one affair after another but never marry. Some, unfortunately, eventually do marry and have children but never stay at home and care for their children. It is probably better that these women do not care for their children but relegate the care to others. Were such a woman to make the attempt the children would suffer more and the woman might become ill with some form of psychiatric disturbance. It would be much better if such women had never had children in the first place. They should have settled for working out some kind of compatible relationship with their husband and let it go at that.

Subsequent to this troubled period which begins at puberty these young women begin to form an interest in some field or another. They are aware of their inability to successfully relate to a man, and they realize they must do something with their lives. Some simply go to work. If they are fortunate enough to have been endowed with a special talent, high intelligence, or both, they eventually find their way into higher education and a business or professional career. The more deeply they become involved in their vocations or careers, the more fixed they become in their way of life.

What I have written is not condemnatory of these women. They are unfortunate; they are denied much that life has to give. But many working or career women make substantial contributions to life, and for this they deserve the respect and the rewards due anyone who contributes to society. This statement applies equally to men who never marry but who contribute to society. Most of these men and women, however, suffer silently—and at times not so silently—from some degree of loneliness and awareness that a part of their nature is not being fulfilled. They are missing out on the joys which can only be found within a family of one's own.

MEN AND CAREERS

If men are going to father children, they must make time for the child and participate in family life in such a way as to make it possible for the child to grow up into normal manhood or womanhood. There is a difference between the effects on the child when mothers work and when fathers do. The difference is due to the fact that mothers are more directly important to babies and very young children than fathers are. The mother needs the love and support of her husband and a secure home, but early in life the role of mothering is primary as far as the child is concerned. The father can be at work all day; the mother should not be. When the work day is over, the man must devote time and energy to his family. Far too many men do not.

The man who aspires to achieve great heights in his work faces certain hard decisions if he intends to have a family, too. He must inevitably face the decision of how to allocate his time and energy. If he has a family he must not neglect it in the human sense. Children need fathers. It is pointless for a man to devote himself solely to his work, make a fortune, and leave that fortune to his children who will be failures because of inadequate fathering. Such a man may have done society a great service through his career, but he should not have burdened himself with a family, nor should he have imposed personality weakness on his children by depriving them of fathering. Ultimately such children tend to become somewhat of a liability to society.

These remarks should not be understood to mean that a man who is highly successful in his work cannot be a good father also. He must, however, take time to be with his children and his family. Children simply will not develop their full potential if their father rarely involves himself in their lives or fails to organize his family along healthy lines.

The observation has been made that the sons of great men tend not to achieve greatness themselves; in fact, many become total failures. While this pattern does not apply to all sons of great men, the tendency is clearly there. This fact can be used as support for the growing body of evidence that fathers are extremely important for family life and for the best personality development of children. Fathers are just as important as mothers.

I have discussed the incompatibility of the career of motherhood and homemaking and a vocational career. A similar incompatibility exists between fatherhood and a career but in a different way and to a different degree.

It should be obvious that a woman can neglect her children by devoting all of her energies to her house. Some women do just that; they avoid their children just as surely as do career women by attending excessively to physical aspects of the home and neglecting the human beings who live in it. Some men do the same thing by expending all of their energy on their work. The personalities of vast numbers of men have become so emasculated that about all they can do is impregnate their wives and then all but disappear from the scene. They are so weak and ineffectual, so filled with unconscious conflicts, that being a husband, father, and head of the home is way beyond them. Other men are worked nearly to death out of economic necessity and have little energy left over for their family. The jobs of some men take them away from the home for too many hours each day, or for too many days at a time. Men in executive positions or those who own and operate small businesses often become drawn more and more deeply into their work and cannot extricate themselves. Their families rarely see them. Men cannot begin to live up to their responsibilities to their families under these various conditions. These are social and economic conditions that must be corrected. Fathers cannot just spend a few minutes a day with their children and expect them to grow into healthy men and women.

I have written very pointedly about women who work. The same advice applies to men. If you are going to invest all of yourself in your work then I think you should not have children. This may be a hard issue for you to face, but face it you must because if you do not, and if you neglect your children and your family life, you will have a heavy millstone around your neck for all of your life. This millstone will be the burden of personal guilt engendered by your perception of having failed your children and family; it will be the enormous drain upon you which will come from attempting to straighten out your poorly adjusted children; it will be financial, for the chances are good that you will have to pay psychiatric bills incurred by the treatment of your children necessitated by any of a great variety of psychiatric disturbances (homosexuality, drug abuse, delinquency, neurosis, psychosis, personality disturbance, and on and on). You will cringe when your children make bad marriages and fail; when they attempt to be successful at their life's work and fail. The chickens always come home to roost, and if you are not a good father the chickens will roost on you.

Think long and hard on the question of whether or not you have what it takes to be a good father and whether you are prepared to order your life in such a way as to make it possible to be one. I said there is no higher calling for a woman than to be a good mother; nor is there a higher calling for a man than being a good father and head of his family.

I have written at some length about why women avoid the full-time career of motherhood. It is just as distressing, and the consequences are just as serious, when fathers fail as when mothers fail. The reasons for this failing are to be found in the unconscious mind. Men who have had poor fathers usually had poor mothers, too. As a consequence they could not successfully pass through the developmental phases of childhood. Many men can be successful at work but cannot succeed as fathers. Rarely are men successful as fathers but not at work. To step into the role of father and do well usually awakens unconscious conflicts of competition with their father. That is, to be the head of the family (their own) has the unconscious meaning of taking father's place in the (parental) family as their mother's mate. Furthermore, these men frequently have strong dependency needs which are destined to be frustrated were they to assume the responsibilities of fatherhood. In addition to having to overcome these internal barriers to being a good father at the head of the family, such men are often opposed by their domineering wives who, on the one hand, want their husbands to fill their rightful place but who, on the other hand, oppose them when they attempt to do so.

These unconscious conflicts in men force them to avoid their family responsibilities in several ways. Some men simply refuse to have anything to do with their children when they are at home, spending all of their time at hobbies, in front of the T.V. set, etc. Such a man frequently turns away from his wife as well and often exhibits jealousy toward her because of the time and energy she devotes to her family.

Other men pour all of their energy into their work when they need not do so. They think their long hours at work are necessary, but in reality they are not. Work provides the means for escaping from involvement with their family.

Some men seek the type of work which takes them away from the home most of the week or for longer periods of time. These men become restless and irritable when they are with their families on weekends. In fact, one of the surest signs that a man is troubled by unconscious conflicts is the irritability and moodiness which appears when he is with his family.

Men avoid their families by "going out with the boys," spending time at bars and at other activities which provide the means for escaping from the family. Frequently a mistress occupies much of a man's time which might otherwise be spent much more constructively with his wife and children.

To summarize, men or women who want to have a child but plan to devote most of their time and energy to their career or job (in the absence of economic necessity) have, I think, revealed their unreadiness for parenthood. Such parents should, in my opinion, abandon the idea of having a child rather than abandon the child after having it. If you do not think being a parent will be satisfying, then don't do it. Don't force yourself into something you are not ready for, and don't impose your immaturities onto your yet-to-be-born children. Children do not "just grow up"—everything you do or do not do, and what you are, has an effect on them. If you are contemplating being a part-time parent, it is better to make the hard decision to be no parent at all. You may continue to mature in the years to come and be ready for parenthood later. If not, you will undoubtedly feel a certain emptiness in your life if you do not have children, but as a consequence of your decision mankind will have fewer psychiatrically disturbed persons—possibly yourself, and almost surely your child sometime in his life. If you cannot do something well, don't do it, is a good principle to live by; none is more applicable to the rearing of children. They are mankind's most valuable natural resource.

Having children is an instance where the principle of doing that which you are afraid to do should be *very wisely applied*, and perhaps it should not be applied at all. I am sure many young people have misgivings about their first child and do perfectly well once the child arrives. However, many do not, and the consequences of unreadiness for parenthood, unlike unreadiness for most other tasks, lead to far-reaching effects on the new child and eventually on society. Never use parenthood as a hoped-for-solution for marital troubles or for personal difficulties.

Society must think long and hard about the present trend which places more importance on work and careers than on a small, high-quality family. Just as serious are those economic conditions which force men to work excessively long work days and force women out of the home and into work. Much attention, support, and prestige is given by society to men and women for their career and work achievement, while practically none is given to those who pursue the most important career of all—the making of a home and a family. *Society had better wake up and provide a great deal more support for those couples who will insure its survival!*

SOME EFFECTS OF CAREER MEN AND WOMEN ON CHILDREN

Unfortunately, far too many children are exposed to certain kinds of career men and women outside the context of the family. Elementary school teachers are a case in point. Some men and women who have not had children of their own do make excellent teachers and have a good effect on children. This is because there is enough masculinity or femininity and uninhibited paternalism or maternalism in them to be able to live up to the human as well as intellectual demands placed upon them in the classroom. Being a teacher provides an outlet for their parental desires. This situation does not place the kinds of demands upon them that family life does. However, many of the teachers of young children are not masculine or feminine or, if they are, they are not fully comfortable with their gender. Some of these teachers are very hostile toward children. Children who come from healthy families can withstand the effects of such teachers, but little boys and girls who are not so fortunate are having their little personalities polluted even further by such teachers.

Women teachers who have personality disturbances which affect their attitude toward their own gender and toward sexuality frequently try to make sissies out of little boys; they stifle their maleness. Even some women who have had families of their own but who teach while their own children are young, out of choice and not economic necessity, impart unhealthy influences on their pupils as well as their own children. Educators would do society a great service if they would hire only men and women who are good teachers *and* who also have masculine or feminine personalities. Teachers are extremely important, not only as transmitters of knowledge but as stimulants for the development of the personalities of the young. Without realizing it, many serve as substitute parents for small children. Homosexual men and women should never be allowed to teach at the elementary, junior high, and high school levels.

I am appalled by the trend of some teachers to adopt teaching styles and classroom attitudes that minimize the differences between the sexes. This is *wrong*. Children should leave school as educated *boys* and *girls*, not as educated sexless beings or confused about sex-role differences. Take a close look at educators who advocate these new trends in blurring sex role differences between boys and girls in the nursery and classroom and you will see women who are not fully feminine and men who are not fully masculine. Their personalities and values influence the young in school, just as the personalities and values of parents influence children in the family, and just as the personality and values of the psychotherapist influences patients. Sex-role differences should be enhanced, not blurred, in all three of these settings. Ideally, those who influence the young, be they parents, doctors, or other career persons, should be as mature as possible. Unfortunately, many are not. For a detailed description of the effects of career persons on children see Patricia Sexton's book *The Feminized Male, White Collars and the Decline of Manliness* (77).

Some of the goals and values of the women's liberation movement are quite valid, realistic, and progressive. However, the tendency to place career objectives above the importance of the family must be strongly and openly opposed. They are doing mankind a grave disservice by inculcating young women with this belief. It is wrong for the leaders of this movement, many of whom are career women, to encourage these young women who have married and have children to reduce their level of responsibility to their family. In this respect the women's liberation movement poses a threat to the family. Many young women who might overcome their difficulties during early years as homemakers are provided an easy way out. The more militant leaders of this movement clearly downgrade the value of a career of homemaking. Instead, they would have women chase after the values of men and compete with them.

One single inescapable fact must be faced. If young women are to be increasingly drawn into the working world through a change in social values, then who will provide care for the children many of these women will have? Making a family and caring for children is a full-time career which only the most mature should attempt. Society will pay an extremely high price if the enormous importance of child care by parents in a home is downgraded or lost sight of. Ever increasing numbers of children will eventually swell the ranks of emotionally disturbed adults. It has been estimated that ten to thirty million children are in need of psychiatric help. Suicide has become the second leading cause of death in the young. Deprive the child of a happy home life and you deprive him of his mental health. If current trends which are eroding the family continue—and those social movements which downgrade the expression of a woman's femininity within a family are prominent among the eroding forces—society as we know it now will end. A strong society comprises strong men and women. Strong individuals come from only one place—from solid families.

Some aspects of the women's liberation movement should be strongly opposed. For society to endorse their antifemininity, their antifamily values, and their competitiveness with men is sheer nonsense. But worse than that the movement places a stamp of acceptability or normality on what is, in fact, a manifestation of psychiatric illness—that is, a social value which reflects the personal illness of a group of individuals. Of even graver significance are the proclamations of major professional organizations to the effect that homosexuality is merely a preferred life style rather than a serious form of psychopathology. Alcoholism, drug addiction, and any other class of psychiatric illness might as well be called preferences too.

Of less impact on the young, but relevant nonetheless, are those career men and women who influence and establish styles in clothing. Many of these people have markedly disturbed personalities; it is well known that some are overtly homosexual. Though styles have changed through the ages, the current clothing and hair styles which blur sex differences are especially clear indicators of the nature of the times. Some of the styles for women diminish or obscure femininity rather than enhance it. Men are having effeminate styles forced upon them and many men seem to eagerly accept these styles. Long hair, scented bodies, handbags, earrings, are the adornments of women. When a man is willing to be influenced by these trends, he is demonstrating his weakness. Women's styles are increasingly sexless or masculine. Note that not only are pantsuits popular for women but that the zipper which was once on the side has been shifted to the front where the man's zipper is placed. I have no doubt whatsoever that the creators of these styles come from disturbed families and are, as a consequence, not fully masculine or feminine. These people have a profound effect on some of the young through their careers.

Young people who are healthy—that means solidly masculine or feminine—will not be affected to any appreciable degree by these styles. However, those who are psychiatrically troubled can be, and I believe are being, influenced by these changes in style of clothing and personal appearance. These adornments tend to reinforce the weakness within them. You can tell a man by the company he keeps, and that company has an effect on him. The same applies to how he dresses and adorns himself. Clothing and hair styles have a feedback effect on the individual and in time will influence his self-concept.

Professional people have a marked impact on society and while a single psychiatrist cannot do much about this I hope you will, after reading this book, keep a close watch on the effects society (and this frequently refers to career women and men) has on you, and especially on your children. Parents can and should influence their school boards to select teachers who will bring out the best in children. Parents should refuse to let their children wear unisex clothing or clothing which reverses the appearance of the sexes. Parents can bring pressure to bear on university teachers who uphold certain values as the new "norm" for society. There are professors in the humanities and other career persons who endorse new lifestyles (sex blurring, open marriage, role reversal in the family, etc.) without any factual basis for doing so. One woman psychologist I know is teaching her class that it is perfectly normal for the father to stay at home and care for the children while the mother works and makes the living. Such a claim is irresponsible and destructive. Teachers who make such claims have overstepped their prerogatives. Their responsibility is to inform their students, not to openly advocate changes in lifestyles in the absence of substantial evidence for the validity of their point of view.

I cannot make a general statement about the personalities of all teachers, university professors, and authors who advocate the new lifestyles—unisex, homosexuality, swinging, open marriage, mate swapping, communal living, etc.—but I invite you to look closely at their personalities. I predict you will find the women to be aggressive, domineering, somewhat masculinized (or at least unfeminine) and the men somewhat short on masculinity. I know this for certain: these self-proclaimed authorities who often say the traditional family is obsolete and that traditional male and female differences are spurious have no scientific basis for their claims and are expressing nothing more than personal opinions. Unfortunately, their academic rank or notoriety as authors places a certain stamp of authority on their pronouncements. Look into their parental history and look into their own family patterns (if they are married) and look at their children, and I think you will have little trouble deciding that these individuals have disturbed personalities. I believe these individuals are recommending for mankind ways of life which they have found to take the strain off their own disturbed personalities. By sharp contrast, what is proposed in my book is backed up by a wealth of solid data and the experience of many serious professionals, including my own. Furthermore, my purpose in telling you something of my personal life and background is so that you can evaluate what I have written in terms of my professional expertise and my qualities as a man. I believe all authors who touch on human values should be required to make similar personal revelations.

It could be argued that I have no right to endorse certain human values and not others. But if mature psychiatrists do not have some knowledge of what is good for people, I don't know who does. It is our business to know; that is what psychiatry is all about. The evidence is overwhelming that certain kinds of parents and family patterns produce children who become strong men and women, and that other parents and family patterns produce sick children or children who will become sick or ineffectual when they reach adulthood. These sick patterns in the family produce certain kinds of people who endorse some of the values of which I am so critical. These values become transmitted to the young and to society in a variety of ways—through music, clothing styles, schools and universities, movies, literature and television, and more directly through interpersonal contact.

I urge you not to accept everything that is being promoted these days by professionals and self-proclaimed authorities whose values reflect their disturbed personalities. Fathers and mothers must stand shoulder to shoulder against many of the current influences on their children. It is your obligation as a parent to protect your offspring from harmful, polluting influences. The human spirit can be polluted just as the environment can. Keep an eye on society and on the professionals and oppose them if you see their influence making your children less responsible, competent and masterful masculine boys and feminine girls. The forces influencing your family are powerful and come from many sources. You should view these forces as disease-producing agents. The onslaught facing parents these days are often nearly overwhelming and do overwhelm some families. Far too many parents have thrown up their hands in despair and have let sick forces in society swallow their children.

The efforts of parents to protect their children will not succeed in every instance because many young people are beyond being influenced constructively. However, you should know that all children and adolescents want their parents to be strong and to set reasonable limits and uphold valid values. Young people often react initially with loud protests and tend thereby to frighten and discourage their parents, but parents should stand firm and hold their ground. *You* set the guidelines and uphold the best values; you can no longer fully rely on the institutions of society to do this for you.

It is my hope that this chapter will help you recognize all the more clearly the necessity for making your family (if you have one) your primary career. Not to do so may cost you and society dearly. When your family disintegrates, all else in life tends to slip, too.

CHAPTER SEVEN

The Castration

of America

In the preface I said this book was born out of a deep concern for the future of America. It is my hope that what I have writteñ will help individuals straighten out their lives, family life in particular, reproduce themselves with healthy children, and thereby insure the future of our nation. It seems to me increasing numbers of men and women are psychologically castrated and naturally their families, if they attempt family life, are castrated. That is, male and female identities and roles are becoming increasingly blurred, personal effectiveness is thereby diminished and the products of such castrated families will be crippled in one or more of a variety of ways.

In this final chapter the focus will be on the relationship between the individual and society, its values and institutions. The family is the key intervening link between the individual and society. The events within the family, the personalities of the parents, the way they relate to each other and to their children is the pivotal point around which civilization turns. The crisis extends to the very roots of our country. Much needs to be done at both the social and individual levels to revitalize America. My book aims largely at individuals; however, efforts can be made at the social level to counteract certain trends and reaffirm solid values.

A major portion of my professional work as a psychiatrist and psychoanalyst has to do with the in-depth study of people for the purpose of correcting what prior influences, largely from within their family, did to them during their developmental years. Such work provides a unique and somewhat rare opportunity to observe the relationship between developmental processes, character and personality patterns, personal values, and social patterns. In short, the personalities of a child's parents, how they related to each other and to the child has a great deal to do with what kind of man or woman the child becomes, how effective he is, what values he holds dear and which social institutions he supports. Profound changes in our social structure, certain laws and in the quality of people we are producing with each successive generation are now in process.

These difficulties began with the coming of the industrial age. Wars and economic pressures have played their part as well. The key element leading to the "castration" of men, women, and families has been the progressive removal of the man from his family. As a consequence, children have been increasingly denied the psychological growth-promoting effect of the presence of an involved, loving, and masculine father. His absence placed many additional burdens on the mother which by necessity took her away from her children. Over the years, wars, economic pressures, the trend toward materialism, the lowered quality of family life in large cities and long commuting distances for fathers have removed men from the home and lowered the quality of family life. The cost has been enormous. Women have had an additional dilemma to deal with, as was discussed in the preceding chapter. Ways of life other than homemaking have become steadily more available to them. With men away and staggered by the additional burdens on them, small wonder the grass has tended to look greener outside the home, especially so when their own readiness for a heterosexual commitment and homemaking has been progressively diminished as a consequence of absent fathers and overburdened mothers when they were developing little girls or as adults whose husbands tend to be away so much of the time.

Currently many men simply abdicate their leadership position in the family, and as a consequence women have been forced to become heads of families or families simply fall apart. Because of the impact of these changes in role function and family stability, characterologic changes have taken place in children so that with the coming of each generation men have tended to become progressively less responsible and more passive, retiring—even effeminate—and women more domineering and aggressive and masculinized. These are *psychological* changes which are contrary to Nature—women's lib movement notwithstanding—and create a contradiction within the individual which not only leads to personal suffering and diminished effectiveness, but virtually insures stresses and strains in heterosexual relationships. Men and women tend to compete with each other rather than live out the marvelous harmony which Nature provides for.

The inability to cooperate, interpersonal competitiveness, irresponsibility, dependence and passivity in the male, and competitive, masculine strivings in the female used to be seen in isolated instances within couples. Now these personal patterns are becoming national patterns. These masses of individuals inevitably and by personal necessity reorder social values. The making of families and the care of children assume a low priority. It is so because people create ways of living which permit them to find a reasonably comfortable fit with the environment. For instance, the more outspoken leaders of the feminist (this term is a misnomer) movement rarely speak of the importance of homemaking, being a mother and wife. Instead, they champion lifestyles which, when examined closely, reveal an underlying envy of the male, a desire to do what he does, indeed to be like him, and at times a deep hostility toward him. A glaring example is the pressure being exerted by the gay lib movement to have their way of life accepted as normal.

The Soviet Union, where millions of men were killed during World War II and where women were pressed by necessity into the work force during the reconstruction period, provides an excellent example of the above-described sequence. Currently 80 percent of the Soviet women work outside the home and the government is desperately trying to induce them to make families but the young women resist. Approximately 33 percent of marriageable Russians remain single. It is my belief that these people, many of whom are products of fatherless homes and often motherless homes too, cannot make a full heterosexual commitment and shoulder the enormous responsibilities of being a parent. Parenthetically, it is here worth mentioning that in Scandinavia, where taxes are so high that women must work, suicide, depression, and alcoholism are highly prevalent as in the Soviet Union. Ironically, some of the taxes support the day-care centers which provide "care" for the babies and children of these working mothers who must work to pay their taxes. Among other things, this illustrates another way governments can seriously interfere with fundamental human processes and in so doing contribute to their own eventual downfall.

It should be recalled that in the early days of the Roman Empire the family was a solid unit with the man at its head. He had absolute authority and commanded great respect. The Roman wife was a magnificent, highly spirited woman, not weak, but strong in the best feminine sense of the word. These families produced the great empire. But the men were taken away as Roman legions expanded the boundaries of the empire and slowly but surely the Roman family changed. The women became "emancipated," families disintegrated, homosexuality flourished. Secret cults sprang up of "women-men and men-women" (homosexuals), whose activities centered on the literal ritualistic castration and destruction of young males; decay was everywhere; sexuality was unrestrained and eventually the empire collapsed. A thousand years of dark ages followed. What is happening in America has happened before.

I have been frequently reminded of the fact that those psychiatric truths about which I have written on family life are clearly described in the Bible. That observations from a psychiatric vantage point should so closely parallel scripture is interesting indeed. Theologians will interpret this finding as evidence of God's work. Those working within a purely scientific framework will see an element of cross-validation in the parallel.

I believe it is now absolutely safe to conclude that it is axiomatic that mature men who by definition are masculine and mature women who by definition are feminine can make families which produce healthy children who become strong men and women. Such individuals made America great. They imposed their strong will on the land and developed the greatest nation of all time.

Now, progressively fewer people can make families and many families that do exist are very sick families or they fall apart. Our land is being flooded by sick people with the coming of each generation. Our values are changing, our laws will change and down we go. Ours is still a great country, but our Constitution, the Bill of Rights, our laws, traditions, and institutions which have made us great and the leading nation in the world will continue to do so only if the individuals within the land are strong and have the opportunity to find personal fulfillment within the framework of our traditions and values. Consider some of the changes which are taking place in America.

Most ominous of all is the fact that marriage and the family is no longer the solid institution it once was. The divorce rate by some estimates has reached 44 percent, a fact which reflects the inability of people to make a lasting heterosexual commitment. Well over one-half of the marriages of young people fail. In California more young people are living together informally than those who are formally married. There are now eight and one-half million children being reared by a single parent, usually a woman; these children are being denied the growth-promoting effects of a family and a home. The number of illegitimate children, particularly blacks, is rising at a shocking rate. The day-care center is supplanting the home for millions of young children as women find vocations other than homemaking, many of them by free choice rather than necessity. Nearly every form of personal disturbance is on the increase, ranging from child beating, delinquency, suicide, drug abuse, alcoholism, crime, homosexuality, to psychosis in both adults and children. One of my colleagues, an expert in child illnesses, estimates there are millions of children in need of psychiatric care.

Now the code is to do your own thing, seek immediate gratification by whatever means is available. One form of sex is as "mature" as another. I read that in houses of prostitution, anal and oral sex is the most sought-after mode. Live singly, in groups, swing, trade off—it doesn't matter, just so you find immediate satisfaction by the easiest means possible. Sex which once served to help cement the relationship between a man and a woman is now as readily available as water and much less meaningful. It has been shown that when society fails to place restraints on sexuality, a cultural decline eventually follows. Further evidence of the lack of restraint on sexuality can be found in the open display of sex on the stage, on film, on television and on the printed page. Pornography is running rampant and focuses mostly on perverted sex of the severest kind. Using children for prostitution and for pornography has become a multimillion dollar business.

The quest for excellence is no longer the burning desire of many young people (or many older ones for that matter) it once was. Our universities, the storehouses and propagators of the best in man's knowledge and achievement, have become infested by a sickness that is tragic. While there are still pockets of excellence in centers of learning, the overall quality of the university experience has declined as well as the level of intellectual development of those entering universities, as has been shown by recent surveys. Even our service academies are having trouble with the honor systems. Now college campuses are hotbeds of drug usage, free-swinging lifestyles; many students have a complete disregard for our best traditions. Students tend to show less regard for personal appearance. Particularly appalling is the appearance of some medical students and young doctors, especially those who enter psychiatry. Now many of these young professionals are shabby and in no way reflect those qualities of self-respect, reliability, responsibility, and competence which provide the very foundation for the field of medicine. This is an especially ominous sign, for physicians have traditionally reflected the highest values of society. Some of the professors at both undergraduate and graduate level, especially in the humanities, are indistinguishable from these students. Regard for one's personal appearance is not limited to the universities. Look on the streets.

Huge numbers of youth are absolutely lost. They literally do not know who they are; they lack goals; they find oblivion in drugs and other forms of escapism; they don't know where to go and, if they knew, they lack the personal resources of self-confidence and masterfulness which would make it possible for them to get there. Pot smoking, by twenty million Americans, is part of this decline. Make no mistake—marijuana contains a very toxic substance. Its regular usage favors retrogression, flight, apathy, the very last kind of human qualities people need in these uncertain times. Many young people have no respect for authority and little regard for the effects of their behavior on others. Their aim appears to be to eliminate what was established by past generations. They seem not to comprehend the great effort it has taken to build this country and how necessary are the values and institutions which give it support and strength and stability. They no longer accept the values that have made this a strong and stable society. The effects on our society of these hundreds of thousands of young people defies estimation. Moral decay is like an abscess in the vital organs of a man.

A particularly ominous sign of our times is the blurring of the differences between male and female, the psychological "castration" to which I have referred. Even Doctor Spock has deleted references to boys and girls in his new book! Anyone who will take the time to observe will immediately recognize this blurring. Charles Winick provides a shocking description of how extensive these changes are in his book, *The New People: Desexualization in American Life*. These changes have also been demonstrated by means of in-depth psychological testing. Winick has pointed out that, in most of those societies which eventually died out and about which knowledge exists regarding the reasons for their decline, sex-role blurring existed.

It is important to recall that Cicero scathingly attacked the pronounced effeminacy of young Roman male aristocrats; no doubt he realized the Roman Empire was doomed with such males inheriting positions of leadership. The painful truth is that sex role definition in our young people is less defined now than twenty years ago. The changes are like a plague sweeping the country. While the individuals themselves are not perishing, their spirits are. These weak people along with others who are weakened in other ways will inherit our land.

Add up all of these changes: increase in crime; mental illnesses, in both adults and children; suicide, the second largest cause of death in young people; alcoholism; drug usage (of epidemic proportion); child abuse (one million instances annually)! In fact, the family is described in a recent study as the most violent place in America; high divorce rate with eight and one-half million children being reared in a single-parent home; juvenile crime; increase in crime among women; minimal restraint on sexuality; decrease in educational achievement in young people; severe sex-role blurring; increase in homosexuality and acceptance of this condition as normal; decrease in parental authority; lowered influence of the church; disregard for all authority by many young people; corruption at all social levels, including an erosion of integrity in high office; the return of scabies and lice (diseases of the dark ages); uncontrollable increase in venereal disease, a large portion of which is transmitted by homosexual acts and by youth as young as twelve years old; a general decline in the quest for excellence especially among the young; disregard for personal appearance including those in positions of responsibility; the absence of national heroes for the young to emulate; the confusion about equal opportunity and equal ability with the associated diminution of quality—and look at the total. All of this spells a serious deterioration in this wonderful nation.

However, the problem does not end there; individual decline does not exist in a vacuum. Society reinforces what is happening to individuals and groups of individuals. Social reinforcement occurs in several ways: (1) individuals of like kind band together and form social movements; (2) leaders of these movements appear from within these groups; (3) society eventually endorses some of these movements by writing new laws. The unsuspecting, uninformed, and the weak give their approval to that which is proposed by the leaders of these movements and we must abide by new laws whether we like it or not.

For instance, the militant feminists are, in my opinion, driven to a large extent by motivations from within their own personalities more than by rational considerations. People usually try to alter the environment to suit their personalities rather than change (mature) in order to be able to meet the challenges and expectations of a mature adjustment. Many of these militant leaders have not been successful in their marriages or as mothers—if they ever married—and some are admittedly homosexual. Furthermore, they enlist the "authority" of renowned professionals to endorse their movements. Margaret Mead, for instance, not only is in the forefront of the women's liberation movement, but she also says that bisexuality should be considered normal. She has endorsed a "marriage" by two homosexual women and their claim that they can be adequate parents to five children.

There are many inequities in our society; however, it remains to be seen whether the women's liberation movement and equal rights legislative efforts do more harm than good overall. These feminist leaders are having a profound effect on developing children as well as on adults. At a time in life when little girls are going through profoundly important developmental stages, militant feminists are urging them to abandon the course Nature intended them to follow (toward womanhood) and enter into intense competition with males, in the various ways I mentioned earlier. No single quality of behavior is more destructive in the relationship between man and woman than competitiveness. What children learn in childhood is carried forth into adulthood. Not to be overlooked is the overall lowering of quality resulting when women try to do what men do best and vice versa.

Another example of social reinforcement of personal psychopathology can be found in the formal position taken by the American Psychiatric Association and the American Psychological Association that homosexuality is merely a variant of sexuality rather than a form of psychopathology. Bear in mind, however, that many psychiatrists and psychologists clearly understand the true nature of homosexuality and opposed the formal position which was taken by these two associations.

How could this incredible declaration by the two major mental health professions have come about? The answer is not difficult to find. Men and women who enter the mental health professions are very commonly troubled within themselves. This fact is well known. As a result, they tend to be sympathetic toward the social aspirations of disturbed persons. Furthermore, health personnel tend to consider the individual before society. As a consequence, when faced by strong lobbying pressures they are more likely to back down rather than stand firm. Our Congress and certain national leaders have demonstrated a similar weakness and as a consequence women are filling positions that only men should fill. There is a certain ''sympathy'' in the more disturbed mental health professionals for homosexuals and from this sympathy comes the mistaken belief that a kindness is being done when they ask society to accept these persons as ''normal.'' Be very careful when you seek help from the mental health profession.

The laws of the land *are* changing as a consequence of these various social movements and the overall quality of life will suffer as a consequence. The fine concept of equal opportunity for everyone is being misread as meaning that everyone is equal. They are not. Men and women are not equal in ability. They are equal in worth but their worth will only be fully realized by *enhancing* not *blurring* their differences. Among men inequality exists; the same holds for women. Greatness for a society can only come when individual differences are recognized, outlets for expression provided, and high performance rewarded. The trend is toward a unisex society and we are close to having this trend reinforced by constitutional amendment. Apparently unaware of the difference between equal opportunity and equal ability, or unable to stand up to pressure groups such as NOW, just as weak men within the family cannot stand up to aggressive wives, the Congress has forced industry and our armed forces to accept women into positions which only men should occupy.

There are tasks women do best and there are tasks men do best. Fire departments will not become more effective when staffed by women, nor will police departments, nor will the fighting arm of the armed forces. No day-care center is equal to a good home. A man cannot become a mother, nor a woman a father. Let us defend this country with the strongest men we have, not with weaklings spaced out with drugs and whose long hair might jam the mechanisms of their weaponry, or with women who are unequal to the man's physical strength and aggressiveness. If our fighter aircraft are ever piloted by women and they encounter well-trained, aggressive enemy males in combat, we are lost; we must have our toughest men manning our ships, planes, and arms.

The picture is clear. Personal psychopathology has led to social pathology and laws are being passed which reinforce personal and social pathology. Remove legal restraints against possession of marijuana, tie the hands of the authority, pass laws which reinforce the blurring of the differences between males an females, and turn us into a homogeneous, unisex society, permit the most depraved behaviors to appear on the screen, TV, and on the street, and encourage the care of children by nonparents rather than reward those who make families and good homes, let women do jobs that men do better, keep pulling the props out from under the family, etc., etc., and the demise of this great country will be assured.

The time has come for individuals to take a strong defensive stand against the trends that are rushing our great country to destruction. Individuals must act first in their own self-interest and make a start somewhere. By so doing, we all collectively may save our way of life.

Begin by looking very closely at the new norms—the wave of the future—and ask, "Do these ways really bring out the best in men and women?" Then look at the leadership of these social movements and ask, "Is that the kind of man or woman I want to be, or want my children to become?" Look at the leadership because there you will find those human qualities which reflect the essence of the social movement. If you don't like what you see, take a stand; protect yourself and your family. Fight off these social forces as if you were being attacked by an enemy.

When you buy clothing for your child, select those items which make your boy look like a male and your daughter look like a female. Encourage your sons to be masculine and for good measure to get a haircut. Encourage your daughter to be feminine and enhance the natural grace of her femininity. Throw out the platform shoes for men, cologne that is really perfume, and effeminate jewelry. If your daughter likes sports, encourage her to play with other girls and not compete with boys. Help her understand that her future happiness and the future of the nation depend on being in harmony with a man and being able to love him and not by competing with him. Teach your sons to be protective toward and thoughtful of women, to love them, but also teach them how not to be dominated by them.

Keep a close watch on your educators from elementary level on. Look at the textbooks, visit their classes, especially those in psychology and sociology, and raise an uproar if what they are taught denies the differences between sexes, advocates the "new sexuality," promotes role blurring within the family, etc. Much of what is being foisted upon the young is pollution of the worst kind, especially that which claims that personal identity can be separated from sexual identity. Above all, remember this, your children will not find in society persons who will teach them the art of parenthood. You are the only teacher they will have. The family finds little support anywhere—some from churches, but even there "God the Father" is being represented by women as more and more churches ordain women. This trend removes the symbolic father figure from many families and individuals whose own fathering is in short supply. Make this your first and highest priority: teach your children to be good parents by example. Fathers and mothers, you have an enormous task facing you! See that you are succeeded by healthy, strong men and women who recognize, appreciate, and fully express their differences.

You may not be able to isolate your children from these pernicious social influences and you may fail in your efforts to directly influence your children, but try hard. Make your family life solid and rewarding; this is your fortress and the fortress of hope for us all. Will Durant said, "The family can exist without the State, but without the family all is lost." Examine closely how much of yourself you put into your family. You men, are you living up to the responsibilities which have traditionally fallen to men? Are you the head of your family? You women, are you doing the same? Are you really committed to your husbands? And above all, are you mothers taking care of your babies and preschool children? Remember, the needs of babies and children have not and will never change. Are you accentuating the differences between your sons and daughters and evoking and reinforcing each child's uniqueness? If not, they will almost surely flock to social movements, and write the laws which will contribute to the destruction of this society. What you do for your family as a whole, for your spouse, and for and with your children determines to a large extent their fate as adults and the fate of society. Those who cannot or choose not to have children deserve society's deepest respect for the sacrifice they make. Save the family and restrict the making of families to healthy and committed men and women and turn out strong men and strong women and we will be on course again. Pioneer families gave us this nation; you who reassert the worth of the family and uphold the best values and institutions in America will save it.

COMMENTS AND
SELECTED READINGS

I have not cited authorities on all of the many issues covered in this book. To have done so would have radically changed the style and the purpose of the book. It was not my intention to undertake a review of the massive amount of literature which deals with the human condition. I have written an account of what I believe to be true; it is observation and opinion based on my own experiences, both personal and professional over a span of twenty-five years, and on the works of others. The case histories and footnotes are presented as evidence to support my beliefs.

Well aware that many of you may desire some additional documentation for what I have written, and for those who might wish to delve more deeply into some particular subject, I mention below some of the most central issues covered in the book, and for your convenience I will refer to a few of the works of others who have written on these topics. These references will serve as a starting place for your further study. The references listed are of the kind which will, in turn, refer to the work of others. These selected readings represent only a sampling of the opinions and facts which have been published.

The profound differences between male and female can be illustrated from several vantage points. On a theoretical level, in Marmor's book Sandor Rado disputes Freud's belief in biologic bisexuality. My paper on Freud attempts to show that Freud's belief was actually an expression and rationalization for his own psychological bisexuality which, in turn, reflected his deep identification with his mother. Stoller's work illustrates the powerful impact of early life experiences on the sexual identity of the child. Gadpaille's excellent review article supports, in my opinion, the notion that male and female have distinct qualities and that these qualities are biologically based. In this connection, you might also read the article by Harris.

For those who are interested in man's evolutionary history, studies in animal behavior are tremendously revealing. Differences between male and female are striking with regard to dominance, sexual activity, territoriality, relationship to the offspring, and to the social group. The writings of Ardrey, Beach, DeVore, Lorenz, and Tinbergen provide the documentation. These works support the view that individuals must develop psychologically in a way which is in harmony with the biological forces within them in order to achieve emotional health.

The vital importance of good mothering is amply supported by both animal and human studies. Neither young animals nor infants develop properly in the absence of mothering or when provided with the wrong kind of mothering. Harlow's pioneering work with monkeys revealed how devastating are the effects on the offspring when the mother is absent. The work of Spitz with infants parallels Harlow's in many respects. Others who have made fundamental contributions to the subject of the mother-infant relationship incude Bowlby, Brody, Escalona, and Klein. Studies such as these should erase once and for all any doubt with regard to the importance of women and the essential function of good mothering for human development. In light of the marked differences between the sexes, it should be equally clear that only women can provide these experiences for infants and small children, and that a strong masculine man and a family offer the best setting for the woman to become a mother.

The structure of the family and the proper role for the man and woman within the family has been written about by many, and from various points of view. Again, the roots of male and female roles in the family can be seen in animal studies. DeVore's book on primates is an example. Basic patterns can be seen further back in the animal kingdom as is illustrated by Lorenz, for instance. All of these studies show that the male is dominant; he lays claim to territory, he protects the female and her offspring, and the most dominant male leads the social group. Goldberg's view on patriarchy is consistent with these observations. Others who have written on the family from various points of view are Anshen, Handel, Lidz, Miller and Swanson, and Parsons and Bales. Anthony and Benedek's book on parenthood covers a wide range of subjects related to family life. Clearly, the family is indispensable and, while there is room for individual variation, the roles of father and mother are well defined, and the effects of optimal family life are amply documented.

There is a great amount of literature which links abnormal human development to disturbed family patterns. The works of Bieber, et al., and Socarides on homosexuals, Green's work with transsexuals, Stoller's work, Bratter's findings with drug users, provide some of the most striking evidence. Fisher has shown the importance of good fathering with regard to the young girl's development. Terms like domineering, aggressive, overprotective, rejecting mother, and weak, passive, remote, tyrannical father appear with clocklike regularity in these reports and in a multitude of papers which fill psychiatric journals. Note how opposite these terms are to the qualities ascribed to male and female in the animal studies, and how opposite to the terms describing male and female qualities in a normal family. The evidence is irrefutable with regard to the kinds of personalities of the father and mother and the quality of family life which turns out boys and girls who become competent men and women. The forty-two case studies included in the book by Voth and Orth give direct clinical evidence for these assertions.

Engel's book illustrates these facts to some degree in the context of the description and discussion of childhood development. Josselyn's monograph describes the process of childhood development clearly and succinctly. Other publications which discuss childhood development, all illustrating in one way or another the importance of the family and of mothering and fathering, are those of Anthony, Bettelheim, Klein, Lesse, and Lidz. The publications listed which have to do with mothering are, of course, also highly relevant to childhood development, as are animal studies.

The psychology of women is described and discussed by Benedek, Bonaparte, Deutsch, S. Freud, Fisher, and J. C. Rheingold. These works are especially important in view of the dramatic changes taking place in women's values and the personalities of so many women. Deutsch's recent book, *Confrontations with Myself*, is particularly illuminating with regard to career women. The publications on abnormal childhood development should provide ample support for the claim that pathological changes within the family (domineering, aggressive, or masculinized mothers, and weak, passive, or absent fathers) make it very difficult, if not impossible, for a girl or boy to become the kind of woman or man who can provide the kind of mothering and fathering necessary for children to become competent adults.

Personality theory is discussed in virtually all of the references having to do with family, development, psychopathology; however, special emphasis on theory can be found in all of the works of Brenner, Anna Freud, Sigmund Freud, Menninger, and Waelder. Freedman and Kaplan, Hall and Lindzey, and Yates discuss theories other than psychoanalytic theory.

There is a vast literature on psychiatric treatment. Ford and Urban, and Freedman and Kaplan describe various therapeutic approaches. Yates's book is on behavior therapy. Menninger's and Greenson's works are excellent descriptions of psychoanalysis. Chessick describes the principles of psychotherapy concisely. The references to Sigmund Freud are all related to treatment, particularly his paper on interminable analysis in volume 5 of his *Collected Papers*. The book by Voth and Orth focuses on the importance of the environment during treatment. My paper entitled "Responsibility in the Practice of Psychoanalysis and Psychotherapy" deals with the pitfalls of treatment when the doctor is poorly trained, irresponsible, or unsuitable by virtue of his own personality. Both Freud and Thompson also discuss the effects of the doctor's personality on treatment outcome.

How the family and personality articulate with society is discussed by Erikson, Kardiner, and Unwin. Winick has described the blurring of sexual differences in our current society and has spoken of the ominous implications these changes have for the future.

The family is the building block of society, and the strength of the latter depends on the strength of the former. The profound changes which are taking place in the personalities of increasing numbers of males and females and within the family, and the increasing number of broken homes, seriously disturbs the development of children, and will ultimately lead to the decline of our society.

SELECTED READINGS

1. Anshen, R. N., ed. *The Family: Its Function and Destiny*. Vol. 5 (rev. ed.). New York: Harper, 1959.

2. Anthony, E. J., and Benedek, T., eds. *Parenthood—Its Psychology and Psychopathology*. Boston: Little, Brown, 1970.

3. Ardrey, R. *African Genesis*. New York: Atheneum, 1961.

4. Ardrey, R. *The Territorial Imperative*. New York: Atheneum, 1966.

5. Beach, F. A. ed. *Sex and Behavior*. New York: Wiley, 1965.

6. Benedek, T. *Psychosexual Functions of Women*. New York: Ronald Press, 1952.

7. Benson, L. *Fatherhood*. New York: Random House, 1968.

8. Bettelheim, B. *The Children of the Dream*. New York: Macmillan, 1969.

9. Bettelheim, B. "Young Radicals Emotionally Ill." *Kansas City Star*, Sept. 22, 1970.

10. Bieber, I. et al. *Homosexuality*. New York: Basic Books, 1962.

11. Bonaparte, M. *Female Sexuality*. New York: International Universities Press, 1953.

12. Bowlby, J. "The Nature of the Child's Tie to his Mother." *International Journal of Psycho-Analysis* 39:350–373, 1958.

13. Bowlby, J. *Attachment and Loss*. Vol. 1. New York: Basic Books, 1969.

14. Bowlby, J. *Separation*. Vol. 2. New York: Basic Books, 1973.

15. Bratter, T. E. "Treating Alienated, Unmotivated, Drug Abusing Adolescents." *American Journal of Psychotherapy* 27(4):585–598, 1973.

16. Brenner, C. *An Elementary Textbook of Psychoanalysis*. New York: International Universities Press, 1955.

17. Brenton, M. *The American Male*. New York: Coward-McCann, 1966.

18. Brody, S. *Patterns of Mothering; Maternal Influence During Infancy*. New York: International Universities Press, 1956.

19. Chessick, R. D. *How Psychotherapy Heals*. New York: Science House, 1969.

20. Chessick, R. D. *Why Psychotherapists Fail*. New York: Science House, 1971.

21. Deutsch, H. *The Psychology of Women*. 2 vols. New York: Grune and Stratton, 1944-45.

22. Deutsch, H. *Confrontations with Myself*. New York: Norton, 1973.

23. DeVore, I. *Primate Behavior*. New York: Holt, Rinehart and Winston, 1965.

24. Engel, G. *Psychological Development in Health and Disease*. Philadelphia: Saunders, 1962.

25. Erikson, E. H. *Childhood and Society*. New York: Norton, 1964.

26. Escalona, S. K. *The Roots of Individuality; Normal Patterns of Development in Infancy*. Chicago: Aldine, 1968.

27. Farber, S. M., and Wilson, R. H. L., eds. *Man and Civilization: The Potential of Women*. New York: McGraw-Hill, 1963.

28. Fenichel, O. *The Psychoanalytic Theory of Neurosis*. New York: Norton, 1945.

29. Fisher, S. *The Female Orgasm: Psychology, Physiology, Fantasy*. New York: Basic Books, 1973.

30. Ford, D. H., and Urban, H. B. *Systems of Psychotherapy*. New York: Wiley, 1963.

31. Freedman, A. M., and Kaplan, H. I., eds. *Comprehensive Textbook of Psychiatry*. Baltimore: Williams & Wilkins, 1967.

32. Freud, A. *The Ego and the Mechanisms of Defense*. New York: International Universities Press, 1946.

33. Freud, S. *The Problem of Anxiety*. New York: Norton, 1936.

34. Freud, S. *An Outline of Psychoanalysis*. New York: Norton, 1949.

35. Freud, S. *The Interpretation of Dreams*. New York: Basic Books, 1955.

36. Freud, S. *Collected Papers*. 5 vols. New York: Basic Books, 1957.

37. Freud, S. *The Complete Introductory Lectures on Psychoanalysis*. New York: Norton, 1966.

38. Gadpaille, W. J. "Research into the Physiology of Maleness and Femaleness." *Archives of General Psychiatry* 26(3):193–206, 1972.

39. Glover, E. *The Technique of Psychoanalysis.* New York: International Universities Press, 1955.

40. Goldberg, S. *The Inevitability of Patriarchy.* New York: Morrow, 1973.

41. Green, R., et al. "Treatment of Boyhood Transsexualism." *Archives of General Psychiatry* 26(3):213–217, 1972.

42. Greenson, R. R. *The Technique and Practice of Psychoanalysis.* New York: International Universities Press, 1967.

43. Group for the Advancement of Psychiatry. *The Joys and Sorrows of Parenthood.* G.A.P. Report no. 84, vol. 8. May 1973.

44. Hall, C. S., and Lindzey, G. *Theories of Personality.* 2d ed. New York: Wiley, 1973.

45. Handel, G. *The Psychosocial Interior of the Family.* Chicago: Aldine, 1967.

46. Harlow, H. F., and Harlow, M. K. "Social Deprivation in Monkeys." *Scientific American* 207:136–146, 1962.

47. Harlow, H. F., and Harlow, M. K. "The Effect of Rearing Conditions on Behavior." In J. Money, ed. *Sex Research: New Developments.* New York: Holt, Rinehart and Winston, 1965, pp. 161–175.

48. Harris, G. W. "Sex Hormones, Brain Development, and Brain Function." *Endocrinology* 175:627–648, 1964.

49. Josselyn, I. M. *Psychosocial Development of Children*. New York: Family Service Assn. of America, 1948.

50. Kardiner, A. *The Individual and His Society*. New York: Columbia University Press, 1939.

51. Katchadourian, H. A. and Lunde, D. T. *Fundamentals of Human Sexuality*. 2d ed. New York: Holt, Rinehart and Winston, 1975.

52. Klein, M. *The Psycho-Analysis of Children*. London: Hogarth, 1963.

53. LeMasters, E. E. *Parents in Modern America*. Homewood, Ill.: Dorsey Press, 1970.

54. Lesse, S. "Jane Doe and Our Future Society—Searching for an Image." *American Journal of Psychotherapy* 17(3):333–337, 1973.

55. Levy, D. M. *Maternal Overprotection*. New York: Columbia University Press, 1943.

56. Lidz, T. *The Family and Human Adaptation*. New York: International Universities Press, 1963.

57. Lorenz, K. *On Aggression*. New York: Harcourt, Brace, 1966.

58. Lorenz, K. *Studies in Animal and Human Behavior*. 2 vols. Cambridge, Mass.: Harvard University Press, 1970–1971.

59. Maccoby, E. E., ed. *The Development of Sex Differences*. Stanford: Stanford University Press, 1966.

60. Marmor, J., ed. *Sexual Inversion*. New York: Basic Books, 1965.

61. Masters, W. H., and Johnson, V. E. *Human Sexual Inadequacy*. Boston: Little, Brown, 1970.

62. Menninger, K. *The Theory of Psychoanalytic Technique*. New York: Basic Books, 1958.

63. Menninger, K., et al. *The Vital Balance*. New York: Viking Press, 1963.

64. Miller, D. R., and Swanson, G. E. *The Changing American Parent*. New York: Wiley, 1958.

65. Montagu, M. F. A., ed. *Culture and the Evolution of Man*. New York: Oxford University Press, 1962.

66. Parsons, T., and Bales, R., eds. *Family, Socialization and Interaction Process*. Glencoe, Ill.: Free Press, 1955.

67. Popenoe, P. "The Fraudulent New 'Morality.' " *Medical Aspects of Human Sexuality* 7(4):159–167, April 1973.

68. Reinhardt, R. F. "The Outstanding Jet Pilot." *American Journal of Psychiatry* 127:732–736, December 1970.

69. Rheingold, H. L., ed. *Maternal Behavior in Mammals*. New York: Wiley, 1963.

70. Rheingold, J. C. *The Fear of Being a Woman*. New York: Grune and Stratton, 1964.

71. Salk, L. "When to Spoil Your Baby." *Newsweek*, March 13, 1972, p. 53.

72. Socarades, C. W. *The Overt Homosexual*. New York: Grune and Stratton, 1968.

73. Socarades, C. W. *Beyond Sexual Freedom*. New York: Quadrangle, 1975.

74. Spiegel, J., and Bell, N. "The Family of the Psychiatric Patient." In S. Arieti, ed. *American Handbook of Psychiatry*. New York: Basic Books, 1959.

75. Spitz, R. A. "Hospitalism: An Inquiry into the Genesis of Psychiatric Conditions in Early Childhood." *Psychoanalytic Study of the Child* 1:53–74, 1945.

76. Spitz, R. A. *The First Year of Life*. New York: International Universities Press, 1965.

77. Sexton, P. *The Feminized Male; Classrooms, White Collars and the Decline of Manliness*. New York: Random House, 1969.

78. Steppocher, R. C., and Mausner, J. S. "Suicide in Male and Female Physicians." *Journal of the American Medical Association* 228(3):323–328, April 15, 1974.

79. Stoller, R. J. *Sex and Gender: The Development of Masculinity and Femininity*. New York: Science House, 1968.

80. Stoller, R. J. "The 'Bedrock' of Masculinity and Femininity: Bisexuality." *Archives of General Psychiatry* 26(3):207-212, 1972.

81. Thompson, C. M. "Interpersonal Psychoanalysis." In M. R. Green, ed. *Selected Papers of Clara M. Thompson*. New York: Basic Books, 1964.

82. Tinbergen, N. *The Study of Instinct*. Oxford, Eng.: Clarendon Press, 1951.

83. Tinbergen, N. *Social Behavior in Animals*. London: Methuen, 1953.

84. Unwin, J. D. *Sex and Culture*. London: Oxford University Press, 1934.

85. Vaillant, G. E. "Natural History of Male Psychological Health." *Archives of General Psychiatry* 31:15–22, July 1974.

86. Voth, H. M. "Some Effects of Freud's Personality on Psychoanalytic Theory and Technique." *International Journal of Psychiatry* 10(4):48–69, 1972.

87. Voth, H. M. "Responsibility in the Practice of Psychoanalysis and Psychotherapy. *American Journal of Psychotherapy* 26(1):69-83, 1972.

88. Voth, H. M., and Orth, M. H. *Psychotherapy and the Role of the Environment*. New York: Behavioral Publications, 1973.

89. Waelder, R. *Basic Theory of Psychoanalysis*. New York: International Universities Press, 1960.

90. Wainwright, W. H. "Fatherhood as a Precipitant of Mental Illness." *American Journal of Psychiatry* 123(1):40–44, 1966.

91. Washburn, S. L., ed. *Social Life of Early Man*. Chicago: Aldine, 1961.

92. Winick, C. E. *The New People: Desexualization in American Life*. Indianapolis: Pegasus, 1968.

93. Winick, C. E. "Sex and Society: Unisex in America." *Medical Opinion & Review* 6(9):62–65, 1970.

94. Yates, A. J. *Behavior Therapy*. New York: Wiley, 1970.

95. Wade, N. "Bottle-Feeding: Adverse Effects of a Western Technology" *Science* 184(4132):45–48, April 5, 1974.

APPENDIX

Those who take the trouble to read a book or article which deals with the human condition and human values have a right to know something about the author as well as his professional background in order to better judge what he has written. What a man or woman becomes is, to a large degree, determined by what influences were brought to bear upon him as a child. We are all products of our past. What we are has a powerful effect upon what we believe; therefore, I will tell you something of the events, people, and experiences, as well as my professional training, which have influenced me the most.

I was very fortunate to have had a calm, gentle, bountiful, and feminine mother. Being a wife and mother completely satisfied her; though educated and a teacher, when she married and began her family she directed all of her energies to her new life. She was devoted to her parental family, to my father, and to me. Although she died following the birth of a little girl before I was six years old, her love and care filled me with a sense of inner goodness, confidence, and optimism which is the inner core of my personality. I was a very lucky boy to have had her for my mother.

The death of my mother however, had its unfortunate effects on my view of life. For many years I was burdened by a sense of insecurity. My deepest concern was that those dear to me might die. Fear would creep over me if my father were late coming home from work. Even today I think I worry excessively about the health and welfare of my wife and children. When parting from friends it always seemed that I would never see them again. Losses and separation later in life affect more deeply those who have suffered the loss of a parent in early life; I have been no exception! But my cautiousness about possible loss made me very vigilant and that has brought about positive results many times.

My father was a strong, self-sufficient, and masterful man. He possessed a keen intellect, a creative and imaginative mind, and a high spirit. He was the head of our family and my mother followed his lead. He and I were very close. He let me work by his side and he taught me what he knew. He also gave me a deep appreciation of Nature. Most importantly, he let me be a part of his life. Ever since I was a boy I have admired him for his ability to do things, to take charge, and to make things happen. He was a very genuine person and the most honest man I have ever known. In addition to being my father, he was my best friend during my adult years.

Father withdrew from everyone to some degree after Mother died. This complicated my continuing development. I harbored too much awe for authority during my adolescence and early adulthood. My personal analysis helped with this but so too did Dad. For despite this sense of awe I have never been intimidated by authority and in particular by my father. We could always talk freely together and did so frequently to his last day. These talks did much to overcome my childhood misperceptions which had been generated by those normal oedipal fears every child experiences and by his withdrawal and, at times, irritability during the years after Mother's death.

My mother's brother Peter and his wife, Bertha, were close friends of my parents. When my mother died, Aunt Bertha and her young son stayed with Dad and me for the entire school year. I shall always cherish the memory of her devotion and care. Uncle Pete and Aunt Bertha opened their home and hearts to me. Their simplicity, genuineness, and acceptance did much to compensate for the loss of my mother. Aunt Bertha is still alive; her cheerful and optimistic quality has not been dampened by old age, physical illness, or by the loss of her husband.

My maternal grandmother was one of the most loving people I have ever known. Grandma Unruh understood boys; knew that what made them feel good was to love them and to reinforce their growing sense of maleness. She too stayed with me for a year after my mother's death. My mind is filled with memories of that year and of later staying with her in the summer, and periodically visiting her, Uncle Pete, and Aunt Bertha through the years. I was always greeted with a warmth and acceptance which I shall never forget, and which now makes it clear why at her funeral her minister referred to her as "The Mother Unruh." One of my last memories of her is rubbing hand lotion into her old and wrinkled hands. I hope she felt during those quiet moments the love and gratitude I felt, and still feel, for her.

Having been cared for by women like my mother, Grandma Unruh, and Aunt Bertha for the first six years of life caused me to have little interest in masculinized, domineering, or otherwise unfeminine women. However, one encounters women like that, and during my early adult years I tended to be too easy on them, believing women to be too fragile to be able to tolerate confrontation. I eventually overcame this misperception of what women are like thanks to the first six years with my mother and father. My personal psychoanalysis which occurred during my psychoanalytic training was of some help in overcoming my caution with women which was based on the fear of loss or rejection. Unfortunately there are many domineering women and passive weak male psychiatrists and psychoanalysts, so that exposure during training to such people on balance was probably more of a hindrance than a help in providing a clear view of what men and women are supposed to be like concerning the qualities of maleness and femaleness. Psychoanalysis was, however, enormously helpful in overcoming a pervasive latent depression which I had never worked out after my mother died.

Although my father's stepmother was hard pressed by the responsibilities of her own large family she always had time for me and was glad to see me. All of her children were good to me and I am grateful for that. One of them, Wanda, seemed especially to sense my need for human warmth after my mother's death and has generously supplied it even to this day.

Dad's sister Martha stayed with Dad and me for about a year after my mother's death. I have a special feeling for her because she had lost her mother at the time of her own birth.

My father remarried when I was nine. We had moved from familiar surroundings and Dad was working hard to support his family and earn his Ph.D. My stepmother was absorbed with reestablishing a family, particularly after my half-brother and half-sister were born. It was wonderful having a brother and a sister and I could not have loved them more. I felt on the outside of things then, but the second family reaffirmed for me the pricelessness of family life. I am grateful to my stepmother for providing a home for me during those difficult preadolescent and adolescent years. I was a shy boy but even so something within always pushed me forward and I could always turn to Dad for advice.

During the summers I visited my grandmothers and Uncle Pete and Aunt Bertha, and though I felt at home with them I was nostalgic too. My mother's death had changed life so much and I felt her absence deeply. The sense of loss was most acute on long quiet summer days. It was fulfilling to see those wonderful people of my boyhood but it saddened me too. Powerful waves of anguish and despair would sweep over me and I would sometimes cry uncontrollably. It was not until many years later that I understood these episodes as reawakenings of my agony over the death of my beloved mother and the many changes that followed as a consequence. Painful as the past has been, these experiences have given me an especially keen awareness of the importance of one's early life and of the fragility of life itself. Even today it is at times almost more than I can bear to witness or read about or hear of the awful abuses suffered by children as a consequence of breakdowns in the family.

During my junior and senior high school years I spent the summers with my mother's sister Katherine and her husband, Harry. These were wonderful, tension-free times; we hunted, fished, and simply felt good together. How vividly I remember the quiet evenings on that peaceful lake, the smell of Uncle Harry's pipe, the sounds of birds, the beautiful sky, the warm air that seemed like the breath of a reassuring presence. Aunt Kate lives with us now. She has been devoted to me and to my family. It is a beautiful sight when she and our youngest son play together; sometimes it seems to me that it is Grandma Unruh with me.

Paul and Eunice Mannen lived near us in Lawrence, Kansas, where we moved soon after Dad remarried. They were childless, and I think I may have filled a need for them as they did for me. We have been close friends ever since. They were like family and I owe them much for their continuous loyalty and devotion. They fulfilled a continuing need for "a home," throughout my entire adult life.

Medical school exposed me again to the fragility and transience of life. The dedication and fine sense of responsibility of the physicians who were my teachers left a deep impression on me. Having experienced the pain and consequences of the loss of my mother, I think I was more aware than most of my fellow students of the preciousness of life. What a privilege I felt it was to become a physician, to have so much trust placed in me. The importance of assuming full responsibility for the lives of patients was engraved on my mind during those years. I am grateful to my associates, analysts and teachers at the Menninger Foundation, the Topeka Veterans Administration hospitals and the U.S. Navy. Those years of psychiatric and psychoanalytic training provided enormously meaningful experiences without which this book could not have been written.

It was during my psychiatric and psychoanalytic training and the years that followed when I began to treat patients, teach younger physicians, and start my own family, that various aspects of my life became integrated in the sense of my achieving maturity. I discovered the relationship of my own past to the present, and the immense importance of family life. I have often wondered whether I value family life too much because of my early experiences. I think not. I think those experiences sharpened my perception of the preciousness of the special kind of humanness that can only be found within the family and without which the family cannot function and the individual cannot develop properly. My clinical work has repeatedly confirmed these impressions as has the work of others.

I owe a great deal to my wife and three sons, ages 21, 18, and 10. Becoming a husband and father can bring out the best in a man. A resonance is created between the present and the past which crystallizes Nature's contribution. I could not have written this book without having participated in their lives and they in mine. I have seen good mothering replayed in my home, and I am forever grateful to my wife for having done and been so much for our three boys and for me. I cannot imagine a richer or more joyful life. They made it possible for me to be a husband and father, and further, to pass on to them and to my patients, students, and to those who read this book the riches that have been given to me.

Harold M. Voth, M.D., is a senior psychiatrist and psychoanalyst at the Menninger Foundation in Topeka, Kansas, where he also serves as the assistant chief of psychiatry for education at the Topeka Veterans Administration Hospital.

He received his medical degrees from the University of Kansas School of Medicine, the Menninger School of Psychiatry, and the Topeka Institute for Psychoanalysis. He is chairman of the ethics committee of the Kansas Psychiatric Association, a charter fellow of the American College of Psychoanalysts, a member of the New York Academy of Sciences, and a fellow of the American Psychiatric Association. Voth, a rear admiral in the Medical Corps of the U.S. Naval Reserve, serves as a consultant to the Surgeon General of the U.S. Navy.

He has written over forty articles for both professional and popular journals, among them the *American Journal of Psychiatry*, *Journal of the American Psychoanalytic Association*, *Modern Medicine*, and the *International Journal of Psychiatry*. Voth is presently writing a second book, *Dimension of Personality*.

Voth, his wife, and three sons now live in Topeka, Kansas.